HITLER AND APPEASEMENT

Hitler and Appeasement

*The British Attempt to Prevent
the Second World War*

Peter Neville

hambledon
continuum

Hambledon Continuum is an imprint of Continuum Books
Continuum UK, The Tower Building, 11 York Road, London SE1 7NX
Continuum US, 80 Maiden Lane, Suite 704, New York, NY 10038

www.continuumbooks.com

First Published 2006
This edition reprinted 2007

British Library Cataloguing-in-Publication Data
A catalogue record for this book is available from the British Library.

ISBN 1 85285 369 7

This edition
ISBN 978 1 85285 527 7

Typeset by Pindar New Zealand (Egan Reid), Auckland, New Zealand.

Distributed in the United States and Canada
exclusively by Palgrave Macmillan,
A division of St Martin's Press.

Contents

Illustrations

Acknowledgements

This book is the product of many years studying and thinking about British foreign policy in the 1930s. But it could not have been written without the help and encouragement of many individuals, not all of whom can be mentioned here.

My biggest debt is to Professor John Charmley, Professor Tony Lentin and Dr Andrew Crozier, all of whom read chapters of the book and commented upon them. They may not agree with all the conclusions reached in it, for which I must of course bear the ultimate responsibility.

I have, in addition, to thank Professor D. Cameron Watt for initial advice and encouragement (not least through a series of very informative letters about the period), Professor Alan Sharp, Professor Michael Dockrill, Professor Geoff Berridge, Professor Peter Beck, Professor Erik Goldstein, Dr Tony McCulloch and Dr Gaynor Johnson. All historians sit at the feet of others, and I was fortunate to be taught by the late Professors F.S. Northedge, Karl Stadler and Ronald Fryer. And those who lay the foundations of an academic career don't always get the credit due to them. I count myself equally lucky to have been taught history at St George's College, Weybridge, by Dudley Woodget. Lastly, I have yet again to thank my wife Phuong Anh for her forbearance while this project came to fruition, and Carol Willis for her secretarial expertise.

The following have kindly agreed to the reproduction of copyright material in the book: the Keeper of the Public Records at the National Archives, Birmingham University, the Archives of Churchill College, Cambridge, and the National Archives of Scotland.

Every effort has been made to contact copyright-holders. If any have been inadvertently overlooked, the publisher will be glad to make the necessary acknowledgement at the earliest opportunity.

Introduction

Appeasement has become one of the most emotive words in historical literature. Its practitioners in the 1930s have become bywords for blundering incompetence and lack of resolution, and have been held up to ridicule. Even now, over sixty years on, it is difficult to shift this stereotypical view. In 1940 Robert Graves and Alan Hodge wrote that, at the time of the Munich Agreement in 1938, 'the umbrella had been mightier than the sword',[1] and there is still a strong perception in the Anglo-Saxon world that appeasement was and is dishonourable and craven. One only has to remember the numerous misleading and ill-informed analogies with the thirties which were made by British and American politicians in the lead up to the recent Iraq War to see this. In 2004, the democratic decision of the Spanish people to vote their government out of office, after having been seriously misled by the previous administration about who had carried out a terrible bombing outrage, was unsurprisingly described by tabloid newspapers as 'appeasement' of terrorism.

Grotesque studies of British policy between 1933 and 1939 still appear that completely ignore or misunderstand the great weight of research done since the 1970s. This has shown that appeasement was, in fact, a rational response to the very difficult position in which successive British governments found themselves.[2] Standard texts, while often offering a more plausible analysis of British policy, are sometimes forty years old and are not updated to take revisionist literature into account.[3] This is not to argue that there is no case against the appeasers, merely to say that the argument is a good deal more sophisticated and evenly balanced than anti-appeasers, who now have the advantage of a great weight of available scholarship and documentation unavailable immediately after the war and in the 1950s, have been prepared to allow.

In part, the problem is about personalities. Winston Churchill is a more colourful and glamorous hero than Neville Chamberlain or Stanley Baldwin. Churchill was also able to influence the historical record in a remarkable way through the first volume of his war memoirs, *The Gathering Storm*. On his own admission, Churchill set out to write his own version of history, and his is the one that has remained with the man and woman in the street, and indeed the media.[4] It is this Churchillian critique which has survived outside academic circles and, to a degree, within them to this day. It has made British, and even more strongly

American, society peculiarly unwilling to forgive the appeasers of the 1930s. Societies which have quickly developed amnesia about the Rwandan genocide, when 800,000 people were massacred in a hundred days while the international community stood by, have been extremely unforgiving about the mistakes made in dealing with Hitler. This may also be related to the centrality of the Jewish Holocaust, the single most catastrophic genocide of the twentieth century in Europe, to the feeling of collective guilt about appeasement. Yet Baldwin and Chamberlain could not have foreseen the unprecedented horrors of Auschwitz and Treblinka where the full evil of National Socialism was exposed.

The shattering Anglo-French defeat in 1940 has also been linked to the inadequacies of the appeasers (both in Britain and France). In fact, the battle was by no means the foregone conclusion that has commonly been suggested. It was, of course, a battle under the control of the French High Command, which made crucial and unnecessary strategic errors and not that of British politicians. Crucially, too, the French allowed their strong air force of 1919 to decline. For all the propaganda put out to the contrary, this was not allowed to happen in Britain.

Any objective study of British foreign policy in the 1930s must surely acknowledge the terrible problems facing the government at the time. Uniquely, Britain found itself facing a potentially hostile combination of three great powers, and trying to calculate what Hitler, Mussolini and the Japanese might do at any given moment was an onerous and dangerous business. Sometimes British intelligence got its estimates wrong; but then, as recent events in the Middle East have underlined, intelligence communities can and do get things badly wrong.

Historians who write about this period in British history may sometimes get the feeling that they are pushing a large boulder up a mountain. However much research is produced, every schoolboy (and schoolgirl) knows that Neville Chamberlain was a silly old man with an umbrella who was duped by a wicked and unscrupulous German dictator. This legend is passed on from generation to generation. Hitler was undoubtedly wicked, but Chamberlain was far from being a foolish old man, as will be demonstrated.

The debate about appeasement is an ongoing one and historians change their minds. A recent example has found a distinguished Canadian scholar, Sydney Aster, moving away from the sympathetic view of appeasement he took in 1973 to a much more critical one by 1989. Another distinguished scholar, the late R.A.C. Parker, came through two studies of Chamberlain and Churchill, both in their way sympathetic, to support the latter's view that a 'Grand Alliance' against Hitler ought to have been constructed but was not because of flaws in British policy.[5]

Nevertheless, the thrust of most work done since the seventies has been towards a more sympathetic appraisal of appeasement. We have to thank the work done by historians such as D. Cameron Watt, Maurice Cowling, Paul

Kennedy and David Dutton in particular for this. In writing this book, I have become more aware of this debt, but also of the tremendous burden that fell upon British Prime Ministers at a time when Britain was a *real* great power with the most daunting of global commitments.

Appeasement, which involves conciliation and attempting to understand rival viewpoints in interstate relations, is in fact the norm in international affairs. Diplomatic services are created to allow relations with other powers to be conducted on a rational and equitable basis. Sometimes this is not possible, and ultimately dealing with the Hitler regime was a case in point. In the post-1945 era, however, the western democracies, with all their experience of pre-war appeasement, still opted to seek accommodation successively with Franco, Salazar, Marcos, Pinochet, Suharto and, lest it be forgotten, Saddam Hussein. They did so not because, as in the case of the former Soviet Union, governments felt inhibited by a nuclear threat, but because the stability offered by right-wing authoritarianism and militarism offered certain attractions. And attempts allegedly to learn the lessons of pre-war appeasement, notably over the Suez Canal crisis of 1956, have been spectacular disasters. Pre-emptive strikes or collusion (replicated in the recent Iraq War) have not always proved effective vehicles for solving international problems.

Britain historically had always been a great power which had preferred to settle disputes by diplomatic means (think of Gladstone paying the United States compensation for damage done by British-built commerce raiders during the US Civil War). In this sense, therefore, appeasement was 'a normal continuation of the British diplomatic tradition of attempting to settle disputes peacefully'.[6] Whether this effort was pushed to unreasonable extremes by British Cabinets in the thirties is a question which this book will attempt to answer.

Armistice

At 6 a.m. on the morning of 11 November 1918 the British Prime Minister, David Lloyd George, was awoken by a phone call. The caller was Sir Rosslyn Wemyss, the First Sea Lord, a member of the British delegation to the Armistice negotiations with Germany. Wemyss told Lloyd George that the German delegation had signed the Armistice in a railway carriage provided by the Allied Commander-in-Chief, Marshal Ferdinand Foch.[1] The news came as a relief to Lloyd George. There had been some doubt about whether the Germans would agree to sign the Armistice terms and end the bloody carnage which had enveloped Europe for four years.

Lloyd George met his Cabinet colleagues at 9.30 a.m. The Cabinet authorised nationwide celebrations, with bells being rung, gun salutes and military bands. But, in this moment of great rejoicing, Lloyd George warned his colleagues about the need for magnanimity. 'The future peace of the world', he told them, 'will depend more on the way in which we behave after victory than upon victory itself.'[2] While he did so, massive crowds were forming outside 10 Downing Street and Lloyd George greeted them from the doorstep shortly after 11 o'clock. After a hasty lunch, he then went to the House of Commons to make a statement, telling its members that the stroke of eleven o'clock that morning had put an end to 'the cruellest and most terrible war that ever scourged mankind'. He went on to utter an immortal phrase, 'I hope that we may say that thus, this fateful morning, came to an end all wars'.[3] Lloyd George then moved to adjourn the House, which went over to the church of St Margaret's Westminster for a service of thanksgiving.

It was Lloyd George's supreme moment. Becoming Prime Minister in the dark days of 1916, he had re-energised Britain's war effort and had become, in the parlance of the day, 'the man who won the war'. Two days before, at the Lord Mayor's Banquet on 9 November, he had been cheered to the echo by those present, who stood on chairs 'yelling and waving as he advanced along the aisle of the Guildhall'.[4] Yet, even in this moment of triumph, Lloyd George had planted the seed of the tree that was to become the notorious appeasement of Germany of the 1930s. For the moment, his plea for magnanimity was drowned amidst the government's stated intention during the December 1918 election that Germany should be squeezed 'until the pips squeaked', and that its fallen Emperor Wilhelm II should be hanged. Nevertheless, a marker for the future had been laid.

Few observers at the time would have guessed that, within four years, Lloyd George himself would fall from power forever when his Conservative coalition partners turned upon him in the autumn of 1922. Or that seemingly insignificant figures on that day in November 1918 would eclipse Lloyd George (who never held political office after his fall) in the struggle to ensure that the horrors of the First World War would not be repeated.

One of these seemingly grey men was Stanley Baldwin, who, in November 1918, was the Financial Secretary to the Treasury, a post he had obtained in 1916 after eight years of solid, if uninspiring, service as a Tory backbencher. Baldwin, born in 1867, had been too old for military service in the war and was acutely aware of the price Britain had paid for victory, writing on the day of the Armistice, 'The strain of the last few days has been great, and I think a good many people are nearer tears than shouting today'. He, too, attended the service at St Margaret's Westminster and found three impressions strongest in his mind: 'thankfulness that the slaughter is stopped, the thought of the millions of dead and the vision of Europe in ruins'.[5] Baldwin, who was a sensitive and humane man, was never to forget the impact of the catastrophe on Britain.

In Birmingham, as in London, the rejoicing was loud and long on Armistice Day. This was the city of the Chamberlains: 'Radical Joe', who had founded the family's fortunes in the nineteenth century, and his son, Austen, the Chancellor of the Exchequer in 1918 and a future Foreign Secretary. But the least promising of the trio (or so it seemed to contemporaries) was to outshine father and half-brother alike. Neville Chamberlain had been Lord Mayor of Birmingham, building upon his father's power and influence in the city, and this role, together with Austen's recommendation, had caused Lloyd George to appoint him as Director General of National Service in 1917. On Armistice Day, Birmingham Council declared a general holiday in the city. The Armistice happened to coincide with the installation of the new Chancellor of Birmingham University, Sir Robert Cecil. Afterwards he and Neville Chamberlain, who had been a strong supporter of the university since its inception, went to Edgbaston to inspect university buildings there which had been taken over by the medical authorities to help house the wounded. Chamberlain observed 'many of the men with white faces and closed eyes, while the organ peeled out a cheerful fantasia and the church bells were ringing'.[6] At this very time, when the nation rejoiced over its military victory, Chamberlain lost his own sister, Beatrice, who died in the cruel influenza epidemic which carried off so many in the last months of 1918. His favourite cousin, Norman, had been killed on the Western Front in December 1917, and as an older man, like Baldwin, Chamberlain was acutely aware of the sacrifice the younger generation had made in the conflict. The only book the future Prime Minister ever wrote was a memoir of his cousin Norman,[7] who had written to him from the Front saying that the horrors of trench warfare should never be allowed to happen again. It was a plea which Neville Chamberlain never forgot, but in November 1918, at the age of fifty, he had yet to enter Parliament. Back in Whitehall, Robert Vansittart, then a junior official, but later to be Permanent Under-Secretary at the Foreign Office, was at work in his office on 11 November. He wrote later that 'someone let off loud crackers outside my office, and girls fainted before they could take cover ... A vast elation reigned; Mafeking Night was nothing to it'.[8] Vansittart was, like everyone, affected by the loss of friends and family in the war, but he was soon, as he noted, to be 'smitten by *mea culpism*' where the subsequent treatment of defeated Germany was concerned.[9]

Miles to the south in the Sussex countryside, Vansittart's colleague, Nevile Henderson, later to be Ambassador to Berlin, was out shooting rabbits on the family estate at Sedgwick when the church bells rang to signal the end of the war. 'I went home at once', Henderson wrote in the second of his two memoirs,

> packed my bag, and travelled up to London that evening. One felt one must be there to see how the people reacted after the long strain of war. I went to a music hall and to a restaurant. It was an unforgettable experience, and I felt myself more like crying than laughing.[10]

Henderson had tried to join the army during the war but the Foreign Office had refused to let him enlist. Nevertheless, like many contemporaries, he became convinced that war was an appalling evil which must be prevented at all costs.

These men had not actually fought in the great conflict, but one who had was Anthony Eden, the son of a minor baronet in County Durham, who had been made the youngest brigade major in the British army in 1918. Eden had lost his younger brother, Nicholas, at only sixteen years old, in the battle of Jutland, just as he was to lose his own son in the closing stages of the Second World War. Looking back at the end of his life in a memoir entitled *Another World*, Eden described how he 'had entered the holocaust still childish and I emerged tempered by my experience, but with my illusions intact to face a changed world'.[11] He even considered a career as a professional soldier before opting for a political career in the Conservative Party.

Eden emerged physically unscathed from the war, but another man with whom his political career was closely linked was not so fortunate. Harold Macmillan was a publisher who had joined the Grenadier Guards in 1914. He was seriously wounded on the Somme in 1916 and invalided out of the army while a serious thigh wound healed. As a result of medical bungling by the army, the wound never healed properly and Macmillan suffered pain from it for the rest of his life. Shell fragments remained in his pelvis and it is probable that only his mother's decision to have him moved to a private hospital in London saved his life. On Armistice Day, Macmillan was still on crutches, having seen out the last two years of the war from a hospital bed.[12]

Macmillan was linked loosely in the thirties to Winston Churchill, who had made an extraordinary comeback by Armistice Day, after the failure of the Gallipoli landings in 1915–16 had seen his removal as First Lord of the Admiralty. He owed his reinstatement as Minister for Munitions to his pre-war friendship with David Lloyd George, but was regarded with distrust by both Liberals and Tories (whose party he had deserted in 1904). The war had excited Churchill, who alone amongst government ministers had actually served in the trenches in France, but, at the point when it ended, his political future was uncertain. He recorded the scene at eleven o'clock on 11 November in his usual vivid prose as he looked down from the window of the Hotel Metropole in London's Northumberland Avenue. 'Victory had come after all the hazards and heartbreaks in an absolute and unlimited form',[13] he noted, but, like Lloyd George, he inclined to magnanimity in victory.

Meanwhile, many hundreds of miles away in Germany, an embittered soldier heard in his hospital ward in Passewalk that the war had come to an end. Corporal Adolf Hitler was an Austrian by birth who had left his homeland in 1913 and joined the German army when war broke out. In October 1918 he had been badly gassed near Ypres in Belgium, and spent the last month of the war recovering from this experience, which left him temporarily blinded. He learnt that the German Empire of the Hohenzollerns had fallen on 10 November and that Germany was now a republic. Already a rabid German nationalist at the age of twenty-nine, the news traumatised him. He recalled his emotions in his book *Mein Kampf* published in 1924:

> I could stand it no longer. It became impossible for me to sit still one minute more ... so it had all been in vain ... Did all this happen only so that a gang of wretched criminals could lay hands on the Fatherland?[14]

Hitler could not accept either at the time, or subsequently, that the German army had been genuinely defeated, and this belief was to central to his whole political philosophy. No one would have believed, however, in November 1918 that this cranky, eccentric individual, whom his comrades in the army had deemed to be a misfit, would haunt all these British politicians and bring about a war more terrible than that which had just ended.

The Birth of Appeasement

The euphoria surrounding the Allied victory in November 1918 put Lloyd George in a position of electoral invincibility. He soon decided to go to the country in an atmosphere of passionate anti-Germanism. The popular call for Germany to be squeezed 'until the pips squeak' and made to pay for the cost of the war resonated throughout the land and throughout the campaign, which resulted in an overwhelming victory for the Lloyd George coalition government. Despite his initial reservations, Lloyd George, consummate politician that he was, never forgot that his mandate was now based on the premise that Germany must be punished for starting the war. The message in the right-wing *Daily Mail* was typical of the sentiment expressed during the December 1918 general election. It was that 'The Huns must pay'.[1] Lloyd George would have agreed. Who else would?

Such vengeful attitudes went against Lloyd George's earlier inclination, for in January 1918 he had renounced any right to impose a financial indemnity on Germany in a speech. As late as the autumn of 1918, the Prime Minister was still saying that the peace settlement must 'not be dictated by extreme men'.[2] But the post-Armistice attitude in Britain changed all that because Lloyd George was above everything a realist. A meeting of the Imperial Cabinet on 26 November decided that a Special Cabinet Committee should be set up to consider the size of any indemnity to be imposed upon Germany. It was, it has been observed, 'a startling change of policy',[3] but one which allowed Lloyd George to win his electoral victory, even if he was still a Liberal leader who relied on Bonar Law's Tory masses in the House of Commons to keep him in power. And the setting up of the Indemnity Committee showed that Lloyd George was in tune with public opinion which demanded German gold instead of more German blood. The last months of 1918 were not a time when generosity to a defeated enemy was likely to prosper.

Yet within just a few years, and certainly by January 1923, when France invaded Germany's key industrial centre in the Ruhr, the British government and British public opinion had made a complete volte-face on the German question. This was despite the fact that France had taken action because Germany had defaulted on some of its reparations payments, which entitled it to respond. The Treaty of Versailles had created a reparations regime and the French were observing the letter of the law. But the British government disassociated itself from French (and Belgian) action in the Ruhr.

How did such a change come to pass? It began imperceptibly in 1919 when, even before the Treaty of Versailles was signed, British leaders began to doubt the wisdom of a punitive approach. As early as March 1919, for example, Lloyd George's government strongly resisted French attempts to continue the blockade of Germany (which had contributed significantly to its defeat) until the peace treaty was signed. Instead, Britain forced the French to agree to suspend the blockade permanently. Already British opinion was swayed by a humanitarian response to reports of German civilians starving because of the blockade.[4] To continue a blockade in such circumstances seemed immoral, and morality was at the heart of the genesis of appeasement.

The real dividing of ways with France came when the terms of the treaty itself were announced in Paris. The immediate reaction inside the British delegation was that these terms were manifestly unfair. The Germans had been given the right to plead their own cause at a later stage, but there was a widespread British perception that the French were being ruthless and unforgiving. Germany was deprived of its colonies and forced to give up territory to France, Belgium and Poland, as well as having to accept military clauses which restricted its army to 100,000 men and prevented its use of military aircraft and submarines. Worse still for some members of the British delegation was the infamous article 231. This obliged Germany to accept responsibility for starting the war and the threat of punitive reparations that might, in the eyes of British critics, cripple the German economy for years to come.

The first and best known of these critics was John Maynard Keynes, the brilliant Cambridge economist, who was disgusted by the way in which the treaty terms had ignored the Fourteen Peace Points produced by President Woodrow Wilson in 1918 (Keynes was equally disgusted by what he saw as Wilson's betrayal of his own principles). These included the principle of self-determination for national and ethnic groups, which Keynes and others believed had been thrown aside by a treaty which deprived Germany of territory in the so-called Polish Corridor and control of the German-majority city of Danzig. (Curiously Keynes opposed the breaking up of the Austro-Hungarian Empire.)

The difference between Keynes and the other British delegates in Paris was that he, unlike his colleagues, was prepared to make his criticisms public. These appeared in his book, *The Economic Consequences of the Peace*, published six months after the Treaty of Versailles was signed in the famous Hall of Mirrors on 28 June 1919. It was a devastating critique of the treaty, especially its reparations clauses. No individuals were spared. Wilson was scathingly dismissed and Lloyd George was described, not entirely flatteringly, as 'this syren, goat-footed bard, this half-human visitor to our age from the hag-ridden magic and enchanted woods of Celtic antiquity'.[5] This view has been recently dismissed as 'romantic nonsense',[6] for Lloyd George was, as he proved during the negotiations, a hard-headed realist. Britain's war aims were achieved with the confiscation of the German High Seas Fleet (subsequently scuttled at Scapa Flow in a last act of German defiance) and colonies, and Lloyd George's adroit insistence that Germany should foot the bill for Britain's war pensions. Only then did he join Woodrow Wilson in criticising France's financial and territorial exactions with their pro-Polish bias in the east.

Keynes dwelt on a higher moral plane. Not for him the sordid compromises that Lloyd George had to make with his allies, and his criticism carried all the greater weight because of his academic reputation and position as the Treasury's Chief Adviser at the Paris Peace Conference. His book, which can rightly be regarded as appeasement's founding text, was as much about morality as it was about economics. Keynes believed that the reparations clauses represented economic insanity (although, as an adviser, he had himself suggested a reparations figure of twenty billion pounds sterling when asked to do so). They would ruin European trade because Germany was an integral part of the continental economy. He also thought that the Treaty of Versailles was immoral because it had flagrantly ignored Wilson's Fourteen Points, conniving in its final form with the old, corrupt secret diplomacy of the pre-war era which President Wilson had affected to despise. For Britain's chattering classes, Keynes soon became the hero of the hour, as much for his witty and insulting references to the 'Peacemakers' as for his devastating assault on the terms of Versailles. In the shadows, however, without the glare of publicity which Keynes had deliberately brought upon himself, was another equally influential figure. This was the South African leader, General Jan Christian Smuts, who has been described as an 'inspirational figure by virtue of his towering integrity, the principled consistency of his critique of Versailles, and his ceaseless efforts to modify and humanise it'.[7] It was Smuts who persuaded Keynes to publish his criticisms of the treaty, and he who coined the memorable phrase that Versailles was 'a Carthaginian peace'. On 28 June, the very day that the treaty was signed, Smuts had protested strongly against its terms to Lloyd George. Smuts had been a guerrilla leader in the Boer struggle against British imperialism between 1899 and 1902, but he admired the magnanimity which the British had displayed towards his people in the post-war settlement. It was for this reason that Smuts had joined the Imperial Cabinet during the First World War to become a trusted and admired colleague of Lloyd George. But he was also a tenacious colleague who led the Empire delegation's strong demand for treaty revision when it met Lloyd George on 31 May after the draft treaty terms had become available. It is with some justice, therefore, that he has been described as the 'leading appeaser' in the British and Empire delegation at the Paris Peace Conference.[8] When Lloyd George made a sarcastic reference to Smuts's eagerness to annex former German South-West Africa under the new League of Nations mandate system (which gave German and Turkish ex-colonies to Allied powers until they were deemed ready for independence), the barb failed to dent Smuts's belief in his mission to save world peace. In Smuts's view, South-West Africa was unimportant compared with the threat to global harmony posed by Versailles.[9]

Smuts, who had been sent by the British government on a mission to Central and Eastern Europe after the war was over, was appalled by the privation that he found there. In Vienna, he and colleagues had eaten lunch at Sachers, a luxury restaurant, which Smuts thought to be a grossly insensitive error. He announced that in future his mission would 'not take anything from those starving countries'.[10] He bristled with indignation about conditions in Budapest but dismissed the threat posed by the new Communist leader, Bela Kun, describing him as a 'little oily Jew, fur coat rather moth-eaten – stringy green tie'.[11]

Smuts could be scathing about those members of humanity unfortunate enough to be outside the boundaries of the British Empire. Slavs in general he described as 'kaffirs', a pejorative term used for blacks in South Africa, and such prejudices certainly flavoured his attitude towards Versailles and its sister treaties of St-Germain, Trianon, Neuilly and Sèvres, which dealt with Austria, Hungary, Bulgaria and Turkey respectively. If Lloyd George became irritated by Smuts's moralism, to Smuts Lloyd George was a disappointment, a man too easily swayed by electoral considerations. Yet Smuts, too, whom Boer leaders nicknamed 'Slim [clever] Jannie', had a realistic streak that was deployed when it suited him. It was he who worked with Lloyd George to make an issue out of British war pensions and to insist that the defeated Germans should pay for them. Although Keynes resigned in disgust from the British delegation before the publication of his book, Smuts remained at his post. Though reluctant to sign the Treaty of Versailles, he persuaded himself that it was his duty to do so while continuing to claim that it was a war treaty rather than a peace treaty. He was contemptuous of realists like the British Foreign Secretary, Arthur Balfour, whom he accused of ruthless pursuit of British national interests. For Smuts, article 231, the war guilt clause, was an insult to German pride, and he refused to sit on an Austrian reparations committee because he thought it ludicrous to penalise a bankrupt state.[12]

Lloyd George refused to consider extensive revision of the treaty. He, after all, had to consider the views of Wilson and the doughty French leader, Clemenceau, whose abrasive response to Wilson's prized League of Nations concept based on his Fourteen Points was that 'the Lord God had only ten'. Nonetheless, Lloyd George's personal contribution to the genesis of an appeasement mentality was considerable. In particular, he provided the celebrated Fontainebleau Memorandum, which ranks alongside Keynes's *Economic Consequences of the Peace* as one of the founding texts of British inter-war appeasement. This document was actually drafted by Philip Kerr, another member of the British delegation and later (as Lord Lothian) a noted appeaser in the 1930s. In it, Lloyd George warned that:

> You may strip Germany of her colonies, reduce her armaments to a mere police force and her navy to that of a fifth-rate power; all the same, in the end if she feels that she has been unjustly treated in the peace of 1919 she will find means of exacting retribution from her conquerors.[13]

Here was prescience indeed which entitles Lloyd George to be categorised as one of Britain's earliest appeasers, although his criticism of Versailles also opens him to the charge of hypocrisy. Britain, after all, had got precisely what it wanted from the treaty; only when it had done so did he castigate others for greed and vengefulness. Above all, the memorandum was a deliberate attack on French policy for deliberately trying to emasculate Germany and storing up trouble for the future.[14]

Lloyd George's apprentice, Philip Kerr, a nephew of the Duke of Norfolk, was one of the most influential of the doubters in the British delegation in Paris. He had been a member of Lord Milner's famous 'Kindergarten' in South Africa, a group of young men (others were Geoffrey Dawson, the editor of the *Times*, and Lionel Curtis, both critics of Versailles) who worked for reconciliation in post-war South Africa, and believed that British magnanimity there should also be applied to Germany. He wanted a 'tough but not a vindictive peace',[15] but he reached this position only after thinking at first that it was impossible to revise the treaty. Such inconsistency has caused Kerr's mind to be compared with 'a weathervane'.[16]

In many respects, Kerr's experience was typical of the experience of those who became mainstream appeasers in the thirties. He had actually drafted article 231 of the treaty as well as its antithesis, the Fontainebleau Memorandum, while also being responsible in June 1918 for the refutation of the official German criticisms of Versailles. But back in London, Kerr came to see the evils of the treaty and its consequences for Germany. He changed his mind and, tormented by 'his own complicity in this blunder, he was burdened by his Versailles guilt complex ever after'.[17] Lloyd George was made of tougher stuff than Kerr. If he had doubts about the treaty, they were linked to the follies of others. He did not agonise in the watches of the night about the wrongs done to Germany.

Kerr came to believe that the French had been vindictive at the Peace Conference, and suspicion of the French and their motives was widespread amongst the Versailles sceptics in 1919. Indeed there was more to it than that, for there lurked in British imaginations a primal fear of the reckless and over-emotional Gallic tendency to exaggerate the German peril. French civilisation itself was suspect, and Robert Vansittart (who was part of the British delegation) told of how his great aunt, hearing that the young man was going to Paris for the first time, threatened to cut him off without a penny if he did so. 'She thought', Vansittart wrote many years later, 'Paris was a wicked place. The Victorian view was that the French practised all sorts of occult forms of sexual intercourse and were the wildest people on earth.' Vansittart thought the British were prone to make the same sort of political judgement about the French. 'If you went to Paris, you would catch some politico-venereal disease. They would infect you with their ideas and guarantees.'[18] Above all, the French wanted an Anglo-American guarantee against German aggression, which Lloyd George promised and then reneged on, when Wilson failed to secure US ratification of the treaty and his country retreated into decades of isolationism.

Nevile Henderson also feared entanglement in French designs. He was present when the Versailles Treaty was signed, being then Second Secretary at the Paris Embassy. Henderson wrote of how 'the Germans were left bitter and resentful' and complained of the numerous and 'violent attacks on us in the French press'. For Henderson, the future envoy of appeasement, 'Fear and Hate, those two worst of counsellors, were the guiding influences so far as the French were concerned'.[19] His view was shared by many others in the British establishment.

There were a few dissenters. Harold Nicolson, whose book *Peacemaking 1919* became a classic account of Versailles, was another member of the British delegation who worried about the treaty settlement. But he could understand French anxieties. 'I quite admit', he wrote in his book, 'that the French cannot see beyond their noses. But they are after all their noses: and my word, what they *do* see, they see damned clearly.'[20] More typical was what the feline Foreign Secretary Arthur Balfour said of the French at the time of their Ruhr adventure in 1923. They, Balfour believed, 'are so dreadfully afraid of being swallowed up by the tiger, that they spend all their time poking it'.[21] By 1923, indeed, the British were no longer convinced that it was not France that was the tiger and Germany the lamb. This was a process which had been underway since 1919, when the British delegation was alarmed not just by the substance of Versailles but also by the manner in which it was imposed, which Nicolson and others thought needlessly humiliated the German delegates during the signing ceremony. For Keynes, Smuts, Nicolson and Kerr, French arrogance was personified by the brusque way in which Clemenceau had conducted business during the framing of the treaty. Nicolson later recorded the French leader's technique, ' "*Y-a-t-il d'objections? Non ... Adopté.*" Like a machine gun.'[22] For this reason, 'a wave of Francophobia swept up many influential people in public life in Britain'.[23]

The fact that there were so many concerns about the settlement led to the formation of what nowadays might be described as a lobby group for appeasement. On 30 May 1919, at about the time that the draft terms of the Treaty of Versailles were presented to the German delegation, a group of like-minded

Foreign Office officials in Paris formed the Institute of International Affairs, better known today as Chatham House, the Royal Institute of International Affairs. The Institute's members were Harold Nicolson, Allen Leeper, Arnold Toynbee and Edgar Abraham. Nicolson left the Foreign Office in 1930 to become a politician and writer (married to another distinguished writer, Vita Sackville-West) and Toynbee became an eminent historian, but Leeper stayed inside the Foreign Office. An important ally was Lord Robert Cecil, who had been Minister of Blockade in the wartime coalition and was another member of the British delegation in Paris. Another was James Headlam-Morley, a historical adviser at the Foreign Office.[24] Chatham House, as the institute became known, was an elitist, frequently pro-German organisation designed to enlighten 'other less discerning members of the same magic circle'.[25] It also had very strong links with Oxford University, many members being Fellows of All Souls. If appeasement needed an intellectual forum, Chatham House provided it. Distrust of Versailles and its ills motivated most of the membership.[26]

It is important, however, to appreciate that revisionism as far as Versailles was concerned went well beyond the narrow confines of the Institute of International Affairs. For when the Imperial Cabinet (composed of members of the British Empire delegation plus members of the British Cabinet) met over the weekend of 30 May to 1 June 1919, everybody there was against the terms of Versailles as then put forward. Present at the meeting were not only the Australian, New Zealand and Canadian representatives (plus Smuts and Louis Botha for South Africa), but also Churchill (Secretary of State for War), Milner (Colonial Secretary), Lord Chancellor Birkenhead, Austen Chamberlain (Chancellor of the Exchequer) and Edwin Montagu (Secretary of State for India). The consensus against Versailles at this meeting has rightly been described as 'remarkable'.[27]

Yet most of these men did not, like Smuts, oppose Versailles on moral grounds. Their reservations were tactical, and they were swayed in particular by the existing international situation which involved problems outside the narrow perspective of the German peace settlement.

Churchill in particular was alarmed at the prospect of a vindictive peace driving the Germans into the hands of the Russian Bolsheviks, who had seized power in November 1917, following the overthrow of Tsar Nicholas II the previous March. He had argued for a swift end to the Allied blockade lest orderly government break down in Germany, thus creating a situation which could be exploited by revolutionary Communism (as it was, there were two Communist putsches in Berlin and Bavaria in 1919).

It was essential in Churchill's view that France should 'moderate her vindictive policy' towards Germany and accept British good offices in creating an improved Franco-German relationship.[28] In a characteristically vivid phrase, Churchill described his policy as 'Kill the Bolshie, Kiss the Hun'.[29] The term 'Bolshie' itself rapidly entered the English language to represent undesirable antisocial behaviour in Britain itself.

Churchill was accused of being obsessive about Russia and he was certainly the greatest enthusiast for Britain's ill-fated intervention there in 1918–20 (Lloyd George was less keen). But Churchill also described Versailles as being 'harsh and excessive',[30] though, like other colleagues in the Cabinet he exaggerated the impact the treaty had on Germany, just as the Germans (predictably) did themselves. When, in 1921, the Allied powers finally fixed the figure for German reparations payments at £6.6 billion in gold marks, there was much German bleating, which conveniently ignored the devastation of northern France and Belgium by the German army during hostilities. But by 1923 certainly, British statesmen were being convinced of French unreasonableness and German victimhood.

Of those present at the meetings of May–June 1919, Churchill, Chamberlain, Birkenhead, Milner and Montagu can all be described as tactical revisionists. They believed not that the Treaty of Versailles was immoral, but that it needed revision in the interest of creating a positive post-war relationship with Germany. Lloyd George's reservations were significant, but in the end he felt obliged to stand by the treaty as 'an instrument of redress, restitution and even of retribution'.[31] By the time he came to write his war memoirs (his memoirs only appeared in the late thirties), time put a different gloss on the 1919 peace settlement, but Lloyd George was more pragmatic at the time than he would later allow.[32] Nonetheless, his Fontainebleau Memorandum had given post-war appeasement a fair wind alongside Maynard Keynes's book and Smuts's behind-the-scenes agonising.

Britain and France had already fallen out over policy in the Near East, when the Chanak Crisis of 1922 found Lloyd George backing the Greek invasion of Asia Minor while France and Italy withdrew in the face of the Turkish revival led by Mustafa Kemal. France's police action in the Ruhr in January 1923 therefore merely compounded Anglo-French tensions. Chanak had brought down the Lloyd George coalition in November 1922, but there is nothing to suggest that he would have opposed the policy that his Tory successor, Andrew Bonar Law, adopted over the Ruhr. Bonar Law and his colleagues believed that France's action was of dubious legality, but otherwise stood aside as Franco-Belgian troops occupied the area.[33] In 1921, by contrast, when Germany had also defaulted on its reparations payments, Britain had joined in Franco-Belgian police action in the Rhineland, although a repeat offence by the Germans in 1922 found Britain refusing to support its allies in taking punitive action. Historians have tended to focus on January 1923 as the greater crisis, but Britain's refusal to act in 1922 was more than a mere straw in the wind, marking as it did a parting of the ways with France over the reparations issue. Conveniently forgotten in Whitehall was the failure to honour the 1919 guarantee to France which was at the root of the latter's insecurity.

Austen Chamberlain, soon to become Foreign Secretary in the Conservative government, was one of the few British politicians to understand French insecurities. Most saw the French as a real and present danger to European security, including the then Foreign Secretary, Lord Curzon, who warned that France's dominant air power and growing submarine fleet would make it 'possible for her to dictate her policy to the whole world'.[34] Some were even convinced by the wild suggestion of the RAF chief, Lord Trenchard, that the superior French airforce could be used to blackmail Britain into supporting French policy. Bonar Law discussed his foreign policy concerns with his new Paymaster General, the fifty-three-year-old Neville Chamberlain,[35] but in May 1923, Bonar Law's poor health forced him to stand down in favour of the Chancellor of the Exchequer, Stanley Baldwin.

Baldwin, whose lack of interest in foreign policy has been frequently exaggerated, thought that at the root of Britain's post-war economic difficulties was the reparations issue and the Ruhr occupation. He vowed on inheriting the premiership to 'try and settle Europe'.[36] Meanwhile in Berlin the British Ambassador, Lord D'Abernon, a Lloyd George appointee with a background in international banking (which reflected Lloyd George's lack of faith in the Foreign Office), was in no doubt where the blame lay over the Ruhr imbroglio. D'Abernon thought that Franco-Belgian action was 'an act of unwarranted aggression against Germany', and that morality decreed that the British government intervene by means of diplomacy, and even by force if need be, to preserve German sovereignty against French rapacity.[37] D'Abernon deserves more recognition as an early appeaser, and his appeal to morality was in tune with an important theme in inter-war appeasement. Britain must protect Germany against the French bully, or at the very least act as an impartial mediator in Franco-German quarrels.

As it was, Anglo-American financial pressure soon forced the French to remove themselves from the Ruhr. Following the London Conference of 1924, the American Dawes put forward a plan which both rescheduled and reduced German reparations payments. In this way, what has been described as 'a curious cycle of dependence' was established.[38] American money subsidised German reparations payments which in turn allowed Britain and France to repay their considerable debt to the United States in respect of wartime loans. The Americans had been unsympathetic about Anglo-French complaints about the level of repayments, their famously taciturn President Calvin Coolidge remarking 'they hired the money didn't they?' But now US loans to Germany created a brief period of prosperity in that country, which seemed likely to make the reparations regime work. British financiers and bankers were as anxious as their American cousins to see Germany restored to its place in the European economy, and French economic planning was based on the assumption that 'the Boche will pay'.

Economic reconstruction coincided with a brief era of hope in great power relations. Its linchpin was the 1925 Treaty of Locarno, as a result of which Germany voluntarily accepted the new Franco-German and German-Belgian frontiers as laid down by Versailles, and also (through Locarno articles 42 and 43) the demilitarised status of the Rhineland's west bank as decreed by Versailles. In the following year, Germany was belatedly allowed to join the League of Nations.

Austen Chamberlain was one of three statesmen (the others being Briand and Stresemann) who conceived the Treaty of Locarno. For his work he subsequently received, as did his fellow statesmen, the Nobel Prize for Peace. Locarno did not, however, require German acceptance of the newly-established frontiers between Germany and its Eastern European neighbours, and in particular, the so-called Polish Corridor which cut Germany in two. Ominously, the Germans referred to the new states of Poland, Czechoslovakia and Yugoslavia as *Saisonstaaten* – implying that, like the seasons, they would be transitional rather than permanent. Austen Chamberlain was not unduly perturbed by such attitudes; for him the Polish Corridor was an issue 'for which no British government ever will or ever can risk the bones of a British grenadier'.[39]

Such a remark should not occasion surprise given the context. Central and Eastern Europe was unknown territory for British statesmen and the territorial settlement there was of very recent vintage. Chamberlain thought the area to be inherently unstable, and agreed with his predecessors at the Foreign Office that its value might lie only in providing the territorial compensation needed to maintain the balance of power in Western Europe.[40] Otherwise, Eastern Europe in particular was a nuisance. In 1914, Queen Mary had talked of war 'for tiresome Serbia'. By 1938, confused Tory backbenchers were still talking about Czecho*slovenia* rather than Czechoslovakia.

This confusion was mirrored by the British government's ambivalence about the area. At the time of Locarno, Chamberlain told D'Abernon that in getting 'additional security in the West, I think we do not in fact lessen the danger of war in the East'.[41] The east harboured the dangerous Bolsheviks with whom few Tories wanted any truck. Paranoia about Bolshevism had after all contributed to the first Labour government's electoral defeat in 1924, when the notorious 'Zinoviev Letter' (now recognised to be a forgery) appeared to show that the Bolsheviks were plotting to subvert British democracy. Meanwhile, there was rejoicing about the new 'spirit of Locarno' which ended Germany's status as a European pariah. The British satirist and MP A.P. Herbert, wrote about 'Locarney Blarney', and a plethora of ballrooms and dance-halls were named after the shiny new treaty throughout Britain.

As the twenties drew to a close, Britain, like numerous states, signed the 1928

Kellogg–Briand Pact (the cornflakes family had spawned a Secretary of State), which renounced war as an instrument of national policy. The reparations regime was modified again in 1929 when the US-sponsored Young Plan rescheduled German debt again right down to 1988. Austen Chamberlain lost office in 1929 when a second minority Labour government came into power. His successor, Arthur Henderson, 'Uncle Arthur' as he was known in the corridors of the Foreign Office, was more sympathetic to the USSR than his Tory counterpart and therefore exercised about European disarmament, but otherwise British foreign policy altered little. The death of the conciliatory German Foreign Minister Gustav Stresemann in the same year proved to be a watershed as far as the unfortunate Weimar Republic was concerned, but most significant of all was the crash of the US Stock Market in New York in a black week in October. In a matter of months, the prosperity of the twenties in the United States turned to ashes, and with it, the long-term prosperity of Britain and Europe.

In 1930, the biggest shadow which lay across Britain in the minds of men and women was the memory of the Great War. Its most potent symbolic form was the Armistice celebration each 11 November, with the whole country brought to a standstill by the two minute silence (a format cast aside after 1945 and then reintroduced, in voluntary form, in the 1990s). Literature too reminded the British of their sacrifice and their disinclination to repeat it. Between 1928 and 1930, for example, Sherriff's *Journey's End*, Blunden's *Undertones of War*, Graves's *Goodbye to All That* and Sassoon's *Memoirs of An Infantry Officer* were all published, the authors all being men who had seen service in the First World War. The poetry of Sassoon and Wilfred Owen (killed in the very last weeks of the war) also cursed the fate of the hundreds of thousands who had indeed been, in Owen's phrase, 'doomed youth'. In Germany, an enraged Hitler, now starting to make his mark in German national politics, castigated Remarque's *All Quiet on the Western Front* for its pacifist defeatism (the book was subsequently made into a distinguished Hollywood film).

Nevertheless, criticisms of the war came not just from front-line soldiers but also from those who had given the orders.[42] Lloyd George's memoirs have already been referred to, but Churchill's *World Crisis*, and the memoirs of Viscount Grey of Falloden, the former Liberal Foreign Secretary, both concluded, like Lloyd George, that the outbreak of war in 1914 had been the result of 'overzealous militarism and excessive secret diplomacy'.[43] But for a man who had not fought in the war or had a place in its high councils, a relative's warning rang out over the years.

Nothing but immeasurable improvements will ever justify all the damnable waste and unfairness of this war – I only hope those who are left will *never, never* forget at what sacrifice these improvements have been won.[44]

So wrote Norman Chamberlain to his cousin Neville in 1917, pulling at the heartstrings of the man who was to become the world's most celebrated and notorious appeaser. Guilt lay at the roots of appeasement, guilt over the young men who had died in their prime, and guilt that a defeated enemy had been treated too severely. To understand this is to begin to understand the desperate struggle to preserve the peace in the 1930s.

3

Hitler Comes to Power

In the aftermath of the Wall Street Crash, the German economy collapsed. American loans to Germany under the Dawes and Young Plans were withdrawn, and the Germans, who had invested in long-term projects such as the electrification of their railway system, soon found that the brief recovery of 1924–28 was in jeopardy. Economic distress (unemployment had reached six million by 1932) was combined with political authoritarianism. The aged President Hindenburg used an emergency decree provision in the Weimar Constitution to rule via a series of personal favourites. The first of these, Brüning, was soon named 'The Hunger Chancellor' because of his deflationary policies; the second, von Papen, was a lightweight ex-cavalry officer with no political support in the Reichstag. The last Chancellor of the supposedly democratic republic, von Schleicher (aptly translated into English as 'creeper), was a general whose manoeuvring failed to counteract the rise of the Nazis, resulting in his dismissal in January 1933.[1]

Adolf Hitler had become the leader of the biggest mass party in Germany with his devastating attacks on Versailles and Weimar. By 1932, the Nazis were polling as many as fourteen million votes and, even though Hitler was defeated by Hindenburg in the presidential election campaign, he clearly had a popular mandate that demanded his inclusion in the government. He was also astute enough to hold out for the Chancellorship rather than accept some lesser post under Papen or Schleicher. Ultimately, President Hindenburg, whose aristocratic pedigree in Prussia made him contemptuous of the 'Bohemian Corporal' (an odd confusion since Hitler was an Austrian and not a Sudeten German), felt obliged to appoint Hitler Chancellor on 30 January 1933.

British reaction to the Nazi phenomenon was mixed. Some observers were impressed by the vitality and élan of the Nazi movement, but Robert Vansittart was not one of them. He had already become alarmed by the state of German politics, noting how 'Germans, no longer able to beat up aliens, rounded on each other ... All Germany was demoralised'.[2] Yet Vansittart, often regarded as the arch anti-appeaser, conceded the justice of many of Germany's grievances. He felt that Germany had a case in 1931 when it pressed for a customs union with Austria (forbidden by article 80 of the Treaty of Versailles), and that German complaints about French unwillingness to disarm were fully justified. He was convinced, in his post of Permanent Under-Secretary at the Foreign Office, that the German case at the Geneva Armaments Conference (which had been dragging on for two years) was 'on every ground of morality and equity exceedingly strong'.[3] In fact, Vansittart was not as anti-German as critics accused him of being, but he was wary of German intentions, especially after Hitler came to power in 1933. Nevertheless, the fact that he could see the justice of Germany's demand for equality in armaments (he also conceded that Germany was 'entirely within her rights' in building the new pocket battleship *Deutschland*, which technically infringed the naval clauses of Versailles), merely underlined the tendency of the British establishment to seek redress for German grievances.[4] Vansittart's emphasis on 'morality' is surprising in view of his later reputation as a professional anti-German, but it also reflects his disillusionment with French policy. Lacking the reassurance of an Anglo-American guarantee, France insisted on maintaining its military superiority over Germany. Vansittart, however, would never be anything other than a tactical appeaser, whereas men like Lord Lothian were thoroughly convinced of the moral evil imposed by Versailles.

Others were concerned about whether Germany could remain stable under the new regime. Thomas Jones, for example, a close associate and friend of Lloyd George, wrote in his diary on 7 February 1933 'that if Hindenburg can be kept alive for another two years, they may escape civil war. If not, there will be civil war at once on his death'.[5] Jones was on equally friendly terms with Stanley Baldwin, then effectively deputy Prime Minister to Ramsay MacDonald in the National Government set up in 1931 to counteract the impact of the Great Depression, and influenced his thinking on Germany.

He was, of course, wrong. Hindenburg's death in August 1934 merely gave Hitler the chance to consolidate his power by merging the positions of Chancellor and President. Some weeks earlier, at the end of June, Hitler had also shown his ruthlessness by executing Ernst Röhm, the head of the paramilitary SA, and others who had shown the temerity to question his regime's behaviour. Jones registered his own disgust that 'an intelligent nation should submit tamely to such a government'.[6] By 1936 Jones had altered his position. In May of that year, he had an interview with Hitler and tried to persuade Baldwin (by then Prime Minister) to meet him. The meeting never took place, but Jones, like others, was seduced by Hitler's apparent modesty. 'He is a complete contrast to Mussolini', he wrote, 'and made no attempt whatever to impress or "aggress" his visitor.'[7] By 1937 Jones was pressing for the removal of Sir Eric Phipps, the British Ambassador in Berlin, on the grounds that he had 'no telephone line to Hitler' because he was too prejudiced against the Nazi regime.[8] Jones had come round to the opinion that, however deplorable the internal policies of the Nazis might be, peace could only be preserved by applying a more emollient policy to Anglo-German relations. Appeasement morality could be applied only to international relations, but this was not an unreasonable position at the time.

Hitler's greatest British conquest was in fact Jones's master, Lloyd George, who had also convinced himself that Versailles was flawed, although not as a consequence of any errors perpetrated by himself. In September 1936 Lloyd George himself, accompanied by Jones, went to Germany and visited Hitler in his mountain retreat at Berchtesgaden. At this point Hitler had already been in power for more than three years and had started to show his hand by making aggressive moves against the Versailles system. In 1933, he had walked out of the Geneva Disarmament Conference and left the League of Nations. By 1935, he was confident enough to announce peacetime conscription and the existence of the Luftwaffe (a clear breach of Versailles). This was followed in March 1936 by an illegal movement of German troops into the demilitarised Rhineland.

It might have been expected that Britain's senior wartime statesman would have castigated Hitler for his flagrant breaches of the treaty. But this was far from being the case. In two conversations with Hitler, the second in the company of his daughter Megan and his son Gwilym, on 4 September 1936, Lloyd George was full of compliments. The invitation to go to Germany, which had come via the newly-appointed German Ambassador to London, Joachim von Ribbentrop, had 'tickled his vanity'.[9] According to Hitler's long-serving interpreter, Paul Schmidt, Lloyd George told the German Führer that 'I deem myself lucky to meet the man who, after defeat, has united the whole German people behind him and led them to recovery'.[10] In the Schmidt account, Lloyd George also appeared to cast doubts about the usefulness of collective security (whose virtues foreign opponents of Hitler constantly stressed) by saying that 'alliances are always dangerous'.[11]

Lest it be thought that German accounts in the period are not wholly reliable (and it must be conceded that they are not), Lloyd George's comments are confirmed by British testimony as well. While it is true that Lloyd George declined Hitler's invitation to attend the annual Nazi Party rally at Nuremberg, saying that such a visit would not be understood in Britain, he was effusive in his praise of the Führer. This is clear both from the account written up by Thomas Jones and that left by Lloyd George's private secretary, A.J. Sylvester.

When he returned from his first talk with Hitler at the Berghof, with its magnificent view of the Bavarian Alps, Lloyd George was described as being in 'a state of elation, enraptured at the success of the talks and infatuated with Hitler'.[12] He reportedly told Sylvester that Hitler was 'a very great man. Führer is the proper name for him, for he is a born leader, yes, and a statesman'.[13] The two men, Lloyd George told his Private Secretary, 'got on like a house on fire'.[14] Another man present on the occasion was T.P. Conwell Evans, the Secretary of the Anglo-German Fellowship, who recorded Lloyd George's emotional response when Hitler presented him with a signed photograph of himself. The former Prime Minister, wrote Conwell Evans, got up: 'with a sob in his throat, he declared that he was honoured to receive it from the greatest German of his age'.[15]

Alarmingly, Lloyd George told Hitler that Ribbentrop's appointment to London was welcomed in London in part because of 'his personal qualities'.[16] When it is remembered that Ribbentrop was a totally inept ambassador who alienated everybody in London (not least by the Hitler salute he gave King George VI at his first audience), to such a degree that he was nicknamed 'von Brickendrop', one is entitled to ask whether Lloyd George's age (seventy-two) had undermined his judgement. This may be too severe. Lloyd George was sincere in his belief that Anglo-German relations should be put on a sounder footing. In this he was at one with the appeasers, and he was a war leader who had railed against the wasteful tactics of generals like Haig for throwing away the lives of countless British young men.

Hitler played on such memories sedulously. He had already charmed delegations of British war veterans with his accounts of his own wartime experiences and with protestations about his desire for peace. Now he turned his attentions to Lloyd George whom Jones records as being told by Hitler that 'it was realised in Germany that if the war was won by the Allies, it was not due to the soldiers, but to one great statesman – Lloyd George'.[17] In response, Lloyd George told Hitler that he was currently completing the last volume of his war memoirs and that he had written of how, if Hitler had been Führer between September and November 1918, 'a better peace would have been negotiated, for the German collapse was so complete'.[18]

In one respect, Lloyd George was guilty of a very serious misreading of Hitler's intentions. He had read *Mein Kampf* but still came back to England saying that Hitler 'has no desire to absorb millions of Slavs, whom he despises and would regard as an offence to the doctrine of racial purity'.[19] The explanation given by his long-standing mistress and personal aide, Frances Stevenson, that this was because Lloyd George only had an expurgated version of *Mein Kampf* which contained no reference to Hitler's desire for living space in Russia, fails to convince, given the plentiful references to such an intention.[20] Miss Stevenson, later to be Lloyd George's second wife, continued to believe thirty years on that Lloyd George could somehow have secured a political agreement with Nazi Germany, had he possessed the necessary political power.[21]

So did Lloyd George himself, who told Conwell Evans in 1937 that the failure to reach an Anglo-German accord in 1935–36 was a result of the 'hesitancy and nervelessness of the Baldwin administration'.[22] Such sentiments go some way to explain Lloyd George's intrigues in the summer of 1940 when he seemed to be prepared to play the role of a British Pétain, should Churchill be forced to resign.

The case of Lloyd George offers an important insight into British attitudes. Here was a man with a wealth of experience of foreign affairs, who though ageing was by no means a spent force, and who still hankered after the post of Foreign

Secretary even in 1935 (Baldwin's massive electoral victory in November destroyed any such possibility.) Lloyd George was also a man who had a low opinion of Baldwin and his successor, Neville Chamberlain. Yet even he, a Prime Minister who had run a war and dealt with men like Clemenceau, could not read Hitler correctly. Small wonder that those less gifted than Lloyd George, with less of a flair for foreign affairs, found the German dictator such a difficult opponent.

Lloyd George was also by instinct an appeaser, a fact his role in bringing down the Chamberlain government in 1940 has tended to obscure. True, he called for more rearmament, but this was part of his appeasement policy also. But his conviction that he alone could have brought about Anglo-German détente was surely a matter of hubris.

If the heavyweight Lloyd George was so impressed by Hitler, it is not surprising that others also found Hitler's protestations of innocence convincing. Winston Churchill denied that he was one of them, and condemned Lloyd George for his credulity. 'No one,' he wrote in 1948, 'was more completely misled than Mr Lloyd George, whose rapturous accounts of his conversation make odd reading today.'[23] Churchill went on to claim that 'All those Englishmen [Lloyd George would not have been best pleased by this attempt to categorise him as English] who visited the German Führer in those years were embarrassed or compromised'.[24]

In condemning what was a private visit by Lloyd George, who was not representing the British government in any way, Churchill was being somewhat disingenuous. He himself visited Germany in 1932 and, while he was in Munich, agreed to a meeting with Hitler, which had been set up by Ernst 'Putzi' Hanfstaengl, a Harvard-educated playboy who had become an intimate of the Nazi leader.[25] The fact that the meeting never took place was due to Hitler's unwillingness to meet Churchill because, he told Hanfstaengl, 'no one pays any attention to him'.[26] Churchill criticised Nazi anti-Semitic policies in conversation with Hanfstaengl, but there is no particular reason to believe that he would have been more resistant (at least at that stage of his career) to Hitler's blandishments than Lloyd George. He had, after all, been greatly impressed by Mussolini, saying that, had he been an Italian, he would have supported him. Churchill seems in his war memoir to have been struck down by a convenient literary amnesia. In 1935, well after Hitler's assumption of power in Germany, he was still unsure whether Hitler

> will be the man who will once again let loose upon the world another war, or whether he will go down in history as the man who restored honour and peace of mind to the great Germanic nation and brought it back serene, helpful and strong, to the forefront of the European family circle.[27]

It is therefore clear that even Churchill himself was not as rigorously consistent on the Nazi issue as he subsequently liked to pretend.

If Churchill remained confused by Hitler, moral appeasers like Lothian were not. He recognised that the Nazi regime was essentially brutal and ruthless, but he thought that Hitler had restored German honour and given the country stability. Nazism, he believed, was a consequence of the inequities of Versailles, and its restless nationalist spirit could only be appeased by recognising the need for concessions. He met Hitler in January 1935 and was told by the dictator that 'war was a great madness'. Lothian was encouraged and thought the solution simple; 'Treaty revision by pacific means, by negotiations between equals'.[28] There was no need to work through the tiresome League of Nations or to cooperate with the equally tiresome French. Lothian's activities were regarded with suspicion by the Foreign Office, who regarded him as an amateur diplomatic pest.

Lothian's house at Blicking in Norfolk was a meeting place for like-minded appeasers. One of them was the influential Geoffrey Dawson,[29] the Editor of the *Times* who, like Lothian, had been a member of Milner's Kindergarten in South Africa. He too lamented Versailles's numerous injustices. When Hitler illegally entered the Rhineland with his forces in 1936, Dawson's leader in the *Times* appeared under the headline 'A Chance to Rebuild'. Even more famously, Dawson told Lothian a year later that he spent his nights 'taking out anything which I think will hurt their [the Germans'] susceptibilities and in dropping in little things which are intended to soothe them'.[30] Dawson spoke with great authority, especially to foreigners, who regarded his newspaper as the authentic voice of the British government (it was true that Dawson was on close terms with both Baldwin and Chamberlain). He was a strong ally of the Government during the thirties, and of its efforts to reach an accommodation with Germany. Waldorf, Lord Astor, and his wife Nancy, the owners of Cliveden, made notorious as a sort of melting-pot of appeasement through the so-called 'Cliveden Set', were also active appeasers. In fact, the set's influence on policy was nothing like as great as opponents of appeasement suggested.[31] Nevertheless, Astor too was impressed by what Lothian told him about his interviews with Hitler (Lothian made another visit to Germany in 1937). He wrote to the sympathetic Editor of the *Observer*, J.L. Garvin, about how Hitler was 'genuinely anxious for understanding with the British Empire'.[32]

Astor owned both the *Times* and the *Observer* and was therefore in a position to influence the reaction of the British public to Nazism, although there is no evidence that he intervened with editors to impose a particular line in the way in which the press barons, Beaverbrook who owned the *Express* papers and Northcliffe who owned the *Daily Mail* did.[33] But the line taken by both the *Times* and the *Observer* had been sympathetic even before Hitler came to power, because both Dawson and Garvin were anxious to help create an Anglo-German understanding. So too was Dawson's deputy editor, Barrington-Ward, who later became Editor of the *Times* himself.

The *Times* believed, under Dawson and Barrington-Ward's stewardship, that a Nazi-dominated government would not do 'any real harm' and, shortly after his appointment in 1933, its view was that Hitler possessed both 'sincerity' and 'personal magnetism'. It went on to say that Hitler was 'ultimately manageable if the proper tactics were adopted'.[34] This proved to be the ultimate problem for the appeasers both in government and outside it. What were the 'proper tactics' for dealing with as mercurial a creature as the German Chancellor? He continued to confuse so that even the liberal *Manchester Guardian* could suggest that the Nazis were merely 'ordinary politicians when in office'.[35] This judgement followed the moderate behaviour of Hitler's underling Wilhelm Frick, the first Nazi to assume office as Interior Minister in the state of Thuringia. It encouraged what became a special characteristic of the appeasement mentality in its dealings with Nazism, which was the idea that some Nazi leaders were 'moderates' who could rein in the extremism of their fellows.

Such thinking was also found in the Foreign Office, where the future Under-Secretary, R.A. Butler, a convinced appeaser, wrote in 1935 of how the Hitler Youth Movement impressed because of its 'public spirit'.[36] Butler was typical of a certain type of Tory who found the Nazi emphasis upon physical exercise and communal activities rather admirable. If the Nazis could be thought of as a kind of rather eccentric Boy Scout movement, they might become more intelligible to a British audience. Even when Nazi behaviour shocked, this was not Britain's business. Internal developments were a matter for the German government not the British. This was an attitude firmly in line with British policy, going back to the days of Cobden and Bright in the nineteenth century. With the advantage of hindsight, it is easy to castigate such a position, but the position of the appeasers was rational. The administration of foreign countries was a matter for foreign governments. If they began to transgress, by menacing other states and threatening British interests, that was another matter.

People in the Labour Party had a different perspective. They thought that the First World War had been caused by greedy capitalists and armaments manufacturers, the merchants of death. They were strong believers in disarmament where the Tories were not. The appearance of Hitler, therefore, put them in a dilemma, especially as he attacked and destroyed the infrastructure of Labour's sister Social Democratic Party in Germany. The first concentration camp at Dachau was full of Social Democrats and Communists by the end of 1933.

Things were made even more difficult for Labour by the fact that the party was split by Ramsay MacDonald's decision to form a National Government to solve the economic crisis in 1931. MacDonald was deserted by the Labour rank and file and branded as a traitor, but the party was slaughtered at the polls in the 1931 election. A few leading Labour figures, including the Chancellor of the Exchequer, Snowden, remained in MacDonald's Cabinet, but he was heavily reliant on Tory support for survival.

MacDonald was replaced as Labour leader by the Christian pacifist George Lansbury, who went to visit the Führer in 1935 and found him to be 'a mixture – dreamer and a fanatic', but free of personal ambition. Bizarrely, Lansbury hoped that 'Christianity in its purest sense might have a chance with him'.[37] By 1935, however, Lansbury's moment had passed and he was attacked in devastating fashion by the Transport and General Workers' Union boss, Ernie Bevin, at the party conference. The issue in this instance was Mussolini's pending aggression against Abyssinia. Bevin accused Lansbury of 'hawking your conscience round from body to body asking to be told what you ought to do with it'.[38]

Christian Socialism of the Lansbury type would plainly not do in dealing with Hitler, but the Labour Party remained in some confusion about how to react to the Nazi dictator. Clement Attlee, for example, who replaced Lansbury as leader he resigned the day after Bevin's assault, was slow to perceive what Nazism was about, even though, as a major in the First World War, he was no pacifist. Only when he went to Germany in 1933 for a conference and was confronted by 'very tough-looking Nazis' did the reality behind Nazism impose itself upon him; and even then, like other party colleagues, he was reluctant to support the rearmament programme which Tories like Baldwin and Chamberlain wanted to implement.[39]

The most celebrated Labour anti-appeaser of the thirties was Hugh Dalton, a former academic at the London School of Economics who had been an Under-Secretary at the Foreign Office during the 1929–31 Labour government. Dalton was in Berlin for four days at the end of April 1933, where he was given ample evidence of Nazi brutality. He met a Jewish professor called Emil Lederer who had been sacked from his post, and who told him that Nazis had ransacked his flat and stolen his valuables.[40] The daughter of another professor (one of some ninety academics sacked by the Nazis), Dalton was told, had been branded on her leg with the Swastika. 'Germany', Dalton concluded, 'is horrible.'[41]

Yet how could Hitler be stopped when the Labour Party, though shocked by Nazi persecution of socialists, opposed British rearmament? It did not trust the Tory imperialists to use armaments wisely, and some Labour supporters did not even trust the League of Nations. (Stafford Cripps, a leader of the sister Independent Labour Party, denounced it as 'the international burglars' union' in 1935.)[42] Dalton was sufficiently alarmed, however, to sponsor a document at the meeting of Labour's National Executive in 1934 that declared Labour to be in favour of collective security while saying nothing about the means to be used (notably rearmament) to resist Hitler. This statement of Labour policy was accepted by a large majority at the 1934 Labour Conference. Nevertheless, despite its detestation of Fascism in all its European varieties, Labour could still not bring itself to vote for the armed services estimates because of its distrust of the Tories. A few of its members, including Dalton and Bevin, came to see that the only language the Nazis understood was force, or the threat of force, but the resistance of the Labour movement to rearmament is not surprising. Pre-war militarism was blamed for the outbreak of the First World War by Labour supporters and, when Hitler came to power, Britain was 'only fifteen years away from the carnage of the Western Front'.[43] In 1933, the Socialist anti-war candidate John Wilmot won an overwhelming by-election victory at East Fulham against a pro-armaments Tory. So strong was the fear of war that, even in establishment Oxford, the students memorably voted for a motion declaring that 'This House will in no circumstances fight for King and Country', despite the efforts of Churchill's son, Randolph, to sabotage the motion. Whatever internal evils Nazism might be guilty of, therefore, British public opinion, be it left or right inclined, was determined to avoid war. Meanwhile, the balding Dr Hugh Dalton, with his booming voice and domineering manner, waged an internal campaign to get Labour to recognise that anti-Fascism needed teeth.

The National Government that took power in 1931 was dominated by the Conservative Party. Tories were, by and large, more likely to be impressed by the rightness of Germany's case against Versailles than the case for disarmament, but, like Labour, they were alarmed at the prospect of another war. The leading Tory in 1933 was Stanley Baldwin, who had survived an attempt to oust him as leader while in opposition. Contrary to myth, Baldwin was not ignorant about or uninterested in foreign affairs,[44] but like others he was puzzled by the Nazi phenomenon. As late as 1935, he was saying 'no one knows what the new Germany means – whether she wants peace or war',[45] but he was not ignorant about what the Nazis were doing in Germany. War was the ultimate horror for Baldwin, who saw it as 'the most fearful terror and prostitution of man's knowledge that was ever known'.[46]

Increasingly, after the National Government was formed, Baldwin was the leading man in the Cabinet, as the intellectual capacity of the ageing Ramsay MacDonald ('the Boneless Wonder' as Churchill cruelly called him) dwindled. Baldwin's main supporter, Neville Chamberlain as Chancellor the Exchequer, also feared war but was never the credulous Germanophile of legend. While on holiday in Germany in the early thirties, Chamberlain wrote of 'how I loathe the Germans'.[47] He was 'the packhorse' of the Conservative Party who took on many burdens, including an interest in defence and foreign policy. As Chancellor, he was concerned that the British economy, which was emerging from a most serious recession, might be adversely affected by an overlarge commitment to rearmament. It is a nonsense to suggest, however, that Baldwin and Chamberlain opposed rearmament, or that the government failed to recognise the German threat. Hitler's behaviour might be puzzling (one of his first foreign policy moves was a cunning non-aggression pact with the despised Poles in January 1934), but the fact that he might be a threat was fully recognised.

The most solid evidence for this was the government's decision to set up a Defence Requirements Committee in 1934. This was a special sub-committee of the Committee of Imperial Defence, convened to determine what impact the international situation would have on the needs of the armed services. On it sat Maurice Hankey (the Cabinet Secretary) representing the government, Vansittart and Fisher (the Permanent Secretary at the Treasury and an ally of Chamberlain's) together with the armed services Chiefs. The Defence Requirements Committee reported that Germany was 'the ultimate potential enemy against whom our "long range" defence policy has to be directed',[48] while Japan, guilty of aggression in Manchuria in 1931, was seen to be a secondary threat. The committee's conclusions were accepted by the National Government at a point well ahead of Hitler's numerous breaches of Versailles. The debate, therefore, was never about *whether* there was a German threat but about the *resources* which could safely be allocated to deal with it. This debate about the relative balance between military and non-military needs is one that must take place in any government.

Most Tory backbenchers agreed with the government line on Germany and continued to do so. One who did not was Harold Macmillan, who was loosely associated with the Churchill anti-appeasement group. Yet even Macmillan recognised as late as 1936 that Britons had a bad conscience about Germany. On 20 March, Macmillan wrote in the *Star* newspaper, 'We remember what we refused to Liberal Germany [and] how far we have been responsible for the triumph of Hitler'.[49] Unease about Versailles troubled even those who came to believe that policy towards Germany was dangerously adrift. One of these was Bob Boothby, who had been Churchill's Parliamentary Private Secretary when he had been Chancellor of the Exchequer in the 1920s. He was a frequent visitor to Germany and wrote in old age of the way 'in which Hitler managed to impart his own hysteria to the vast audiences which he addressed'.[50] Boothby's concern, however, was 'less about the character of the Nazi regime than air superiority'.[51] This was actually a position which placed Boothby closer to government supporters than he might have recognised. Government policy was to be more and more concerned about the German aerial threat. In 1933 this was puny, but the government already knew (as did the French) that the Germans had been blatantly infringing the Versailles clauses relating to air forces for years. As early as November 1932, Stanley Baldwin made his famous statement that 'the bomber will always get through',[52] underlining official concern about British vulnerability to air attack. This anxiety added another dimension to an appeasement policy initially fuelled by guilt over the peace settlement, and fear of another great conflagration in Europe. It explains the persistent British attempts after 1933 to secure German agreement to a pact to reduce air strengths.

Macmillan and Boothby would not have considered themselves to be in the Conservative mainstream on Anglo-German relations. One MP who was, Henry

'Chips' Channon, was a wealthy American socialite who reflected both the anti-treaty and anti-French tendency in the Tory Party. On 16 March 1935, Channon wrote in laconic style in his diary, 'Today's big news is that Germany has decided to rearm, and has ordered conscription. This means the end of the Treaty of Versailles. I think France, as usual, is to blame.'[53] Somehow, in Channon's mind, a German breach of Versailles could be blamed on French unreasonableness. If not entirely logical, Channon's comments show how many Tories held the French refusal to disarm to blame for Germany's illegal decision to rearm (which in reality had been made years before Hitler came to power in 1933). This meant that, in the minds of appeasers, Versailles was indefensible. All that could be attempted was an ordering of the concessionary process, so that Germany would not use violence to achieve redress.

The last bastion of conservatism in Britain was as ever the monarchy, and George V reflected the feelings of his people in the 1930s. In 1935 he told the then Foreign Secretary, Sir Samuel Hoare, 'I am an old man. I have been through one world war. How can I go through another? If I am to go on, you must keep us out of this one.'[54] George had many German relations, some of whom (like the Duke of Saxe-Coburg-Gotha) were overtly Nazi, and he had only avoided acute embarrassment in the First World War by changing his family name to Windsor from the Teutonic-sounding Saxe-Coburg-Gotha. Once the war was safely over, however, George V 'embraced an extreme pro-appeasement stance which was to percolate through his family'.[55] This was not because of pro-German sentiment, as both George and his German-born Queen Mary of Teck worked hard to create an image of loyal Britishness. Both his sons knew about the horrors of war, as the Prince of Wales had served in France and Italy (although not as a front-line soldier), and he had seen at first hand what trench warfare could mean. Prince Albert, the future George VI, had taken part in the Battle of Jutland. All the royals believed that a disaster like the First World War must be prevented at all costs.[56]

Recent suggestions that Edward, Prince of Wales was some sort of crypto-Nazi fail to convince. This dashing young man was politically gauche to an extreme, but, even as someone who had been shielded from active participation in the war, he was haunted by the needless deaths of many young men of his own generation. As King Edward VIII in 1936, he raised absurd Nazi hopes that he might become some sort of British Quisling.[57] Forced to abdicate in December 1936, as a result of his ill-fated relationship with the American divorcée Mrs Wallis Simpson, the Duke of Windsor, as he became, subsequently embarked on a thoroughly ill-judged visit to Nazi Germany in 1937, clearly against government wishes. The visit included an interview with Hitler at Berchtesgaden that was widely condemned in Britain, although Hitler (as ever when he wanted to impress foreign visitors) was 'conspicuously affable'.[58] There is more than a suggestion of pique about the visit as retaliation for George VI's decision not to accord the Duchess of Windsor the normal title of 'Her Royal Highness'. But one of Edward VIII's biographers concludes, probably fairly, that 'the worst that can be said about the German visit is that the Duke closed his eyes to most of what he did not wish to see, and allowed himself to be paraded as an admirer of the economic miracle'.[59] Edward, like many of his class and type, was a man of increasingly right-wing views who found the order and community spirit brought by Nazism attractive. In part, this was because, like many right-wingers, he had a morbid fear of Soviet Communism, and tended to see Nazism as a counterweight to it. But he was no pacifist and supported rearmament. When pacifists criticised the Officer Training Corps in public schools, Edward retorted that it was a mystery to him

> that a certain number of misguided people ... should feel that the only way in which they can express the feeling we all have of abhorrence of war ... is by discouraging, and if they are in authority prohibiting, any form of healthy discipline and training.[60]

The Duke of Windsor's visit to Germany was an embarrassment, particularly in the light of George V's efforts to establish the Britishness of the Windsor dynasty. But his successor, George VI, and his wife, Queen Elizabeth, were equally sympathetic to the policy of appeasement pursued by Baldwin and Chamberlain. Neither expressed the sympathy for Nazi achievement that the Duke of Windsor misguidedly did, but they admired Chamberlain and, in equal measure, disliked Churchill, who had not helped himself by creating, or trying to create, a 'King's Party' to defend Edward VIII in 1936. The views espoused by the royal couple were, however, in no sense shocking. They reflected the views of the mass of the British people in their fervent desire to avoid war.

The British reaction to Nazism, therefore, reflected the anxieties of the day. Guilt about Versailles remained deeply etched into the British psyche, and with it the hope that Hitler's protestations about his desire for peace would turn out to be genuine. Even those like Churchill who later won plaudits for seeing through the German dictator were not in fact quite as perspicacious about Nazi Germany as they later claimed. And Lloyd George, who denounced Chamberlain as a dullard and a good Lord Mayor Birmingham in an off year, still found much to admire in the German Führer in 1936 when his transgressions against the 1919 peace settlement were already clear for all to see. Yet in the minds of the appeasers, and the group included journalists, civil servants and royals as well as politicians, such transgressions were in themselves seen to be a result of the unjust Versailles Treaty. Redress of German grievances, it was believed, would surely result in more emollient behaviour in Berlin, and harmony in Europe.

In the meantime, the British government watched events warily. Lacking US support for military intervention, the British felt unable to act against Japanese aggression in Manchuria in 1931, while Hitler's behaviour seemed at the outset to have positive and negative features. In October 1933, Germany withdrew from both the Disarmament Conference at Geneva and the League of Nations. Yet in January 1934 Hitler signed a non-aggression pact with Poland, which was a surprising act for an extreme nationalist known for loathing the Versailles Treaty and all it stood for.

The British government was keen to secure German agreement to treaty revision. In January 1934, it proposed that Germany be allowed an army of three hundred thousand men, and an air force which would be half the size of the French one. As the British failed to offer France any further guarantee of its own security, the new Domergue government refused to agree to the British proposal. Then, in July 1934, Hitler encouraged Austrian Nazis to try and overthrow the Austrian government in Vienna, and the Chancellor Dollfüss was murdered. The attempted coup failed, and Hitler had to hand over the murderers of Dollfüss for punishment. Was this failed coup an indication of aggressive intent on Hitler's part? At the time, no one in London was sure, as the extent of the Führer's involvement was unclear. Nevertheless, the possibility that Hitler was working to undermine the Versailles system was accepted. This was why the Defence Requirements Committee had recognised Germany as the primary threat to Britain, while also noting the possible danger posed by Japan in the Far East.

Between 1931 and 1934 the global context in which British foreign policy was operating had, therefore, changed profoundly. Imperial Japan was becoming an aggressive and rapacious power in Asia, while Nazi Germany had to be recognised as a potential threat to European security in a way Weimar Germany had never been. A xenophobe like Hitler was never going to accept the status quo in Europe, but would judicious concession persuade the German dictator to avoid violent unilateral solutions? Storm clouds had begun to appear on Britain's horizon, and there was no certainty that Europe's other dictator, Benito Mussolini, with his Mediterranean ambitions ('our sea' the Italian Fascists like to call the Mediterranean), would observe the norms of international behaviour.

The British appeasers peered into an uncertain future, but it would be a nonsense to maintain that they were dismissive of potential threats. As early as 17 May 1933, the then Foreign Secretary, Sir John Simon, referred in a Cabinet paper to Germany as the 'mad dog' of Europe and said that Britain must call its bluff.[61] While it is true that Simon's hard line would only follow a German refusal to pursue disarmament talks, the Foreign Secretary's tough talk sits ill with the callow and craven image of him in more traditional anti-appeasement accounts. Simon and his colleagues, including the then Prime Minister Ramsay MacDonald (although his powers were on the wane), could not, and would not, ignore the threat posed by Hitler, whose intention to dismantle Versailles and expand eastwards had been made clear in *Mein Kampf*, *unless* a conciliatory British policy could persuade him to recognise the perils involved in such aggression.

Four Appeasers

The four men who dominated the process of foreign policy formulation in the 1930s were Stanley Baldwin, Neville Chamberlain, Anthony Eden and Edward Wood, Viscount Halifax. A fifth man, Ramsay MacDonald, Prime Minister from 1929 to 1935, was influential in the first half of the decade, but by the time the external threat had been clearly identified his powers were waning, making him the despair of his colleagues. Their characters and values form an intrinsic part of the background to appeasement.

Stanley Baldwin seemed to be the most quintessentially English of Prime Ministers. 'The Squire of Bewdley', as he was often nicknamed, personified the English virtues of quiet dignity and moderation, and the dignified pipe-smoking individual who peeps out at us from contemporary newsreels cultivated the image of the country-loving Englishman throughout his political career.[1]

Born in 1867 in Bewdley, Worcestershire, Baldwin's origins were industrial rather than rural. His father, Alfred Baldwin (photographs show a splendidly hirsute Victorian figure), was a third-generation ironmaster. Nor was Baldwin wholly English, for his mother, Louise MacDonald, was half Welsh and half Highland Scot. His love of poetry and literature can perhaps be attributed to his Celtic blood. There was a dreamy, introspective side to Baldwin's nature that manifested itself in a deep spiritual faith. His mother was the daughter of a Methodist minister and remained a loyal Methodist all her life, but Alfred Baldwin abandoned Methodism to become a high church Anglican. Throughout his life Stanley Baldwin, though an Anglican himself, valued his Free Church heritage.[2]

From his father, Stanley also inherited his Conservatism. Alfred Baldwin was Tory MP for the Bewdley division of Worcestershire from 1892 until his death in 1908. He was a patriarchal figure who got on well with workers in the family forge in Wilden, and Stanley acquired valuable skills as a manager while working for his father. Alfred also prized family relationships, being one of six children. One sister married Lockyard Kipling (the father of Rudyard) and the two men became close friends. Another married the painter, Edward Burne-Jones.

Stanley Baldwin did not look back on his schooldays as the happiest days of his life. He first went to Hawtree preparatory school near Slough before being sent to Harrow (to his surprise, as he had expected and hoped to be sent to Eton). At

Hawtree, the young Baldwin showed considerable intellectual promise. He continued to do so at Harrow, winning prizes in History and Mathematics. His father had great hopes for him, but at the end of his third year, Baldwin was involved in a damaging scandal that concerned the writing of juvenile pornography. The headmaster of Harrow, Montagu Butler, chose to make a *cause célèbre* of the episode, not so much because Baldwin (like others) had been caught in typical adolescent misbehaviour, but because he had sent a sample of his naughtiness to his friend Ambrose Poynter at Eton. He had, therefore, become the boy who 'supplied Harrow filth to Eton'.[3] Butler chose to send for Alfred Baldwin about the incident Stanley was flogged and was never made a school monitor as expected. Thereafter his academic performance declined, perhaps as a consequence of a feeling that he had been unjustly treated. He left Harrow a year early in 1885.

Baldwin was not the first great man to suffer from a miserable experience at public school. It is dangerous, therefore, to read too much into the Harrow episode, save perhaps to reflect on Baldwin's later aversion to dictatorship of any sort. And the powers of an English public school headmaster before 1914 were as absolute as that of any tyrant. At all events, a pattern of academic underperformance continued. When Baldwin went up to Trinity College, Cambridge, he began well with a First at the end of the first year, but got a Second at the end of the second and an unimpressive Third at the end of his final year. This erratic scholarly performance was combined with a surprising failure to make any impact in college. Baldwin made few friends and his total failure to contribute resulted in a request for him to resign from the Trinity debating society. The arrival of Montagu Butler as Master of Trinity a term after Baldwin went up to Cambridge may not have helped his prospects, as relations with his former headmaster remained tense. It probably affected Baldwin's decision to drop Classics in favour of History, which, in turn, may have affected the class of his degree. Sharp disappointment over his son's failure at Cambridge may have occasioned the uncharacteristically bitter comment by Alfred Baldwin that he hoped Stanley wouldn't 'have a Third in life'.[4] Alfred was not, however, the savage critic of his own son that Lord Randolph Churchill was of the youthful Winston, and the two men were to work together amicably enough until the elder Baldwin died. For twenty years, Stanley laboured in the family firm as second-in-command to his father without complaining unduly about his lot. After a period in a rented house in Wilden (from which he used to cycle to the family forge), Baldwin moved to Astley Hall, near Stourport, where he lived in some style until his own death in 1945. A new wing to the house was built and as many as ten gardeners were employed.

In 1892, Stanley Baldwin married Lucy Ridsdale, whom he had met while staying with the Burne-Joneses at Rottingdean in Sussex. Lucy was a more extrovert character than her husband and did not share his intellectual interests or his penchant for long country walks. By contrast, she had considerable talent as a cricketer and carried out the duties of a political wife loyally. Sophisticated Londoners may have sneered at Lucy Baldwin's odd hats but she was 'on the whole a very satisfactory wife'.[5] This was very important, as Baldwin, an uxorious man, was also prone to periods of lassitude and depression. The impression created by those who knew the couple well is that Lucy could 'jolly' Stanley along when one of these periods of introversion oppressed him.

Stanley and Lucy had six children, the eldest of whom, Oliver, proved to be a sore trial to his father (a difficult son was something he shared in common with Churchill). Oliver joined the Labour Party and broke with his father at the time of the 1923 general election which Baldwin lost. He went on to be an MP, but the breach with his father was finally healed and he ended his career in the ultra-respectable post of Commander-in-Chief of the Leeward Islands. The second son, Windham, or 'Bloggs' as he was known in the family, was an altogether less controversial figure. He had links with the literary world, while one of Baldwin's three daughters, Betty, wrote a book about her time in a nunnery.

In the period before his father's death, Baldwin lived the life of a respectable Tory gentleman. He was a committed Anglican like his father, a Justice of the Peace and a member of Worcestershire County Council. He also began to make a few political speeches in his father's Bewdley constituency. In 1904, he was adopted as the Conservative candidate for the neighbouring Kidderminster constituency. His political timing was unfortunate, however, because 1906 was the year of the great Liberal landslide and Stanley Baldwin was defeated. By contrast, Alfred Baldwin hung on to his seat.

Stanley did not enjoy the campaign, being drained by the experience, as he was not one of nature's natural baby kissers. He had to go on a walking tour in the Cotswolds to restore his energy, a period of recuperation which was to be typical of his political career, with bouts of hectic activity followed by lengthy spells of recovery. His character was finely tuned, and the roughhouse of politics had to be combined with lengthy breaks in the English countryside or on the Continent (especially at his beloved Aix-les-Bains).

When Alfred Baldwin eventually died, in 1908, Stanley was the natural heir to the Bewdley seat. With almost indecent haste, he was adopted as the new Tory candidate only two days after his father's death, and returned unopposed by the end of the month by a by-election. This followed a humiliating rejection for the City of Worcester seat, despite the personal recommendation of the great Joseph Chamberlain, who treated the nearby city of Birmingham as a personal fiefdom. Baldwin complained about being rejected 'in my own county town in favour of a stranger'.[6] His consolation was Bewdley, where he remained, his majority never threatened, for the next thirty years.

A solid if unspectacular period as a backbencher was followed, as has been seen, by a period as Financial Secretary at the Treasury, before he was catapulted to the post of Chancellor of the Exchequer in the wake of the collapse of the Lloyd George coalition. Senior Tories, including Austen Chamberlain, Balfour and Horne, were excluded because of their reluctance to serve under Bonar Law. This created unexpected opportunities for relative unknowns like Baldwin.

Baldwin presented just one budget in an unusually short speech, in which he brought income tax down from five shillings to four and six pence in the pound, and further pleased the working man by reducing the tax on beer and abolishing the one on cider altogether.[7] Five weeks after he gave his budget speech, Baldwin was Prime Minister, Bonar Law's poor health forcing him to stand down. Baldwin was preferred to the prima donnish Foreign Secretary Curzon, who also had the disadvantage of being a peer.

Baldwin was only in post for little over a year when he made one of the most audacious, and seemingly reckless, decisions of his long political career. In December 1923, he called a general election over the issue of tariff protection, with the result that the Tories lost eighty-six seats (although it is noteworthy that the actual Conservative vote only went down by half a per cent). Baldwin was concerned about the rising level of unemployment in post-war Britain, but his motive for calling the election does not appear to have been primarily economic. Baldwin had wanted to 'settle Europe' but the intransigent behaviour of the French Prime Minister, Poincaré, who sent French troops into the Ruhr in January 1923, prevented this, and Baldwin was heavily criticised for his foreign policy decisions. He also thought that tariff reform would help to reunite the Tory Party, bringing back the supporters of Austen Chamberlain, who had resented the way unknown figures like Baldwin had engineered the fall of the Lloyd George coalition in 1922. The decision to go to the country was in fact primarily political, an attempt by Baldwin to strengthen his authority, based on the belief in Conservative Party Central Office that the Tories could win.[8]

As it turned out, Baldwin had made a major blunder in underestimating the degree to which free trade was still a sacred cow in British politics. He himself had been a victim of Joseph Chamberlain's attempt to impose so-called 'stomach taxes' on the electorate in 1906 (the Liberal cry was that the Tories would force up the price of staples like bread), but seems to have forgotten this lesson in 1923. The Tory defeat in December 1923 meant that a minority Labour government, reliant on Liberal support, took office in January 1924. It did not last long and was voted out of office again in October 1924, when the Liberals deserted it.

Baldwin now began his most successful administration, while the foreign policy arena was fleetingly benign. He once again showed a capacity for the unexpected by appointing Winston Churchill as Chancellor of the Exchequer. Many Tories were appalled by the appointment, as Churchill had left the Tory Party in 1904 and had only recently rejoined it, but Baldwin felt that it was better to chain Churchill to Cabinet responsibilities, although it has also been suggested that he was swayed by Neville Chamberlain's disinclination to take the post (he preferred to retain his previous post of Health Minister). Churchill was surprised but grateful at the unexpected gift, telling Baldwin that he had 'done more for me that Lloyd George ever did' (Baldwin must have been gratified by this gibe against a man whom he loathed).[9] As matters turned out, Churchill was not a bad Chancellor, although he was misled by his professional advisers over the issue of the return to the gold standard.

Baldwin's Foreign Secretary was Austen Chamberlain, who was known for his pro-French sympathies. But the Cabinet would not endorse any firm commitment to a military pact with the French, although Baldwin fully backed Chamberlain's scheme for a four-power guarantee of Germany's western frontiers that was enshrined in the 1925 Treaty of Locarno (though the absence of any underwriting of the *eastern* settlement proved to be equally crucial in the long run).[10] The Cabinet Secretary, Maurice Hankey, was especially opposed to any additional guarantees being given to the French, but it is clear that Baldwin personally endorsed Chamberlain's policy before it was put before the Cabinet early in March 1925. It was therefore, unfortunate, from Chamberlain's point of view, that the illness of Baldwin's mother prevented him from being present at Cabinet to support his Foreign Secretary. This meant that the four-power pact would not include any permanent military commitment to France. More than that, there was a clique in the Cabinet, comprising Curzon, Balfour, Amery, Churchill and Birkenhead, opposed to any idea of continental commitment.[11] Baldwin's support for Chamberlain was, therefore, crucial and ultimately ensured that the Treaty of Locarno was signed by Britain.

This point needs emphasis, as it has become an historical myth that Baldwin was uninterested in foreign affairs. He had plenty of domestic concerns, such as the issue of the gold standard and the 1926 General Strike, but the documentary evidence does not support the view that Baldwin neglected his responsibilities with regard to foreign policy. Naturally he left the lion's share of responsibility to Austen Chamberlain, but Baldwin played his part in a context where, it has been observed, the government was divided between those who

> saw the empire as the primary focus and Europe as a secondary area, and a little Englander school which paid only marginal attention to the Empire and wished for no binding commitments to Europe.[12]

In this situation, Baldwin supported his Foreign Secretary's desire for a more pro-active policy as best he could. But even Chamberlain regarded Eastern Europe as being beyond the pale of British responsibility. Hence his celebrated comment about the Polish Corridor not being worth 'the bones of a British grenadier'. He never showed any real interest in negotiating an eastern Locarno, and this view reflected Baldwin's instincts as well. What followed in the 1930s, therefore, was a logical continuation of traditional British reluctance to get involved in faraway European commitments. Ultimately, however, Neville Chamberlain was to be castigated for *moving away* from his half-brother's injunction and intervening directly in the affairs of Central and Eastern Europe.

It was during his first administration between 1924 and 1929 that Baldwin published a little book of essays, under the title *On England*,[13] which gives us some insights into his views about politics and government. In it Baldwin's faith in the British democratic system shines through. Democracy he defined as

> government of the people by the people through their freely elected representatives, and unless the responsibility for that Government is felt throughout the length and breadth of the country, from top to bottom, by men and women alike, democracy itself will fail.[14]

The system demanded hard work, Baldwin believed, and a need for 'higher education, for further vision than any form of government known in this world'.[15] Totalitarianism was a personal affront to Baldwin because it destroyed democracy and human dignity; already in 1926, its tentacles were ensnaring the people of Mussolini's Italy.

Baldwin does not have the reputation for being a great imperialist in the way in which Churchill does. He nevertheless had a quiet pride in the Empire, and its indivisibility, which his cousin Rudyard Kipling would have recognised. The Empire was 'this great inheritance of ours, separated as it is by the seas, we have yet one home and one people'.[16] More than this, Baldwin looked to the Empire as 'the means by which we may hope to see that increase of our race which we believe to be of such inestimable benefit to the world at large'.[17] If the imperialistic tone jars with the modern reader, Baldwin's words reflected a pride in Empire which would have echoed with many of his fellow countrymen and women. With it went the assumption that British ways were best, and that Britain had a special role to order the world when its resources allowed it to do so. But already by 1926 Baldwin was learning how finite those resources were.

Baldwin had a proper English middle-class disdain for the press. When he was defeated at the polls in 1929, his leadership came under threat over the issue of India, which he saw as a key issue for mainstream moderate Conservatism. For, despite his love of the Empire, Baldwin came to see that India must be conceded some form of autonomy, a view which was bitterly contested by Churchill, who left the Shadow Cabinet over the issue. Churchill's allies in his campaign against Baldwin were the press barons, Rothermere and Northcliffe, both of whom saw Churchill as an alternative leader of the Conservative Party. In the spring of 1931, it seemed that Baldwin would have to go. On 1 March, Neville Chamberlain actually told his Cabinet colleague, Sir Samuel Hoare, that Baldwin had resigned.[18]

He little knew his man. Baldwin had no intention of standing down and horrified Chamberlain by threatening to stand in a by-election in order to reassert his authority. In doing so, Baldwin did just this, causing the *Times* hurriedly to withdraw a leading article entitled 'Mr Baldwin Withdraws'.[19] Baldwin's devastating dismissal of the press barons as men who had 'power without responsibility, the prerogative of the harlot throughout the ages' is well known. Less celebrated is his certainty that he would see Northcliffe and Rothermere off. Later Baldwin remarked, 'the Lord ... delivered Rothermere into my hands'.[20] In the end, it was little surprise that Baldwin's emollient qualities, together with a steely political spine, defeated the maverick brilliance of Churchill, whom many Tories continued to regard with suspicion, despite his recent Chancellorship. These steady Baldwinesque qualities were demonstrated at their best on the radio where, according to Hoare (later Lord Templewood), he 'gave the impression of an English countryman sitting at the end of the day in a comfortable chair in friendly conversation with two or three of his old friends'.[21] This was precisely the image that Baldwin was trying to create in the minds of his fellow countrymen and countrywomen.

Nothing could have been more alien to the pipe-smoking, cricket-loving Baldwin than Hitlerite Germany. He struggled to understand Nazi totalitarianism, telling his close associate Thomas Jones in September 1933, 'the world is stark mad. I have no idea what is the matter but it is all wrong and at times I am sick to death of being an asylum attendant'.[22] Despite his preference for the domestic agenda, Baldwin was quick to see the similarities between Fascism, Nazism and Communism,[23] and to recognise the need for rearmament. The problem, in Baldwin's view, was that Britain was a democracy and 'a democracy is always two years behind a dictator'.[24] This meant that the peace-loving British, with their vivid memory of the carnage associated with the Great War, would be reluctant to support great armaments. Such a programme, Baldwin knew, would arouse fears that war was inevitable and, as a political leader, he believed that rearmament needed the democratic consent of the British people. This was why he made his subsequently notorious pledge that there would be 'no great armaments' in an election speech in 1935.[25] He did not deserve the venom of Churchill's accusation in his war memoirs that he had put party before country,[26] because he valued Tory re-election above national security.

After Baldwin, Neville Chamberlain was the second man in the Tory Party, but he was a man of very different temperament. Some of Chamberlain's difficulties arose from the fact that, unlike Baldwin, he was not an emollient man of the people. He had a hard, abrasive edge that antagonised people, especially those who happened to be members of the Labour Party.

Neville had a difficult legacy. His father Joseph Chamberlain, arguably the ablest politician in the late nineteenth and early twentieth century not to become Prime Minister, did not have a very high opinion of his second son's abilities. Austen was the obvious politician in the family, while Neville seemed destined for a lifetime spent running the family businesses. But he had a particularly hard and wounding apprenticeship when he was sent by his father to grow sisal in the Bahamas at the tender age of twenty-one. The venture failed (losing Joseph about a million pounds in modern terms) after Neville had spent seven hard, grinding years on the island of Andros, where he was one of just three Europeans among eight hundred black labourers (with whom he apparently got on well).[27] At the age of twenty-seven Neville, who was never offered the opportunity of attending university, must have felt himself a failure. His half-brother was already an MP and a rising star at Westminster.

If this experience is added to an unhappy time at Rugby School, which Neville Chamberlain detested, it is not fanciful to speculate that later complaints about his spiky, public persona overlooked the difficulties that he had experienced as a youth. Baldwin, Eden and Halifax were all Oxbridge men (the last becoming a Fellow of All Souls College). By contrast, Neville Chamberlain was only allowed by his father to study Metallurgy and Engineering at Mason College in Birmingham. He lacked the social assurance of his peers, did not marry until he was forty, and arguably covered a sensitive personality with a combative outer shell. In the security of his domestic circle, Chamberlain was a different man, as those who knew him well attested,[28] and his marriage to Annie de Vere Cole, the daughter of an army officer, was a successful one. They married in 1911 and remained together for thirty years until Chamberlain's death, the marriage producing a son and a daughter.

The image of Chamberlain as the narrow-minded provincial business-man who should have remained content with the position of Lord Mayor of Birmingham dies hard. But the accusation that Chamberlain was ignorant about foreign places and foreign ways (linked to his notorious 1938 radio broadcast about Czechoslovakia being 'a faraway country') cannot be sustained. He loved Italy, which he visited frequently on holiday, and also travelled widely in France, Germany, Egypt, the United States and Canada. Although averse to politics as a very young man, he took an increasing interest in international affairs. He was critical, for example, of Britain's pre-war ententes with France and Russia, showing a distrust of collective security which prefigured his appeasement policy in the 1930s. 'The real enemy is Germany', he wrote to a friend in 1908, 'and they [the agreements] are even worse than useless against her. It seems to me that they may very possibly drag us into a war but will be little help if war should come.'[29] Far from being the pacifist of legend, Chamberlain was infuriated when the then Liberal Government refused to lay down four extra dreadnought battleships.[30]

At the centre of Chamberlain's political life lay the conviction that he was carrying through his father's legacy. Joseph Chamberlain had been a Liberal until he defected to the Tories over the issue of Irish Home Rule in 1886. But Neville, like his father, always felt himself to be a Liberal Unionist rather than a Tory. The marriage between the two groupings was one of convenience rather than conviction.

After his father's incapacitating stroke in 1906, Neville Chamberlain began to move slowly and somewhat unwillingly towards involvement in national politics. He was an effective Lord Mayor of Birmingham during the First World War, and his achievements there (together with the judicious application of influence by Austen Chamberlain, who was by now a Cabinet Minister) brought him to the attention of David Lloyd George, the leader of Britain's wartime coalition government.

So began, after Andros, the most searing episode of Neville Chamberlain's life to that point, which resulted in a lifelong feud between Lloyd George and himself. Lloyd George wanted a Director-General of National Service who was supposed to be responsible for the voluntary recruitment of men and women for war work (it did not involve dealing with the military). Chamberlain's first problem was that Lloyd George did not like him. According to Leo Amery, then Assistant Secretary of the War Cabinet, Lloyd George fancied himself as a phrenologist who could judge a man's potential by the size of his head. When he met Chamberlain, Amery reported Lloyd George as remarking, 'When I saw that pin-head, I said to myself he won't be any use'.[31] But the decisive factors were more prosaic. Chamberlain was not an MP, so he could not fight his corner in the House of Commons, let alone in the Cabinet. He was also constantly obstructed in his work by other departments, notably the War Ministry and the Ministry of Labour. In seven months starting in December 1916, Chamberlain recruited just three thousand men and women for essential war work. Angered by the futility of his task, he then resigned in disgust, family members urging him to seek a safe parliamentary seat instead. The legacy of this failure was an abiding detestation of Lloyd George and all his works, which was fully reciprocated. As late as 1940, Lloyd George refused to join Churchill's wartime coalition government when he heard that his appointment would be dependent on the approval of Churchill's predecessor, Neville Chamberlain.

The First World War left Chamberlain with a real horror of war and its consequences. He, like Baldwin, was too old to fight in it, but he was deeply affected by the death of his cousin Norman in Flanders. The two men were extremely close, having served together on Birmingham Council, and Chamberlain wrote that Norman's life 'was devoted to others and I feel a despicable thing beside him'.[32] The policies pursued by Neville Chamberlain as Prime Minister reflected both his hatred of war and the memory of Norman's death in 1917.

Norman's entire company of Grenadier Guards was killed by German machine gunners.

Norman's death strengthened Chamberlain's desire to get into Parliament, as did Lloyd George's treatment of him. In the general election of December 1918, therefore, when entering his fiftieth year, Chamberlain stood and was elected Member of Parliament for the Ladywood Constituency of Birmingham. He was a late starter in national politics, but he soon began to make up for lost time.

Circumstances favoured him, as they had Baldwin, when the government of his arch-enemy Lloyd George fell after the Tory back-bench revolt of November 1922. Austen chose to remain loyal to Lloyd George and so excluded himself from office, but for Neville the premiership of the little known Andrew Bonar Law offered new opportunities. First as Postmaster General and then as Minister of Health, he demonstrated great administrative competence, impressing both Bonar Law and Baldwin. When ill health forced Bonar Law to stand down, Baldwin made Chamberlain his Chancellor of the Exchequer. So began a partnership which was to dominate British politics for the next fourteen years.

Somewhat surprisingly, when the Tories returned to power in 1924 (after the first minority Labour government had been defeated at the polls), Chamberlain rejected the post of Chancellor, preferring instead to become Minister of Health once more. This had the effect of creating an opportunity for Churchill at the Exchequer, to the surprise of everyone including the recipient. Chamberlain himself thought that he might be a very successful Minister of Health but would only make a second-rate Chancellor.[33] As it was, Chamberlain proved to be a first-rate Health Minister between 1924 and 1929.

When the Tories lost the 1929 general election, there were threats to Stanley Baldwin's leadership of the party. Chamberlain had worked closely with Baldwin, but he was sometimes irritated by what he saw as Baldwin's lassitude. The thought that he might replace him as the party leader must have occurred to him. In March 1931, he actually told Baldwin that most of his colleagues thought he should resign. Baldwin ultimately declined to do so, and there were suspicions about Chamberlain's loyalty. Neither was he universally popular in the Conservative Party. One Conservative wrote that 'If you searched the whole world, you could not find more unsuitable man for his present job [Party Chairman], or one less qualified to be a leader of men'.[34] All his life, Chamberlain had a capacity to make enemies, just as his abilities brought him admirers.

When the Tories returned to power once more in 1931, Chamberlain's reinstatement as Chancellor was inevitable, particularly as Churchill had fallen out in spectacular fashion with Baldwin over the issue of India. In this capacity, Chamberlain was at the very heart of foreign policy-making and defence planning, a fact which effectively undermines the accusation that as Prime Minister he knew nothing of such matters.

At the point, therefore, where the challenge of the aggressor states began to emerge in the early 1930s, Chamberlain was a politician of wide political experience, albeit also a man with a strong aversion to the prospect of war. But he had no philosophical objections to the principle of rearmament, in the wake of the growing threat from Germany, Italy and Japan.

Anthony Eden differed from Baldwin and Chamberlain in several ways. He was a generation younger than the other two and had fought in the First World War. He also liked (most vehemently in old age) to regard himself as an anti-appeaser. The passage of time, however, and the release of papers under the new 'Thirty Year Rule' in 1968, has increasingly undermined this claim.[35] Eden rightly belongs in the ranks of the appeasers.

Eden was born in County Durham in 1897. His father, Sir William Eden, was a baronet and the family could trace its ancestry back to the sixteenth century. Anthony grew up at the family seat of Windlestone Hall near Bishop Auckland (the family also spent time in a London town house) as the third of four sons, but his childhood was blighted by his father's eccentricity and uncertain temper, which, it has been remarked, 'verged on insanity'.[36] Such a trivial event as a boy whistling in the street might cause Sir William to break a window with a flowerpot. His sons lived under the shadow of Sir William's irrational outbursts.

Anthony Eden followed the classic educational pattern for one of his class in the early twentieth century. Preparatory school was followed by Eton, which Eden did not like (although paradoxically he sent his own two sons there) and where he made no impact. His last year was in any case blighted by the death of his eldest brother, John, at Ypres, and the death of his father early in 1915. Eden then joined the King's Royal Rifles and made what was for him a crucial transformation. By 1918 he was a brigade major and the holder of the Military Cross, having turned from 'a callow youth into a confident and self-assertive man'.[37] Eden, unlike Baldwin and Chamberlain, knew about the realities of war from personal experience, although the war does not seem to have affected him so profoundly as it did his contemporary Harold Macmillan. Later, in 1934, Eden was to feel that his experience as a soldier enabled him to establish a personal rapport with Adolf Hitler. The war also demonstrated a mastery of detail and organisation that was to become Eden's hallmark as a politician.

Eden rejected the army as a prospective career in favour of one in the Diplomatic Service. To this end, he went up to Christ Church, Oxford, at the age of twenty-two, to read Oriental Languages. At Oxford, as at Eton, Eden did not stand out. He obtained the desired First Class Honours degree but avoided student politics.

This is all the more remarkable because, in 1922, Eden changed his mind and, making use of a personal recommendation from the Marquess of Londonderry (who knew the Eden family), secured the Tory candidature at Spennymoor. It was an unwinnable seat that Labour won comfortably in the General Election of 1922, but his experience led to his nomination for the safe Conservative seat of Leamington and Warwick. Eden was duly elected for the seat in 1923, retaining it without difficulty, even in the Labour landslide year of 1945, until he left the House of Commons in 1957. Eden saw himself as a 'One Nation' Tory who was tenaciously, some said embarrassingly, loyal to the Conservative leader, Baldwin.

Eden was blessed with good luck throughout his career up until its disastrous climax in the 1956 Suez Crisis. The resignation of a colleague soon gave him an opportunity as Parliamentary Private Secretary to the Foreign Secretary, Austen Chamberlain, because Baldwin recommended him in 1926. So began Eden's thirty year association with the Foreign Office. It was his natural home, as he knew little about domestic affairs, where his initiatives were sketchy and poorly thought out. In the Foreign Office Eden showed the deference to his elders and betters which made no enemies and accelerated his promotion up the political ladder. Some resented Eden's precocity, and Robert Vansittart was later to write that Eden 'said the right thing so often that he seemed incapable of saying anything else'.[38] Vansittart's view was perhaps jaundiced in that it was written twenty years after his own sacking as Permanent Under-Secretary in 1938, but it contains a germ of truth nonetheless. Blessed with film star good looks, young Eden could seem to be too good to be true in his rapid ascent to power and influence. He loyally followed Austen Chamberlain's line at the Foreign Office, showing himself, like his master, to be keen on imperial ties but no internationalist, and to be a man who wanted British overseas commitments to be limited rather than open-ended.

The line to Baldwin was always kept open and, in 1931, Baldwin's influence secured Eden another promotion as Parliamentary Under-Secretary at the Foreign Office, briefly under Lord Reading and then under Sir John Simon. He had embarked on the road to the Foreign Secretaryship, which he was to obtain at the early age of thirty-eight. Inevitably, lacking as he did the rounded experience of Baldwin and Chamberlain, Eden could seem callow and superficial, although he proved to be a formidable negotiator on occasion. A sensitivity to criticism and a tendency to limit himself to a narrow clique of friends were Eden's Achilles heels.

Edward Wood, third Viscount Halifax, had moved seemingly without effort from a traditional Yorkshire squire's upbringing to the highest councils of the land. His family had been respectable merchants in York who has done well enough to be able to purchase an estate near Doncaster, which happily sat on the great Barnsley coalfield. The family's fortunes were thus secured for generations. Nobility was then achieved by the granting of a viscountcy to Edward's grandfather, Charles Wood, who served both as Secretary of State for India and Chancellor of the Exchequer.

Edward's father, the Second Viscount Halifax, was clearly something of an eccentric, if of a different genre from Anthony Eden's father, Sir Robert. He was an almost fanatical supporter of High Anglicanism (he had been at Oxford during the later phase of the religious renewal in the Church of England associated with that city), but was also a writer of ghost stories and a keeper of emus and kangaroos in the park at the family home at Hickleton. By contrast, his wife, Lady Agnes, was a calm counterweight to her husband's vagaries.

Edward was one of six children, none of whom, save himself, lived to be twenty-five years old. This made him the repository of his father's hopes and ambitions, which were considerable. Life was not easy for young Edward in a physical sense either. He was born without a left hand, and had to rely on an artificial hand with a thumb on a spring, becoming increasingly dextrous at operating it with the passage of the years. He also suffered from a lisp which, it has been claimed, made the deep tones of his voice more attractive to listen to.[39] Great height was his other most striking physical characteristic. He was to tower over political colleagues in successive administrations in the twenties and thirties.

His father's expectations must have been a considerable burden for the young Edward to carry. At the tender age of eleven, his father wrote to him that 'You know when you are big you are to get a First Class in History at Oxford and do all sorts of grand things'.[40] Others found Edward to be a serious-minded child, but, given the weight of parental expectation, this was hardly surprising. He arrived in Eton in 1894 (both his father and grandfather had been Etonians), but his time there proved that he would never be a good classical scholar, as he was bored by Catallus and Horace. Fortunately for Viscount Halifax's ambition, his son had already shown a flair for History, and his physical disability did not prevent him from taking up sports like tennis. Edward was also allowed a bicycle by the school authorities because of his disability. The best word for his time at Eton, chosen by Halifax's most distinguished biographer, is 'blameless'.[41] Edward ruffled no feathers at Eton and neither did the formidable headmaster Warre have the sort of negative influence upon him that Montagu Butler had on Stanley Baldwin. Yet he seems to have left the school with few regrets. Not for him the romantic attachment which Winston Churchill had for Harrow.

Edward Wood went up to Christ Church, Oxford, in 1899, where his father had been before him. At Christ Church, he obtained the desired First Class in History while still finding time for attendance at many High Anglican services (this devotion being an inheritance from his father) and country sports like beagling. He found no apparent contradiction between his developing love of blood sports and his Christian beliefs. He made several strong friendships at Oxford, though few of his close friends were to survive the carnage of the First World War. The future Cabinet Minister did not take part in the debates at the Oxford Union, concentrating in an admirably systematic fashion on his academic studies. His academic triumph in 1903 was underlined strongly in November of that year when he was elected a Prize Fellow of All Souls. Edward's triumph was all the more remarkable because he was not a natural intellectual. His achievement reflected rather a capacity for hard work which stayed with him for the rest of his life.

After spending some time at All Souls as a Junior Fellow, young Wood took his father's advice and went on a Grand Tour of the Empire, which included a visit to India, which was to figure so prominently in his later life. In 1907, he returned to All Souls and dedicated his time to writing a worthy but somewhat dull biography of John Keble of the Oxford Movement, a particular hero of his father. This was published in 1909, the year in which Halifax married Dorothy Onslow.

Dorothy clearly played a key role in Halifax's life and career. She came from a distinguished family, three of whom had been Speakers of the House of Commons, and her father had been Governor-General of New Zealand. She was an ideal political wife for that era, supportive but never presuming to interfere in matters of policy.[42] Very early on in her married life, she learnt that her husband's career came first, for the couple's honeymoon was cut short so that Edward could stand for the vacant seat of Ripon as a Conservative. This was not an obvious development, as the Woods had been members of the old Whig Party. This had been subsumed by Gladstone's Liberal Party by the turn of the century. Edward's ideological affiliation to the Tory Party can only be described as loose, but he was certainly a member of its progressive wing in 1909.

Young Wood had little time to make a name for himself in the House of Commons before war came to Europe in 1914. A man who had a serious disability could easily have been excused from military service, but he insisted on enlisting in the Yorkshire Dragoons and served until 1917. As a dismounted cavalry squadron, Wood's men had little front-line fighting to do, spending most of their time on mundane tasks such as repairing roads and escorting prisoners of war. But he was under fire in the trenches on several occasions and showed himself to be 'a man of exceptional physical courage'.[43] For this reason, he was mentioned in despatches in 1917 before he returned to Britain to take up the job of Deputy Director of Labour Supply in the Ministry of National Service. He had taken advantage of various periods of leave to make speeches in the House of Commons between 1914 and 1917.

Wood's background of distinguished military service is important, because it helps to give the lie to suggestions that the appeasers were men who knew nothing of war. Indeed, a quite perverse attempt had been made recently by the historian, Andrew Roberts, to suggest that Halifax did not fight in the war at all. Thus we are told that the

> senior anti-appeasers all had fine war records – Duff Cooper, Anthony Eden, Harold Macmillan, Winston Churchill ... while National Government ministers who advocated appeasement – Baldwin, MacDonald, Chamberlain, Hoare, Sir John Simon, Lord Halifax and Sir Kingsley Wood – had not themselves seen action.[44]

In Halifax's case, this comment is just plain wrong, and it was hardly the fault of men like Chamberlain and Baldwin that age precluded them from fighting in the war. Ramsay MacDonald was, in fact, a conscientious objector who was imprisoned during the war, but Edward Wood fiercely attacked such objectors in wartime speeches. He also wanted the toughest possible peace to be imposed upon Germany once the war was over. Hence the danger of seeing the appeasers in simplistic terms as enfeebled cowards who shirked a fight. Another prominent appeaser, Barrington-Ward, the Deputy Editor of the *Times*, which strongly supported Baldwin and Chamberlain, won the Military Cross in the war. Neither should Eden be placed in the category of anti-appeaser as his record clearly demonstrates. The history of appeasement shows clearly enough, and Halifax is an outstanding example, that those who wanted to mete out tough treatment to Germany in 1918 were often the same men who wanted an accommodation with it twenty years later. Such a change in attitude did not depend on whether they had seen war service or not.

War service for Edward Wood was significant because it sharpened his paternalist instinct, as well as giving him an appreciation of the qualities of the lower classes. Wood was a popular officer who looked after his men but was also known to be a strict disciplinarian. And a good war record was a distinct asset for a Tory politician in the post-war period.

Wood first entered the government in 1921 as Under-Secretary of State at the Colonial Office, working under Winston Churchill. Churchill, whose bark was usually worse than his bite, initially refused to see him until Wood stormed into his office and demanded to be treated like a gentleman. 'After that the two men co-operated well.'[45] Wood served in the Lloyd George Coalition but soon developed the same antipathy towards the Prime Minister as his mentor, Stanley Baldwin. By contrast, Baldwin epitomised the tolerant mainstream Toryism which appealed to Wood. Together with another Conservative MP, Geoffrey Lloyd, he wrote a book called *The Great Opportunity* that championed causes like votes for women and national unity. Its tone was bland but the book had a considerable success.

In 1922 the Lloyd George government fell, with Wood voting against the Prime Minister at the famous meeting of the Conservative Party at the Carlton

Club on 19 October. The refusal of senior Tories like Birkenhead and Austen Chamberlain to serve then gave Wood the chance of rapid promotion, just as it did Baldwin and Neville Chamberlain. Wood was appointed President of the Board of Education with the task of implementing H.A.L. Fisher's 1918 Education Act.

He still found time to play the role of the country squire in Yorkshire. His duties at the Board of Education were not unduly onerous, and he was able to go hunting twice a week. He became Master of the Middleton Hunt and it was noticeable that hunting metaphors and allusions filled his conversation.[46] Weekends were often spent at the great houses of other great aristocratic families, including the Percies, with whom Wood was friendly.

When Baldwin made his celebrated gaffe by calling an election over Protection in 1923, Wood found himself in Opposition for eleven months. After the Conservatives returned to office in 1924, he was sent to the Board of Agriculture, where he served without great distinction until Baldwin offered him the post of Viceroy of India in October 1925. There was a show of diffidence before Wood accepted. This sort of modesty annoyed others who doubted its genuineness. Beaverbrook was to call him a 'sort of Jesus in long boots',[47] and his emollient line in India was to earn him the dislike of the Tory right led by Churchill.

India, where Gandhi's non-violent approach concealed the real threat of a violent upsurge against British rule, presented the new Viceroy, who now held the new title of Baron Irwin of Kirby Underdale (his eighty-seven-year-old father still held the title of Lord Halifax), with a considerable challenge. Irwin and his wife left for India in March 1926. Once there, Irwin tried to follow a middle way between conciliation and repression. He was prepared to sign death warrants, if he thought the occasion demanded it, but also earned Gandhi's respect as a man of principle. Irwin was surprised, however, by the vehemence of diehard Tory reaction when he announced in 1929 that 'the natural issue of India's constitutional progress ... is Dominion status'.[48] Churchill denounced him (he was later to call Gandhi a 'naked fakir'), but Irwin had the support of the new Labour government and also, after some hesitation, of Baldwin. On this issue, Irwin put country above party. He thought the concession of Dominion status in the long run was the right course. And his winning over of Gandhi, despite differences, was crucial. He described the Indian leader as 'logical, forceful, courageous with an odd streak of subtlety', qualities which he had in abundance himself.[49]

Irwin was careful to avoid imprisoning Gandhi, despite his campaign of Civil Disobedience, until disruption in India made it inevitable. His achievement was to persuade the Indian leadership of British *bona fides* where Dominion status was concerned. Had there been a national uprising in India in the 1930s, at a time when Britain's defence resources were thinly stretched, the consequences could have been fatal. Irwin was accused of appeasement over India by the right-wing press in Britain, but his policy was fully vindicated.

Irwin returned from India in 1931, but for a year kept out of politics. He even rejected the Foreign Secretaryship that Baldwin, as the major figure in the new National Government, had in his gift. Baldwin persuaded him to return to government in 1932, in his old position as President of the Board of Education, although he also had a significant watching brief over the India Bill, which was to concede a degree of autonomy to India in 1935. Irwin showed more and more interest in the field of foreign policy, but always with the moral 'squint' which caused Churchill (who was good at nicknames) to call him 'The Holy Fox'. Irwin gave critics the impression that he thought his views had the approval of the Almighty. This may have been unfair, and the common view in the Tory Party was that Irwin was a safe pair of hands. His previous experience, especially as Viceroy in India, had prepared him, in the eyes of the party leadership, for the high office that was to come his way in the late 1930s, although he lacked knowledge of European affairs. Irwin became the third Viscount Halifax on the death of his father in 1936.

5

Italy and Japan

The overwhelming focus of the literature of appeasement on relations with Nazi Germany makes it easy to underestimate the problems caused by the existence of two other potentially hostile great powers in the 1930s. But successive British governments were acutely aware of Britain's weakness in a global context, where war with either Italy or Japan might also be a possibility. Should these powers unite with Germany, the consequences for Britain and its Empire were likely to be catastrophic. It was essential, therefore, the appeasers reasoned, to maintain reasonable relations with one or preferably two of the authoritarian dictatorships which confronted Britain during the period. It was indeed hoped that Mussolini, by the late thirties clearly the junior Fascist dictator, could be used to moderate Hitler's excesses.

Mussolini had come to power in Italy in 1922 with the connivance of the monarchy, the church and the army. His Fascist 'revolution' had its admirers in Britain, where the political right saw him as a possible bulwark against Bolshevism. One was Winston Churchill, who said in 1927 (to the Duce): 'If I had been an Italian, I am sure I should have been wholeheartedly with you in your triumphant struggle against the bestial appetites and passions of Leninism'.[1] Other admirers included Austen Chamberlain and especially his wife, Ivy, who acted as an intermediary between London and Rome when Neville Chamberlain became Prime Minister.

Admittedly it was easier to admire Mussolini in the twenties, when he was not such an obvious menace to international peace and stability as he was in the decade that followed. The Duce was constrained by the need to stay on reasonable terms with Italy's former allies, Britain and France, and only his attack on Corfu in 1923 (following the murder of an Italian general for which he held the Greeks responsible) gave an indication of the sort of lawlessness which was to come. Even so, some British observers had doubts about Mussolini, the diplomat and historian Harold Nicolson commenting in 1923 on 'the exuberant petulance of Mussolini's language'.[2] But this petulance was generally reserved for a domestic audience. Foreigners noticed that when abroad Mussolini tended to restrain his language. At home, both his language and his actions could be brutal and unscrupulous (political opponents were murdered and, by 1925, Italian democracy had been effectively destroyed). In Britain's Rome Embassy, Howard Kennard, a future Ambassador to Poland, noted that Mussolini's recklessness might end with 'some rash and impulsive step which might greatly react on the people of Europe'.[3]

In 1925, however, Mussolini courted international opinion at the Locarno conference, although journalists boycotted him after a Fascist outrage against Liberal opponents days before. He agreed that Italy should act with Britain as a guarantor of the agreement which emerged at Locarno, and even hoped (vainly) that he himself might be nominated for the Nobel Peace Prize alongside Austen Chamberlain, Briand and Stresemann. There was tension with Yugoslavia, Italy's new post-war neighbour, but British leaders hoped that Mussolini, despite his violent rhetoric, would settle in as a respectable member of the European family. They were prepared to overlook diplomatic gaffes, such as Mussolini's insistence on wearing his Fascist Party badge when he had an audience with King George V at Buckingham Palace in 1923 (he had already created an incident at Claridge's Hotel by claiming that the French delegation to the London Conference on German Reparations had been allocated better rooms that the Italians).[4]

Grounds for optimism where Mussolini was concerned remained until 1934 at least. In that year, Mussolini had an interview with Alfred Duff Cooper, who served as War Minister and First Lord of the Admiralty in successive administrations and found him 'nicer than I expected – simpler, more humorous and completely lacking in pose. We talked chiefly about disarmament and were quite in agreement'.[5] Duff Cooper amused the Duce by saying that to blame armaments for wars was like saying that umbrellas produced rain. Normally regarded as an anti-appeaser, although he remained in government until 1938, Duff Cooper was one of those politicians who, though fearful of Nazism, thought agreement with Fascist Italy possible.

In Fleet Street, Geoffrey Dawson, now Editor of the *Times* was equally taken with the Italian dictator. Mussolini, he told a correspondent, was 'most impressive. No one can go there without being struck by what he has done ... the trains run and the streets are swept'.[6] Dawson's friend, Lord Lothian, was also prepared to give the Duce the benefit of the doubt. His claims on Ethiopia could be justified, Lothian believed, because of that country's feudal barbarism and encouragement of slavery. Italy's militarism under Mussolini should be played down.[7] Churchill, for his part, still thought Mussolini to be a 'Roman genius ... the greatest lawgiver among men'.[8] Thus admiration for Mussolini was still commonplace in the Conservative Party and the hopes placed in him in the international context seemed plausible enough.

In 1934, after all, Mussolini stood with Britain and France against the threat of Nazi aggression in Austria, which Mussolini regarded as being within the Italian sphere of influence. Article 80 of the Versailles Treaty also banned union between Germany and Austria, although this would not have unduly impressed the revisionist dictator. But when, in July 1934, Hitler encouraged Austrian Nazis to mount a coup in which the Austrian dictator, Döllfuss, was shot and left to bleed to death in his office in Vienna, an enraged Mussolini sent troops to the Brenner Pass. His anger was increased by the fact that Frau Döllfuss and her children were staying with him in Rome at the time. It was Mussolini who had to tell the unfortunate woman that her husband had been assassinated, and he denounced Hitler as 'a horrible sexual degenerate, a dangerous fool'.[9] Italian disapproval was formalised together with that of Britain and France at Stresa in April 1935, when the three powers effectively warned Hitler off Austrian territory. He had already been forced to return the murderers of Döllfuss for execution in Austria. Up to this point, therefore, the hopes placed in Mussolini seemed reasonable enough. Vansittart was to write later that Mussolini's 'intelligence and character were disparate, but he had both more imagination and more knowledge of the world than home-keeping provincials like Hitler or Stalin'.[10]

As it turned out, Stresa marked the high-point of Anglo-French cooperation with Mussolini, as the two sides drifted apart over the issue of Abyssinia (now Ethiopia). Yet even here there had been a disposition to accommodate Mussolini long before the crisis which followed Italy's attack on Abyssinia in October 1935. In the 1920s, Lord Curzon, the then British Foreign Secretary, had sided with the Italians over the issue of Abyssinian suitability for membership of the nascent League of Nations. Writing to the head of the British delegation at the League headquarters in Geneva, Curzon said that he personally had no doubt that 'Abyssinia is quite unfit to be admitted and that her admission will neither redound to the future credit of the League or promote the interests of Britain'.[11] In fact, the Ethiopians were admitted to the League against Curzon's wishes and the blame for this has been placed on Robert Cecil, the British delegation head.[12] But British goodwill towards Fascist Italy was demonstrated by the cession of Jubaland to it by Ramsay MacDonald's first Labour government in June 1924 (showing that the British Left as well as the Right was prepared to do business with Mussolini). Nevertheless, the Italian aspiration to annex Abyssinia, the scene of their humiliating military defeat at Adowa in 1896, remained. Ten years later, this aspiration was to bring about a crisis in Anglo-Italian relations. Fascist ideology was in tune with a widespread Italian belief that Britain and France had used the League of Nations mandate system to enlarge their empires, leaving Italy with nothing. The cession of a small territory like Jubaland did not mollify Italian envy or anger.

The British government was, of course, fully aware of Mussolini's designs on Abyssinia, which Italian propaganda portrayed as a barbaric and aggressive society that was a menace to its neighbours. It was true that Abyssinian tribesmen had invaded Kenya, the Sudan and Eritrea, which were under British and Italian control respectively. Slavery was also endemic and was even supported by the church. But what really exercised Mussolini was the fact that the Abyssinian Emperor, Haile Selassie, was attempting to modernise his country and had even obtained arms in Europe (Hitler was an enthusiastic provider). Reform might endanger Italy's case for annexation.

The British government, which was in 1935 still led by Ramsay MacDonald in the last phase of his career, tried to reach an accommodation with the Duce. In May 1935, Sir John Simon, a National Liberal Foreign Secretary in a Tory-dominated government, sent Mussolini a message which referred to the 'deep feeling which is entertained in the United Kingdom in support of promoting the peaceful solution of international disputes by the League of Nations'.[13] This was a coded way of saying that Britain would support an arrangement over Abyssinia which would be acceptable to Mussolini and Haile Selassie, and which could then be presented as a League of Nations' solution.[14] But within the confines of the Foreign Office Vansittart as Permanent Under-Secretary was prepared to use quite brutal language. 'Italy will have to be bought off', he minuted on 8 June 1935, 'let us use and face ugly words – in some form or other, or Abyssinia will eventually perish'.[15] Vansittart wanted to trade away British Somaliland, rather than Abyssinia, to appease Italian appetites. To do otherwise would be to undermine the credibility of the League.

The other factor in British government calculations was the state of British public opinion, which in 1935 was strongly pro-League and anti-war. Early in 1935, the 'Peace Ballot' organised by the League of Nations Union found that ten million Britons supported non-military sanctions against an aggressor; a further seven million wanted collective military security measures only. This was no climate for unilateral military action against Mussolini should he go ahead and attack Abyssinia following an alleged Abyssinian provocation at Wal Wal in December 1934 on the frontier between Italian Somaliland and Abyssinia. When Stanley Baldwin won the November 1935 general election, his confidant Thomas Jones wrote in his diary that 'he has strictly confined the extent to which he was prepared to move against Italy and distinguished Mussolini from the Italian people'.[16] As it was, Mussolini had already invaded Abyssinia in October, having convinced himself that the absence of any Anglo-French public statement about that country at Stresa could be interpreted as connivance in such aggression. Private British warnings about the consequences of such aggression were ignored by the dictator, as were offers of territorial concessions outside Abyssinia in East Africa which Vansittart had advocated. This was appeasement pure and simple, which Vansittart's admirers have been reluctant to recognise.

The process of appeasement was carried a step further in December in the notorious Hoare–Laval Pact, which offered Mussolini about two-thirds of Abyssinia in return for the evacuation of Italian troops. Its British author was the new Foreign Secretary, Sir Samuel Hoare, who had made what was regarded as an enthusiastically pro-League speech at Geneva on 12 September in which he said that 'the League stands, and my country stands with it, for the collective maintenance of the Covenant in its entirety, and particularly for steady and collective resistance to all acts of unprovoked aggression'.[17]

Hoare was regarded in government as a safe pair of hands (although Churchill had embarrassed him over the India Bill by accusing him of doctoring evidence to the Select Committee from Lancashire cotton manufacturers) and was a senior Tory with much Cabinet experience, but this reputation was about to be exploded in dramatic fashion. Part of Hoare's problem was that, although Baldwin encouraged him to make pro-League noises at Geneva, as did MacDonald who was a keen supporter of the organisation, Tories in general were sceptical about collective security. In 1935, Churchill shared this mentality, whatever he may have said later.

Behind the scenes, therefore, once Baldwin had become Prime Minister on 7 June 1935, moves were afoot to appease Mussolini even after his invasion of Abyssinia. Vansittart was the driving force behind this initiative, but there is no evidence that the junior Foreign Office Minister, Eden, opposed it and Hoare was fully in support. 'I believed', he wrote in his memoirs, 'and still believe, that the plan was the best possible, or should I say, the least bad in the circumstances.'[18] It is clear that the plan had Cabinet approval because, although the Cabinet collectively thought that too much was being conceded, it avoided a war with Italy in which French support could not be guaranteed. The French had already been affronted by the Anglo-German Naval Treaty in June 1935 which allowed the Germans to build up to 35 per cent of British and imperial tonnage. The French had not been consulted about this piece of British appeasement and they (not unreasonably) thought Hitler to be a much greater threat than Mussolini. By contrast, the British were anxious about their vulnerability in the Mediterranean, where Malta was virtually defenceless, and Baldwin's low opinion of the Royal Navy has been referred already.[19] The Chiefs of Staff were particularly adamant that Britain was in no position to go to war. Britain, therefore, tried to follow a tenuous double policy. Public loyalty to the League combined with efforts to bring Mussolini to the negotiating table (it was known that the Duce was becoming impatient with the slow Italian advance in Ethiopia, where the ferocity of Abyssinian resistance unnerved his Commander-in-Chief, the veteran Fascist de Bono).

The French were even more enthusiastic about talking to Mussolini and it was agreed that Hoare, who had been ordered to take time off by his doctor, would stop over in Paris on his way to an ice-skating holiday in Switzerland. Laval, the French Foreign Minister, personified almost everything Baldwinesque Tories like Hoare disliked about Frenchmen with his 'greasy hair, dirty white tie and shifty look'.[20] His task was to keep France out of a war for which his countrymen had no appetite, and he had already had long talks about Abyssinia with Hoare on 10 and 11 September.

Hoare duly met Laval on 8 December and an agreement emerged whereby Abyssinia, though much reduced in size, would have a corridor to the sea. Mussolini seemed disposed to accept the package, telling his Ambassador in London, Count Grandi, that he might abandon his demand for the whole of Abyssinia.[21] This was no great concession, as the rump Abyssinian state was unlikely to survive for long on its own.

The scheme was scuppered, however, when details of the Hoare–Laval Plan were leaked to opposition French newspapers in circumstances which still remain controversial. When the details became known in Britain, there was uproar. Mussolini was already regarded as an unprincipled bully by the public, and the *Manchester Guardian* had noted that, within a week of the invasion in October, he was being booed when he appeared on cinema newsreels.[22] Even those who have been regarded as the most spineless of appeasers by some historians reacted strongly both against Italian aggression and the Hoare–Laval Pact. Dawson had little time for the League, but he wrote a sharply critical leader for the *Times* about Hoare–Laval under the title 'A Corridor for Camels'. His deputy, Barrington-Ward, was even more outraged by what Hoare had done, saying that he felt 'utterly humiliated and dispirited and ashamed of my country'.[23] Dawson blamed Vansittart, whom he felt to be 'quite unsuited to his present position', for the fiasco.[24] Lothian was more belligerent, wanting to block the Suez Canal, which would have been an act of war as such action would have breached the 1888 convention regulating the operation of the Canal, and so sever links between Italy and East Africa. Mussolini subsequently admitted that such action would have put the Italian war effort in grave jeopardy.

Meanwhile Hoare had proceeded on his way to Zuoz in Switzerland largely unaware of the storm that his agreement with Laval had unleashed. A keen skater, he had arranged for a local rink to be placed solely at his disposal but fell and fractured his nose in two places when he ventured onto the ice. When he returned to Britain, Hoare was prevented from attending Cabinet by his doctor's fear that his fractures might lead to infection. According to Hoare's account, Baldwin came to see him and said, 'We all stand together'.[25] In fact, as Baldwin well knew, the Cabinet was far from united on the issue once the terms of the Hoare–Laval Pact had produced consternation in the country. As late as 11 December, the Cabinet still seemed determined to stick by the terms offered to Mussolini, but in subsequent meetings public opinion began to make an impact. When the Cabinet met on 18 December, J.L. Thomas, the Secretary of State for the Colonies, told his colleagues that he 'was receiving most terrible letters from his constituency', and Baldwin himself said that there was 'a worse situation in the House of Commons than he had ever known'.[26] Lord Halifax also told colleagues that, although the

Hoare–Laval Plan had his support on its merits, circumstances made it inevitable that Hoare should resign. It was this meeting which decided Hoare's fate and the next day, feeling very self-conscious because of his bandaged nose, Hoare made his resignation speech in the House of Commons.[27]

Hoare had reason to feel aggrieved in the light of the Prime Minister's assurances, and the strength of public reaction against him may well have been exaggerated by Baldwin. This allowed Baldwin to cover up the differences in his Cabinet over Abyssinia, and the fact that Hoare had been inadequately briefed before being sent to Paris. Baldwin told the House of Commons on 19 December that 'something has happened that has appealed to the deepest feelings of our countrymen',[28] but it was one of his least convincing parliamentary moments. In his defence, it can be said that Baldwin was determined to bring Hoare back into government and that he did so shortly afterwards. The whole débâcle gave rise to one of King George V's few known jokes: 'No more coals to Newcastle,' he quipped, 'no more whores to Paris'.

Robert Vansittart was infuriated by the way an outbreak of British righteous indignation had jeopardised his policy of trying to keep Mussolini out of the arms of Hitler by making colonial concessions. Instead, the ill-feeling generated over the Hoare–Laval fiasco had the opposite effect. The British, he wrote, long after the event, 'suddenly all became knights without armour, eager to kill Musso with their mouths'.[29] Churchill agreed with him at the time, telling the Commons that 'We are not strong enough – I say it advisedly – to be the lawgiver and spokesman of the world'.[30] The historical irony is that we now know Mussolini to have been a paper tiger, and one of the strange features of the period is the regularity with which British military and naval intelligence overestimated Italian strength. In 1935, for example, Italy had no aircraft that could reach the main British Mediterranean naval base at Alexandria. Neither did the Italian admirals share Mussolini's confidence that they could neutralise the Royal Navy in the event of war. British intelligence was also consistently to exaggerate the potency of the Italian long-range bomber, the Savio Marchettie 81.[31]

Nevertheless, and however flawed British perceptions of Italian military strength might be, the Baldwin government faced a considerable dilemma over the Abyssinian War. The Italian Fascists were guilty of odious atrocities in Abyssinia, massacring and gassing hundreds of thousands of half-armed tribesmen as their Duce sought military glory. This gave opposition to Mussolini a moral dimension, but it was in the teeth of the appraisal offered by military leaders at the time that Britain was in no position to take Mussolini on. It would have been a brave Prime Minister who would have rejected such advice, especially when, despite the spasm of moral outrage against Italy, public opinion showed no real stomach for a fight. It placed its faith in the League which Conservative politicians and Royal Navy admirals alike had little confidence in. Neither was there any real belief that France would support Britain in a war against Italy on the issue of Abyssinia, which the French regarded as a secondary one. If the two powers disagreed, as subsequent differences over oil sanctions showed, the League would be rendered impotent.

The other important aspect of the Abyssinian crisis was that it showed how nuanced appeasement was. Those like Churchill, despite being always portrayed in stereotypical terms as anti-appeasers, opposed the use of military force against Mussolini. So did Baldwin, Chamberlain and Eden, despite the latter's unde-served post-war status as an anti-appeaser. In Fleet Street the *Times* journalists Dawson and Barrington-Ward were critical of government policy towards Italy, although they approved of the appeasement of Germany. Vansittart, notoriously anti-German by repute (although not in fact as anti-German as his critics maintained), favoured the appeasement of Mussolini, whereas he had major reservations about the attempts to reach accommodation with Hitler. Lothian, whom Vansittart despised, wanted strong action to be taken against Mussolini over Abyssinia, yet until 1938 was one of the strongest advocates of the appease-ment of Germany. Supporting appeasement of one totalitarian power did not, therefore, preclude the advocacy of coercive measures against another. When Mussolini was completing his conquest of Abyssinia, Baldwin fully recognised the evil behind both varieties of Fascism. In April 1936, he told Thomas Jones, 'With two lunatics like Mussolini and Hitler you can never be sure of anything. But I am determined to keep the country out of war'.[32] Faced with Fascist barbarism in Abyssinia, Baldwin did not lack a moral dimension, but he had to face the realities of Britain's international situation.

The Baldwin-Hoare-Vansittart policy of trying to keep Mussolini out of the clutches of the Nazis was probably doomed to failure anyway. The Abyssinian War, which was over by the summer of 1936, smashed the Stresa front and fatally strengthened Mussolini's militaristic delusions. The evidence also suggests that Mussolini was putting out feelers to Berlin even before the outbreak of the war in October 1935. Early in 1936, he told the German Ambassador in Rome, von Hassell, that he would not object to Austria becoming a German satellite as long as its independence was preserved, a clear volte-face in Italian policy towards its neighbour. Neither did Italy take action at the time of Hitler's reoccupation of the Rhineland in March 1936, despite the fact that Mussolini was supposed to be a guarantor of the Locarno Treaty.[33]

The outbreak of the Spanish Civil War in July 1936 accelerated the process whereby Italy drifted into the German camp. Hitler also supported the rebel leader Franco, but to a markedly lesser degree than Mussolini. In November 1936, German-Italian ideological affinity was underlined in the so-called Rome-Berlin Axis. All this took place in a context of British efforts to avoid a serious rupture with Mussolini. Where Spain was concerned, this also meant keeping Britain's ally France from actively assisting the Spanish republic. This would have been the natural inclination of its left-wing Popular Front government led by Léon Blum. But Eden was determined to prevent such an association taking place. It has, therefore, rightly been observed that: 'Official British reaction to the Spanish Civil War provide another instance of the appeasement of the fascist powers in action.'[34]

The outbreak of the war in Spain caught the Foreign Office by surprise, but Baldwin immediately told Eden that 'on no account, French or other, must he bring us into a fight on the side of the Russians'.[35] This was because the Soviet Union, a pariah state for Tories, was an overt supporter of the Spanish republic, whose government contained Communists from the outset. But Eden's natural inclination was to remain neutral and to avoid an open rift with Mussolini, despite the latter's flagrant pro-Franco bias. In a speech in the House of Commons on 5 November 1936, Eden stressed that there was no reason that British and Italian interests in the Mediterranean should not be compatible. It should 'be possible', Eden told his fellow MPs, 'for each country to continue to maintain its vital interests in the Mediterranean not only without conflict with each other, but even with mutual advantage'.[36] If Britain was not prepared to take on Mussolini over Abyssinia, it was even less prepared to risk war for the left-wing Spanish Republic. Spain might be a *cause célèbre* for left-wing intellectuals and trades unionists (hundreds joined the famous anti-Fascist International Brigades), but the Baldwin and Chamberlain Governments were resolutely determined not to antagonise Mussolini or Hitler by supporting the republic.

On 2 January, Eden signed the Anglo-Italian Gentleman's Agreement which reaffirmed the compatibility of British and Italian interests in the Mediterranean, and included an exchange of notes undertaking 'not to alter the status quo as regards national sovereignty of territories in the Mediterranean area'.[37] This policy also reflected the desire of the armed service ministries to eliminate Italy from their list of potential enemies. Eden may have had doubts about Mussolini's sincerity, but he saw the advantages of 'a détente in the Mediterranean while British rearmament proceeds'.[38] The dangers that Mussolini posed were not, the British knew, confined only to the western Mediterranean. In March 1937, Mussolini visited the Italian colony of Libya, and on 18 March, in a typical piece of Fascist militaristic symbolism, he was presented with the Sword of Islam and reiterated the pledge he had given six days before that 'Moslems may rest assured that Italy will always be the friend and protector of Islam throughout the world'.[39] This declaration had a sinister ring in London where the British government was already grappling with problems caused by the revolt of the Palestinian Arabs in 1936, nascent Egyptian nationalism and a Kurdish uprising in Mesopotamia. British policy always had to be formulated through the prism of global military and strategic threats.

British attempts to keep Italy on side continued through 1937 and 1938, despite a constant flow of Italian volunteers to Spain in breach of the principle of non-intervention which Eden had laboured to establish. At home, Spain was not the divisive issue it might have been. On the Right, only a few die-hards supported Franco (one being the eccentric historian, Arthur Bryant), and in 1936 and 1937 successive Tory Conferences barely made reference to Spain.[40] There was no real suggestion either that had Labour, the main Opposition party, been in power British policy on Spain would have been markedly different. The British government could not prevent republican volunteers going to Spain and Labour might have winked at it, but a real military commitment was another matter.

British hopes that Mussolini could still be used as a moderating influence on Hitler were to be rudely shattered by events in 1938 and 1939. Mussolini's ideological drift towards Nazi Germany was already evident in the 1937 Anti-Comintern Pact, even if this was primarily an anti-Soviet device, but the real evidence that British hopes for him were an illusion came with a dramatic shift in his policy towards Austria. Before Hitler invaded Austria on the night of 11–12 March 1938, he had already secured Mussolini's approval, and the Duce had signalled that he regarded the issue of union between Germany and Austria as a 'German problem'. Hitler was effusively grateful and Mussolini's son-in-law and Foreign Minister, Count Ciano, recorded his view that *Anschluss* (union) between the two states was inevitable.

In Britain, Neville Chamberlain, who had succeeded Baldwin as Prime Minister in May 1937, thought an opportunity had been lost as far as an Anglo-Italian détente had been concerned. On 12 March, as German troops poured into Austria, he told Cabinet colleagues that Britain had been 'too late in starting conversations with Italy'. Next day he wrote to his sister about how the *Anschluss* might have 'been prevented if I had had Halifax at the Foreign Office earlier'.[41] Chamberlain was deceiving himself about the likelihood of success where Mussolini was concerned. Nevertheless, the attempt to achieve an accommodation with Mussolini was worthwhile given the perceptions of the time which recognised Germany and Japan as the greater threats. The misappraisal of Italian military strength was not Chamberlain's fault but the responsibility of military intelligence, and it was surely sensible to try and keep the line to Rome open, even though Mussolini's behaviour was increasingly hostile towards Britain and especially France.

Mussolini had little love for the Czechs who were to be Hitler's next victims in Central Europe. As the only democracy in the region with strong ties with France, it was hardly to be expected that he would object to German attempts to undermine Czech autonomy in the summer of 1938. There has been recent debate about whether Mussolini seriously considered going to war with Hitler over Czechoslovakia in September 1938 (even though there was no formal military alliance between Italy and Germany at that point).[42] He certainly provided diplomatic support for the German position, but once again Chamberlain relied upon him as an arbitrator who would hold the ring between Germany and the two Western democracies at the Munich Conference in late September. This settled the fate of the Czech Sudetenland, which was given to Germany, and Mussolini's connivance in the result. The proposals which he put forward as a basis for discussion at the four-power meeting at Munich (the wretched Czechs were not even invited) were actually drafted for him in advance by the German Foreign Office.[43] Chamberlain and Halifax did not know this of course; had they done so, they might not have invested so much time in trying to maintain good relations with Fascist Italy.

Even after Munich, Chamberlain maintained his hope that Mussolini might be used as a counterweight to Nazi extremism. But he now had another problem. This was Mussolini's increasingly strident demands for territorial concessions in French North Africa. Abyssinia was not enough for the Duce. Nevertheless in October Halifax still believed that it was possible 'to increase Mussolini's power of manoeuvre and so make him less dependent on Hitler, and therefore freer to resume the classic Italian role of balancing between Germany and the Western Powers'.[44] In its anxiety to keep Mussolini friendly, the British surrendered to Italian demands for the ratification of the April 1938 agreement, even though Mussolini had not honoured its stipulation that Italian forces should be withdrawn from Spain. In January 1939, Chamberlain and Halifax visited Rome in an effort to harness what they wrongly believed to be Mussolini's influence over Hitler. Chamberlain thought that the visit had been a success as Mussolini was 'emphatic in his assurances that he intended to stand by his agreement with us and ... wanted peace'.[45] This was far from being the Italian assessment of the talks. 'How far away are these people. It is another world. These men are not made of the same stuff as the Francis Drakes and the other magnificent adventurers who created their empire',[46] wrote Count Ciano.

Ciano's reaction was exaggerated. Both he and Mussolini were flabby, overweight libertines, but his comment demonstrated the way he and his father-in-law, the Duce, were thinking. Britain and France were categorised as effete and timorous democracies overtaken by the new Fascist dynamic in Italy and Germany. But Chamberlain was not in fact so lacking in backbone that he would support strident Italian claims on French Tunisia (the British visit coincided with a vociferous anti-French campaign in the Italian press). As Mussolini flatly refused to withdraw such claims, or to offer any reassurance about the behaviour of his Nazi friends, the consequences of the Anglo-Italian meeting were insubstantial. As has accurately been observed, Chamberlain did not find a doorway to improved Anglo-German relations in Rome in January 1939, 'not a doorway, not a key, not even the vaguest of directions'.[47] Any hope that Italy was capable of holding the balance between Hitler and the West as hoped for by Halifax, three months before, had long gone. Mussolini would bargain with the Anglo-French for compensatory territorial scraps but his orientation was now firmly fixed towards Berlin.

All that could be said by way of encouragement to British hopes was that Mussolini was angered by Hitler's coups being carried out without any prior consultation with him (the *Anschluss* being the exception). On 15 March 1939, Hitler sent his army into Bohemia and Moravia while Mussolini lamely complained that 'every time Hitler occupies a country he sends me a message'.[48] Three weeks later, on Good Friday, 7 April 1939, Mussolini responded by sending his own armies into the tiny neighbouring state of Albania. He had already snubbed Chamberlain's attempt to get him to intervene after Hitler had occupied Prague. Italy, Mussolini told the British Prime Minister, could not intervene until 'Italy's rights had been recognised'.[49] Nevertheless, and despite Mussolini's unwarranted aggression against Albania, the Chamberlain government continued to seek an accommodation with Rome. But it did so in a more realistic spirit. Chamberlain told his sister that 'Musso has behaved to me like a sneak and a cad ... he has carried through his smash and grab raid with complete cynicism'.[50] The British were not sure about whether Germany and Italy were in collusion over these consecutive acts of aggression (Ciano, by contrast, thought Italy was asserting its independence of Germany). It was clear, however, that Mussolini could not be relied upon to help preserve the status quo in Europe, and that British policy had to proceed on this assumption. In the Mediterranean, British eyes began to focus on Turkey as a possible counterweight to an unreliable Italy.

The pro-German drift in Mussolini's policy was confirmed when he signed an offensive–defensive treaty with Hitler in May, known to historians as the 'Pact of Steel'. The failure of British policy here was demonstrated by the fact that Italy bound itself to assist Germany in almost any circumstances, including an unprovoked attack on another power (which, in fact, Hitler was preparing against Poland). Ironically, though, it was at this eleventh hour that Chamberlain's faith in Italy as a counterweight seemed briefly to be justified. Ciano was appalled by the realisation that Hitler did indeed intend to attack Poland, even though the Duce had included in the Pact of Steel the stipulation that Italy would not be ready for war until 1943 at the earliest. In the last hours of peace before Hitler's offensive began on 1 September, Ciano did act as a mediator at the request of Halifax, who was trying to get the Germans to agree to direct talks with Poland about Danzig and the Polish Corridor. Ciano then came up with the idea that Mussolini should convene a great power conference on 5 September with a brief to revise the Treaty of Versailles.

This time it was the British who refused to agree to such a proposal. Chamberlain to his credit thought it improper to hold a conference while armies were fully mobilised for war, while Halifax thought that, even if direct Polish-German talks could be set up, the conference would be irrelevant. If Hitler rejected direct talks, as he had done consistently throughout the month of August, then (Halifax believed) war would surely follow. It was also true that Mussolini himself was convinced that Danzig was indisputably German and not worth a war. But he also thought that nothing could be achieved unless he, as intermediary, could offer Hitler the city. Ciano's last-minute flirtation with the British (his conference idea was also supported by the British Ambassador in Rome, Sir Percy Loraine) had come too late. Neither was France interested in such a conference.[51]

Chamberlain had placed too much faith in Mussolini's influence in Berlin, even though the Italian Foreign Minister, Ciano, had belatedly realised the truly reckless element in Hitler's plans. Ciano could not convince his master that war would be a disaster for Italy, while the British had taken too long to realise that Mussolini had been thoroughly seduced by the idea of military glory. (In fact, even Mussolini was sufficiently aware of Italy's military deficiencies not to risk going to war until France was on its knees in June 1940.) It was also evident from Mussolini's rhetoric over the years, boasting for example that the Mediterranean would become *mare nostrum* (our sea), that British and Italian interests were becoming increasingly incompatible. Nonetheless, it was clear to the British government that Italy was the lesser threat, and Chamberlain was not alone in his desire to maintain a good relationship with it. Churchill was not unsympathetic towards Mussolini, and the same was true of other senior Tory figures like Leo Amery. But just as British policy towards Germany foundered on the assumption that alleged 'moderates' in the Nazi hierarchy (such as Göring) could influence Hitler, so London consistently exaggerated the influence that the senior Fascist dictator could exercise in Berlin. Britain's parlous international situation in the 1930s decreed, however, that the attempt had to be made to use Mussolini, and the latter took advantage of this. That appeasement of Italy involved the doughty Vansittart was the ultimate demonstration of its necessity. Nevertheless, there was considerable disillusionment with Mussolini in establishment circles. When he treacherously attacked the stricken French on 10 June 1940, Thomas Jones had already recorded a conversation with a friend who said that Italy

> is behaving like the 'kept woman' of Europe. Mussolini's 'kept woman' I understand is a German at this present moment [this seems highly unlikely]. A friend of mine recently back from a mission in Rome, describes Ciano as a tough, Balbo as a crook.[52]

Bismarck had famously described the Italians in similar terms. It was a measure of Mussolini's diplomatic ineptitude that he had single-handedly recreated such an image.

In 1941, the British diplomat Sir Owen O'Malley visited Japan at the end of a tour of duty in Budapest. He wrote later of how, through all the areas he visited, which included Japanese-occupied Manchuria, all the British consuls and other British subjects were 'loud in their complaints of the inefficiency and suspicious and disobliging behaviour of the Japanese'. O'Malley and his travelling companions, by contrast, found the Japanese to be 'courteous and obliging'.[53] These conflicting responses reflected perhaps traditional British admiration for the Japanese and exasperation over their increasingly belligerent and confrontational behaviour in the 1930s. For Britain had been an ally of Japan between 1902 and 1922, and the 1902 Anglo-Japanese Friendship Treaty had been the crowning achievement of the Emperor Meiji, who had worked to modernise Japan by aping western technology and institutions. Japan had sided with the Entente Powers in the First World War, seizing the chance to annex German concessions in China and the Shantung peninsula.

After the First World War, however, Britain found itself in difficulty where Japan was concerned. Its main priority was to maintain cordial relations with the United States, which was becoming increasingly alarmed by the growth of Japanese power and influence in the Pacific. A particular issue was Japanese naval power, which was addressed in the 1921–22 Washington Naval Conference. This resulted in the Five Power Naval Treaty which was signed by the United States, Britain, Japan, France and Italy. Under its terms, the tonnage ratio between the Americans, British and Japanese was fixed at a ratio of 5:5:3 for so-called 'capital ships', that is those with a displacement of 10,000 tons and over which were armed with eight-inch guns. This meant that the Japanese could have a capital fleet 60 per cent of the size of the Royal Navy and the US Navy. The Washington Naval Treaty, as the Five Power Naval Treaty is more commonly known, coincided with Britain's decision to abandon the Japanese alliance because the Americans were so hostile to it. Both decisions were bitterly resented in Japan, where they were linked to accusations of white racism. Although Japanese policy was directed by relatively moderate politicians in the 1920s, such grievances were to fuel the aggressive Japanese nationalism of the following decade.

The British for their part were curiously complacent about the Japanese threat in the 1920s, none more so that the then Chancellor of the Exchequer, Winston Churchill. In 1924, Churchill thought the idea of a Japanese threat in the Pacific was 'nonsense'. He did not believe Japan had 'any idea of attacking the British Empire, or that there is any danger of her doing so for at least a generation to come'.[54] The passage of time, and concrete evidence of Japanese intentions (such as the attack on Manchuria in 1931), did little to alter Churchill's attitude. Ten years later, in 1934, Churchill was still saying that the Japanese posed no threat. By contrast, the new Defence Requirements Committee, set up by the government in the same year, identified Japan as a threat second only to Nazi Germany. Yet again stereotypical anti-appeasers are shown to be vastly less consistent than they are commonly portrayed as being, while the damned appeasing faint-hearts like Baldwin and Chamberlain turn out to be more prescient than usually allowed for (the latter in particular took a keen interest in the work of the committee).

Had Churchill been more perceptive, he would have recognised the warning signs when he was still Chancellor in the period 1924 to 1929. Japan had a chronic overpopulation problem (its population was rising by a million every year), combined with a lack of raw materials other than silk which could be exported. Its industries were dependent on imported raw materials, the Home Islands did not grow enough food, and the Japanese had to pay for imported food with manufacturing exports. Emigration quotas imposed by the USA and 'White Australia' did little to assist Japan's predicament.

Matters came to a head in 1931, as a result of the global depression following the Wall Street Crash, which hit Japanese exports hard. Militant nationalism became a feature of younger officers in the army and navy, and successive Japanese governments were willing to raise arms spending. Moderate politicians became an endangered species, and political assassinations at the hands of the xenophobic Right became commonplace (a typical episode being the butchering of Finance Minister Takahashi in February 1936 while one of the assassins apologised to the victim's servants 'for the annoyance I have caused').[55] All this was added to lingering Japanese resentment about naval disarmament and the way the Anglo-Saxon democracies had, in native eyes, coerced them in 1922.

It came as little surprise, therefore, that Japan's road to war was precipitated by rebellious elements in the military in 1931. The location for this event was the province of Manchuria, in theory part of China but where Japan already had considerable influence through its control of the South Manchurian Railway. Claiming Chinese provocation, the Kwantung army seized control of the whole province of Manchuria, and in March 1932 Japan announced the setting up of 'Manchukuo', supposedly independent but actually run by the Japanese behind the façade presented by the puppet ruler Pu Yi, the last of the Manchu Emperors of China.

Manchuria was the first great crisis to confront the League of Nations and its supposed protectors, Britain and France. It also put to the test British hopes that cooperation with the United States would be fruitful, although successive governments had become disillusioned by the effects of US isolationism in both Europe and Asia. Vansittart voiced British anxiety when he minuted in 1932 that 'we are incapable of checking Japan in any way if she really means business'.[56] The Chiefs of Staff shared this assessment and feared that Japan could endanger the security of India, Australia and New Zealand, especially as the planned new British naval base at Singapore was a long way from completion. The view from London, given fears about the revival of German militarism, was already bleak.

The British Foreign Secretary in 1932–33 was Sir John Simon, an unpopular figure who craved affection but was incapable of inspiring it. Ramsay MacDonald wrote that Simon had 'a terrible manner and smile which robs him of the appearance of sincerity'. He did not hit it off with his American counterpart, Stimson, whom he 'displeased ... by looking as if he had just got out of a cold bath',[57] and a legalistic mind set made Simon's solutions to the Far Eastern imbroglio seem unduly Byzantine. History has probably been unkind to Simon,[58] but he seemed, to contemporaries, to be trying to be all things to all men, that is, appearing to be pro-League while simultaneously courting Japanese, American and Chinese favour. This policy was, of course, unworkable.

Simon faced a real dilemma over Manchuria. Any forcible response to Japanese aggression relied upon American assistance, which was plainly not going to be forthcoming. Stimson, the US Secretary of State, relied on the utopian assumption that condemnation of Japan in the court of world opinion would shame the Japanese militarists (this term seems to be more appropriate than the more pejorative 'Fascists') into repentance.[59] The British found this attitude frustrating, as they also wished to protect their considerable financial and commercial interests in China at a time when Chinese nationalists resented foreign interference, be it Japanese, European or American. The United States, too, had a large financial stake in China.

In Whitehall, an ongoing debate went on about whether Japan should be appeased or faced down over Manchuria and over subsequent issues in Anglo-Japanese relations. Neville Chamberlain, as Chancellor of the Exchequer, believed that an accommodation with Japan was both possible and desirable. He was strongly supported by the Permanent Under-Secretary at the Treasury, Sir Warren Fisher, who had a reputation for being strongly anti-American just as Vansittart had one for being anti-German. In fact 'Van' could be just as caustic about the Americans.

It is questionable, however, whether any other British Foreign Secretary would have done better than Simon, given the circumstances with which he was faced. Despite being condemned by the Lytton Commission set up by the League of Nations, Japan went on to launch an attack near the international settlements in Shanghai in January 1934 (where all the great powers had areas of sovereignty). Although a cease-fire was negotiated between Japan and China in March over Shanghai, the Japanese went on to attack the province of Jehol and occupy it.

The Japanese assault in Shanghai made the Far East an issue in British politics.[60] There was no renewal of Japanese aggression in China until 1937, but the British government remained acutely aware of the threat which it posed to British interests in the Far East. Japanese behaviour had already caused the British to rescind the Ten Years Rule in 1932.

Japan remained a threat for a number of reasons. First, it was a threat to British investment in China. Secondly, Britain's great naval base at Singapore was still under construction and, without it, Britain's only response to possible Japanese aggression was to hazard sending units of the Home and Mediterranean fleets to the Far East, thus depleting its naval forces in Europe. Thirdly and crucially, the Manchurian crisis showed that the USA would not risk a war with Japan, and had opted merely for a policy of so-called 'non-recognition' which Tokyo could safely ignore. Vansittart's verdict on this situation was tart: 'we must be done for eventually unless the United States are prepared to use force'.[61] The need to appease Japan arose from the recognition that US administrations, even under the supposedly sympathetic Franklin Roosevelt, were not going to be party to a policy of coercion. Subsequent US criticisms of appeasement in the post-war era have tended to ignore America's complicity in the policy, precisely because of its unwillingness to wrestle with the Japanese threat. Britain faced by multiple threats in Europe and Asia was in no position to take on Japan single-handed. Its only other hope was that Soviet–Japanese antagonism in the Far East over Mongolia might rein in Japanese militarism or divert it into a war with the USSR (as briefly happened in 1939).

The renewal of the Sino-Japanese war in July 1937 was a result of accident rather than design. Chinese troops fired on Japanese forces near the Marco Polo Bridge near Peking, where they were quite legally stationed under the terms of the Boxer Protocols following the celebrated uprising of the Society of Harmonious Fists against the foreign powers in 1900. This relatively trivial incident need not have led to a general war, but, because of a leadership failure on the Japanese side, it did so. Prime Minister Konoe Fumimaro, appointed a month before the Marco Polo Bridge clash, was expected to be able to control the army but was instead persuaded by the generals to step up the war in China. While it is true that Konoe fundamentally agreed with most of the army's aims, and supported the idea of a Great Asia Association which would be dominated by Japan, he did not want war with the European powers or the USA. But Konoe was chronically indecisive. A fellow Minister remarked that 'Whenever any difficult questions arose, he frequently said, "I want to give up"'.[62] Konoe's frailty gave the warmongers in the Japanese army their head. Shanghai fell to the Japanese and in December, then Nanking was captured after a horrific massacre in which the Japanese killed, tortured or raped 250,000 people. International opinion was horrified, but China was to receive little assistance from the outside world until the United States entered the Second World War in December 1941. Meantime, guerrilla resistance by the Communists, rather than action by the corrupt Chinese leader, Chiang Kai-shek, prevented a complete Japanese conquest.

According to his admirer and Parliamentary Private Secretary, 'Chips' Channon, Chamberlain did 'not like the Japs'. Channon noticed that Chamberlain would amend answers 'to Japanese questions [in the House of Commons] and make them terser'.[63] This may well have been the case, but Chamberlain remained convinced, nonetheless, that appeasement of Japan was necessary. Like Fisher at the Treasury, Chamberlain was dismissive of the Americans, confiding to his diary his belief that 'the USA will give us no undertaking to resist by force any action by Japan, short of an attack on Hawaii or Honolulu'.[64] This prescient comment on 6 June 1934 prefigured the Japanese assault on Pearl Harbor seven years later, and it was starkly accurate. Chamberlain's anti-American prejudice, which partly derived from cultural snobbery, can rightly be criticised, but no one can fault his appraisal of US policy at the time.

Five years later, when the murder of a Japanese office in Tientsin was used as an excuse to humiliate (and even strip search) British subjects, Chamberlain was pleased when the Americans renounced their trade treaty with Japan, but when the Senate refused to amend the Neutrality Act to ban arms exports to Japan, he wrote to the Governor-General of Canada, Tweedsmuir, that it was 'enough to make one weep'.[65] Neither did the vacillating policy of Prince Konoe make the evolution of British policy towards Japan an easy matter. It may be the case that Japan blundered into war as a result of arrogance and the deluded hope that one more victory would see off its enemies, and solve all of its problems,[66] although controversy remains about the responsibility of Emperor Hirohito for its aggrandisement.[67] But such blundering would not make its behaviour easy to interpret in London, where it could easily be taken for an Asian version of Hitler's *Lebensraum*. Japan's links with the Axis powers through the 1937 Anti-Comintern Pact further muddied the waters.

The central focus of British foreign and defence policy in the 1930s was upon the threat posed by Nazi Germany. But the threat from the other two authoritarian states was never taken less than seriously. Given what we now know, it is of course possible to argue that a war against Italy in 1935 could and should have been fought and won. Indeed, it is further possible to argue that the Abyssinian War, rather than the reoccupation of the Rhineland as subsequently suggested by Churchill, was the point where a line should have been drawn in the sand as far as the dictatorships were concerned. The appeasers, therefore, could be castigated for not initiating coercive action against Mussolini to prevent both British and League of Nations prestige from being fatally undermined. This accepts the premise that the worldwide depression of 1929 to 1931, and the consequent focus on domestic economic troubles in the democracies made the likelihood of action against Japan over Manchuria remote.

It is easy, however, to find crucial flaws in such a case. British and French policy differed significantly in 1935 and 1936, with France always seeing Hitler rather than Mussolini as the greater threat. This made the French always more receptive to the idea of a deal with Mussolini, a position which the British government itself had adopted by late 1935. The belief that Mussolini might carry weight with Hitler was subsequently shown to be wrong, but a war with

Italy in 1935 would have created even greater opportunities for Hitler in Central Europe than Britain's ambiguous stance did. And Britain's primary focus on the Anglo-German relationship was underlined by the 1935 Anglo-German Naval Agreement signed *before* Mussolini attacked Abyssinia. This angered the French, and made the French generally unreceptive to any British suggestions that action should be taken against Fascist Italy. The appraisal of Mussolini's military strength in 1935–36 may have been inaccurate, but military intelligence can often be faulty and civilian politicians can hardly be blamed for being influenced by it.

As it was, British policy was influenced by the public's moral disapproval of Mussolini's behaviour to the point where, in late February 1936, the Cabinet did consider the imposition of oil sanctions through the League as a method of punishing the Italian dictator (however late in the day). Baldwin told colleagues that he 'thought his own position as Prime Minister would be much affected ... a refusal to impose an oil sanction would have a disastrous effect both now and at the next General Election'.[68] The Cabinet approved the imposition of oil sanctions by the League, a policy turnabout, from the time of the Hoare–Laval Pact, and one which infuriated the French. The French demanded an assurance that if their support was given over oil sanctions, Britain would undertake to support France in the preservation of the Demilitarised Zone in the Rhineland, even if the French acted alone against a pre-emptive move by Hitler. Baldwin was not prepared to give any such undertaking; and, once Hitler had sent his troops into the Zone on 7 March, there was no prospect of French support for a sanctions policy against Mussolini. By May 1936, Abyssinian resistance to the Italians had effectively collapsed, apart from some guerrilla activity. A possible chance to punish Mussolini had foundered, not on the pusillanimity of the British, but on rival Anglo-French perceptions of the national interest. Fundamental British scepticism about the effectiveness of the League as a defender of international order, and a preference for a bilateral arrangement, was underlined by Neville Chamberlain's celebrated remark on 10 June that the actual retention of sanctions against Italy would have been 'the very midsummer of madness'.[69] Britain could not go it alone on such an issue and go to war, but the government had, in fact, supported some measures against Mussolini, using the limited means at the disposal of the League, whose covenant made no provision for a standing armed force.

6

Three Crises

When he came to power in 1933, Adolf Hitler had certain clear-cut foreign policy goals partly reflecting traditional German grievances against the Versailles Treaty, but which also involved grandiose and reckless ambitions that would have appalled Western statesmen had they fully understood them. As astute a politician as David Lloyd George had been taken in by Hitler in 1936, and the tendency in Britain to see Hitler as a revisionist statesman who might be conciliated by territorial concessions died hard. Part of the strategy involved looking at the issue of colonies, bearing in mind that Germany had lost its own in 1919. Another was to look at those territorial or military aspects of the Versailles settlement which could be altered in the hope that Hitler might become a responsible member of the international community. One of these was the status of the Demilitarised Zone in the Rhineland, where Allied troops had remained until 1930, but where Germany was forbidden from stationing members of the Reichswehr, although it retained sovereignty over the area.

The Rhineland crisis of March 1936 occupies a central place in what has been described as the 'Churchillian critique' of the origins of the Second World War and Britain's role in it. The Anglo-French failure to react to Hitler's illegal occupation of the zone (which breached both the Versailles and Locarno Treaties), on 7 March and thereafter, was seen by Churchill as a decisive turning point. Writing in 1948, he was sure that 'had His Majesty's Government chosen to act with firmness and resolve through the League of Nations, they could have led a united Britain forward on a final quest to avoid war'.[1] The inference is that the then Prime Minister Baldwin and his Cabinet were guilty of dereliction of duty. It is a seductive thesis, given Germany's military weakness at the time (France's army was vastly bigger), but one which ignores inconvenient facts. To be fair to Churchill, he never pretended that the account of the 1930s given in *The Gathering Storm* (the first volume of his war memoirs) was anything other than highly subjective. But his verdict on the Rhineland crisis dominated thinking on it well into the post-war period; as did his vivid portrayal of the effect of this crisis on his Foreign Office helper and admirer Ralph Wigram, who, on the news of the German move, went back to his house in North Street in London and, according to his wife, sat down in a corner of the room where he had never sat down before, and said to me, 'War is now inevitable and it will be the most terrible war there has ever been ... Wait now for bombs, bombs on this little house'.[2]

Wigram died on the last day of 1936, killed, according to Churchill, by his country's failure to react to the German provocation. In this way Churchill managed to conflate Wigram's personal tragedy with the wider one of failing to stop Hitler in 1936.[3]

The records now available to us show that the British government had long since written off the Demilitarised Zone as a defensible entity. As early as 14 January 1935, the British Cabinet, then headed by Ramsay MacDonald, had decided that the Rhineland Zone was not a vital British national interest.[4] Two months later Ralph Wigram himself minuted that 'Nothing is less certain than that we would be ready to resist ... an open violation of the Zone'.[5] He and Foreign Office colleagues agreed that Hitler was likely to take advantage of any differences between Britain, France and Italy over the Abyssinian crisis to re-enter the Zone by force. Eden did not accept Wigram's warnings about the imminence of any Rhineland coup by Hitler, but both he and Baldwin believed that British rearmament, though necessary, must be accompanied by concessions which might link a change in the status of the Rhineland Zone to an air pact. As it was, articles 42 and 43 of the Versailles Treaty prevented Germany from erecting fortifications in the Zone or stationing troops there.

The Cabinet rejected Wigram's pleas for a warning to Hitler about the consequences of violation of the Zone, believing that such a move would be provocative. The Rhineland was, after all, German territory, and the Versailles Treaty placed no obligation on any other power to enforce the application of articles 42 and 43 should Hitler unilaterally break the treaty. The Cabinet preferred a policy of keeping the Germans guessing about the likely British response to treaty transgressions, a policy which it continued to favour until 1938. Eden set out his position in early January 1936, when he told the Cabinet Committee on Germany that:

> It would be preferable for Great Britain and France to enter betimes into negotiations with the German Government for the surrender on conditions of our rights in the Zone while such a surrender still has got a bargaining value.[6]

This statement also drives a coach and horses through Eden's anti-appeasement credentials, for days later, on 17 January, he told the same committee that Hitler's foreign policy involved destroying the 1919 peace settlement (as it surely did), and re-establishing German dominance in Europe.

Eden's Permanent Under-Secretary in the Foreign Office, Vansittart, thought that Britain should consider making colonial concessions to the Germans. In the same memorandum (written on 3 February) he recognised that the Versailles system had broken down and that the best course was to 'try and come to terms with Germany before, as is otherwise virtually certain, she takes the law into her own hands'. Vansittart's proposed solution found sufficient favour with the Cabinet for a special Cabinet Committee, consisting of MacDonald, Chamberlain, Eden, Halifax, Simon, Thomas and Sir Walter Runciman, to be set up. Chamberlain and Thomas (the Colonial Secretary) wanted to offer Germany Tanganyika, the former German East Africa, but the committee could not reach a conclusion on this issue.[7]

Hints had already been dropped by the British government about its attitude to the Zone to their German counterparts. When the German Foreign Minister, Konstantin von Neurath, came to the funeral of George V in January, Eden told him that Britain was interested in linking an air pact, with agreed front-line aircraft figures, to a re-examination of the status of the Rhineland Zone. At the same time, Eden told the Soviet Ambassador in London, Litvinov, that Britain was not capable of decisive intervention in any crisis caused by unilateral German action against the Zone. This appears to have been a slip of the tongue by Eden, but it reflected the view of the Cabinet.[8]

By the beginning of March, the unwillingness of the British Cabinet to support any police action against Hitler over the Rhineland issue was manifest. At its meeting of 5 March 1936, the Cabinet concluded that 'the reality of the situation was that neither France nor England was really in a position to take effective military action against Germany in the event of a violation of Locarno'.[9] This position was fully endorsed by those in leading military circles. Colonel H.R. Pownall, the Military Assistant to the Committee of Imperial Defence, wrote in his diary on the 8 March, the day after German troops entered the Zone, about how Hitler 'will get away with it ... We are certainly in no position (even if we wanted to) to use force – nor are the French though they will squeak and sulk and ask for help'.[10] Pownall's Francophobia was common in the British political and defence establishment, but his comments underline the point that the Chiefs of Staff were also quite unwilling to assist France if it acted to enforce the Versailles Treaty.

When Hitler's long expected move into the Rhineland took place, on 7 March, there was unanimity in Britain. Lothian's remark, 'After all, the Germans are only going into their own back garden', is well known. Less celebrated is a later passage stating that 'we shall never get peace in Europe till Germany is strong enough to demand her rights from France'.[11] Lothian's friend, Dawson, ensured that the *Times* came out with a sympathetic leader under the title, 'A Chance to Rebuild'. German action might be regrettable, but it offered an opportunity to build a new Anglo-German relationship. Across the political spectrum the view was that Britain could do nothing. In his memoirs Hugh Dalton, the most robust

Labour anti-appeaser, concluded that 'it was the practically unanimous view of the Labour Party and of a vast majority of the British people at the time, that we could not apply sanctions to Germany over the Rhineland'.[12] Even Churchill had to concede in *The Gathering Storm* that the comments made by Lothian were 'a representative British view'.[13] How in this context therefore could Churchill twelve years later castigate the British government for inaction? Especially as Hitler had astutely sugared the pill by combining his move into the Rhineland with offers of twenty-five-year non-aggression pacts to France and Belgium, together with an indication that Germany might re-enter the League (which he had left in 1933 after complaining that France was refusing to disarm).

It was still possible to coordinate an Anglo-French response after 7 March, but military wisdom dictated otherwise as far as Britain was concerned. On 11 March, the Chiefs of Staff warned that most British naval, air and ground forces were concentrated in the Mediterranean, and it would take time to recall them to the European theatre. Only two army divisions were actually available to send to France in March 1936 and it was calculated that it would take three weeks to get them there. No tanks were available, nor were there any anti-tank guns or mortars. Even if they had been available, Britain's response was secondary to that of France, and it is here in particular that Churchill's post-war analysis was badly adrift. His assumption was that France ought to have been able and willing to react with force against any move by Hitler into the Rhineland. The evidence suggests otherwise.

The French military was much more concerned that the Abyssinian War would cause a permanent rift with Mussolini than it was about the long-expected German move into the Rhineland. If there was concern, it was that reoccupation might be combined with some larger attack on France itself. Neither were French politicians prepared to raise the issue of what was to happen if German troops did appear in the Zone. Not a single French politician spoke or wrote about this question, and there was no parliamentary debate on the subject in the months and years before March 1936.[14] This silence spoke volumes.

It has been argued that because the French army was in a costly process of re-equipment in the mid-1930s, the Rhineland episode was therefore 'a manufactured crisis with a predictable outcome. It figures in no sense as a turning point of the 1930s'.[15] French Cabinet Ministers had ample warning about German intentions from the Deuxième Bureau (French military intelligence), but no one pressed for a plan to deal with such an emergency. Traditional attempts to make much of the fact that the caretaker Saurrat–Flandin government was in office on 7 March (thus allegedly demonstrating France's internal chaos), do not convince therefore. Foreign Minister Flandin went through the motions of convening a meeting of the Locarno powers (and he is prominent in the Churchill narrative) but France had in fact long written off the Zone. It knew that

British assistance would not be forthcoming, and Mussolini also indicated that he would not support any police action about remilitarisation. France was the power pre-eminently concerned about the status of the Rhineland Zone, but, as it was not prepared to fight for it, it was rather absurd to expect Britain to react in the manner which Churchill seemed to expect. Neither can French failure to respond somehow be blamed on Britain's appeasers. They did not welcome the prospect of a French resort to force but were in no position to prevent it (any more than they had been in January 1923 at the time of the Ruhr occupation). France had been reluctant to support Britain over Abyssinia; now Britain could not see the status of the Zone as a vital national interest to fight for. Neither, more crucially, could the French themselves. At the time, Baldwin feared that the French might let 'loose another Great War' by intervening, and he thoroughly disliked France's pact with the USSR (ratified in February 1936). He thought that a Franco–Soviet victory over Germany in a future war might 'result in Germany going Bolshevik',[16] which showed a degree of prescience. He exaggerated the solidity of the Franco-Soviet alliance, but his fear that the Rhineland issue might lead to a general war was not maladroit. The Rhineland was manifestly not worth a war, and no one could have persuaded the British people otherwise in 1936.

Assumptions that an Anglo-French riposte must have inevitably led to the collapse of the Hitler government remain as they have always been, just speculation, however vividly they are presented in the pages of Churchill's book.[17] Hitler, after all, had survived the setback of July 1934 when he had prematurely encouraged the anti-Döllfuss coup in Austria, and by March 1936 he was winning Mussolini over to his side. The 30,000 German troops who entered the Zone on 7 March (not the 295,000 bizarrely estimated by the French) had orders not to flee if attacked but to retire in good order. The British Military Attaché in Berlin reported that any Allied invasion of the Rhineland could expect 'very determined resistance'. His Ambassador, Sir Eric Phipps, thought that the Germans would 'fight to the finish'. So much for the assumption behind the Churchillian thesis that an Anglo-French response would have led to a rapid and successful conclusion.[18]

The disappearance of the Rhineland Zone took away one of the British government's bargaining ploys, but the colonial issue remained. Restitution of German colonies could perhaps be linked to a more general European settlement, and the Hitler government seemed disposed to consider this. This at least was a possible interpretation of talks which the German Economics Minister, Dr Schacht, had in Paris in August 1936. Schacht had the reputation of being the financial wizard who had saved the German economy from inflationary disaster in the 1920s. He was not a Nazi Party member, and had become concerned about Hitler's grandiose foreign policy objectives in Europe and particularly his stated intention to achieve 'living space' for Germany in the east, which Schacht thought could only lead to war. It was much safer, in Schacht's view, to try and achieve living space by means of a restitution of Germany's colonies. Schacht had written an article in the prestigious journal *Foreign Affairs* in which he declared that the colonial problem was 'simply and solely a matter of economic existence ... There will be no peace in Europe until this problem is solved'. He encouraged the French Premier, Léon Blum, to acquaint the British government with his views.

The British were not unduly impressed by Schacht's suggestion. It was not clear that he had Hitler's authority to place such emphasis on a colonial readjustment, but in a speech on 20 January 1937 the Führer himself stated that 'Our demand for colonies ... will be put forward again and again'. His odious Ambassador in London, Joachim von Ribbentrop (soon to become Foreign Minister) also spoke of Germany's 'small territory ... on the poor soil of Northern Europe'.[19]

The British had favoured examination of the colonial issue in the context of a five-power conference which could effectively renegotiate Locarno, but the Germans showed little enthusiasm for this. Nevertheless, Neville Chamberlain, who had increasing influence on foreign policy evolution as Chancellor, wanted to react more positively to Schacht's initiative and he persuaded Eden to agree. Sir Frederick Leith Ross, the Government's Chief Economic Adviser, was despatched to Germany in February 1937 to talk to Schacht. Little that was new emerged from Leith Ross's visit.

Nevertheless, Eden thought it worthwhile to circulate a record of the Leith Ross visit to the Cabinet Foreign Policy Committee. He hoped to get some sort of consensus about the nature of any British reply to the Schacht proposals. Germany might be persuaded to take part in a more general settlement if some attempt were made to redress its colonial grievances first. When the Foreign Policy Committee met on 18 March, Chamberlain talked of restoring Togo and Cameroon, partitioned between Britain and France, to Germany. It was agreed that there ought to be joint Anglo-French exploratory talks with Germany. But Chamberlain also insisted on conditions. Germany must sign up to non-aggression treaties in place of Locarno (Hitler had, of course, offered these to France and Belgium in March 1936) and rejoin the League of Nations. Neither would Britain agree to return Tanganyika. Chamberlain's strategy has been accurately described as pushing the colonial question into the background; if such a contoversial issue were given a position of importance, it might destroy the chance of general talks.[20] Colonial appeasement offered a chance to build bridges with Germany, but it became increasingly clear that the British preferred other colonial powers to make the major territorial concessions. Even in the case of Togo and Cameroon, it was France that would be ceding the most territory. This suited the national interest admirably. No one could accuse Chamberlain or Baldwin (now in the last months of his long parliamentary career) of giving away Britain's colonial territory lightly. South Africa, too, led by Smuts, showed no disposition to return former German South-West Africa, despite the overtly pro-German sentiments of its settler population.[21] Smuts wrote later to Lothian 'we do not mean to stick to all the ex-German colonies'.[22] What this meant in practice, however, was that (Togo and Cameroon apart) the colonial powers who might have to concede territory were Belgium and Portugal rather than Britain and France.

To Chamberlain's disappointment, the French were opposed to the cession of Togo and Cameroon, but, as Prime Minister from May 1937 he insisted that colonial appeasement be kept on the agenda, and that Dr Schacht should be used as an intermediary between the British and German governments. He could not know that, when he met Göring and the armed forces leaders on 5 November 1937, Hitler would tell Schacht, who was also present, that he favoured waiting until Britain was 'in difficulties', as only then would it be prepared to make real concessions.[23] This ambiguous statement (Britain was after all in real enough difficulty given the behaviour of the aggressor states) seems to have only been an effort to relegate the colonial issue to a subsidiary role in the formulation of German foreign policy. The meeting on 5 November documented in the so-called 'Hossbach Memorandum', after the colonel who took the minutes at the meeting, was significant mainly because it gave a clear indication of Hitler's long-term objectives in Europe. Germany was to be ready, the Führer told his generals and admirals, to take advantage of favourable situations in Austria, Czechoslovakia and even France, where some thought civil war a possibility given the poisonous hatred between left and right.

When the Lord Privy Seal Lord Halifax made his celebrated visit to Berlin later in November, Hitler only made vague pronouncements about colonies. He told Halifax that it was outrageous that 'certain nations did not have sufficient space to live', an obvious reference to his doctrine of *Lebensraum*, but did not provide his British visitor with any detail about exactly what colonial concessions Germany wanted. The most Halifax could elicit from Hitler was a reference to Germany's 'former properties', and a declaration that Germany was not interested in obtaining any territory around the Mediterranean or in the Far East because those areas were too troublesome.[24] Schacht, who had also been invited to the meeting at Berchtesgaden, took the opportunity to say that Germany wanted Togoland and Cameroon back, but that this concession should be combined with the creation of a German mandate from parts of Angola and the Belgian Congo. Schacht's proposal presupposed that Germany would rejoin the League, which was highly unlikely, and Hitler gave no support to his former Economics Minister's proposal. On the British side, it was made clear to Hitler that Tanganyika would not be given up.

Despite his efforts after the war to pretend that he disapproved of Halifax's visit, Eden was pleased by Halifax's sensitive handling of the colonial issue at

Berchtesgaden. But at the Cabinet meeting on 24 November, Eden noted that the Germans had 'given no indication of any quid pro quo for any colonial concession. Germany clearly did not wish to connect Central Europe with the Colonial question'.[25] Given the nature of Hitler's extreme expansionist aims in eastern Europe, this was unsurprising.

Halifax had been unable to extract any meaningful statement from Hitler about colonies but Chamberlain continued to see the issue as a possible means of bringing Germany into a more general European settlement. Sir Nevile Henderson was recalled from Berlin for consultations at the end of January 1938, being accorded the rare privilege of sitting in on the meeting of the Foreign Policy Committee on 3 February.[26] The committee decided to continue the colonial initiative, although Henderson had warned Eden that the German government was likely to be unenthusiastic about his efforts to use colonial appeasement to secure a general settlement with Germany.[27]

Henderson returned to Berlin on 4 February to find himself in the midst of the notorious Blomberg crisis, when Hitler's Defence Minister, General von Blomberg, was found to have inadvertently married a well-known former prostitute. Hitler had been a witness at the marriage ceremony, and the episode was highly embarrassing for him. It has also been suggested that the Gestapo were well aware of Frau von Blomberg's seamy past, but it served as a pretext to get rid of moderates in the regime who might disapprove of his foreign policy excesses. Blomberg was removed from his post, and so too was the Foreign Minister, von Neurath, and the Army Chief of Staff von Fritsch (the last falsely smeared about an alleged homosexual affair).[28] All this meant that Henderson was not able to secure an interview with Hitler until 3 March. And his personal *bête noire*, Ribbentrop, was appointed Foreign Minister.

When Henderson did eventually see Hitler, he talked for some ten minutes about the need to link a colonial agreement with a limitation on armaments, and a restriction on aerial bombing, as he had been instructed to do. According to Henderson's personal account, Hitler 'remained crouching in his armchair with the most ferocious scowl on his face' throughout his presentation of the British case.[29] He showed little interest in the colonial question and said that it could wait for another ten years if need be. In the context of colonial readjustment, therefore, the Hitler–Henderson interview of 3 March 1938 has been rightly described as 'a complete disaster'.[30] Thereafter the looming Austrian crisis meant that Hitler's attention was focused elsewhere. He was never to show as much interest in the colonial issue as the British did.

The events of July 1934 in Austria have already been traced. But the successor to the murdered Chancellor Döllfuss found himself under increasing pressure from Germany, not least because of changes in Italian policy towards Austria. The so-called 'Gentleman's Agreement' of July 1936 between Austria and Germany highlighted Austrian vulnerability because it forced von Schuschnigg to take the crypto-Nazi Glaise-Horstenau into his government in the key post of Minister of the Interior. At the same time, the paramilitary pro-Italian Heimwehr, an obstacle to Nazi ambitions in Austria, was dissolved. Mussolini allowed these developments to pass unchallenged. Von Schuschnigg's position was further weakened in 1937 when the Austrian Nazi Seyss-Inquart was appointed to the Austrian State Council.

There has been some debate about the degree to which Hitler was following an 'evolutionary' policy with regard to Austria. As an Austrian national himself, he could be presumed to favour union (*Anschluss*) between his homeland and the Reich. And the events of 1936–37 certainly suggest that Austria was forced into a pro-German subordinate national status. Perhaps Hitler could afford to be patient. Certainly sending the wily conservative ex-Chancellor von Papen to Vienna as the German Minister suggested that Hitler was disposed to be patient. In December 1937, Hitler told von Papen that he wanted to avoid the use of force in Austria to prevent international repercussions.[31] Göring also believed that Hitler might put off action on Austria until the spring or summer of 1938.[32] Papen suggested to von Schuschnigg that a meeting between the two Chancellors would be helpful.

On the Austrian side there was alarm about what seemed to be heightened subversive activity by the Austrian Nazi Party. Raids by the Austrian police at the end of December 1937 had uncovered evidence that the party was planning nationwide sabotage and provocation (Austrian intelligence had broken the Nazi cipher), allegedly to be followed by further demands from Hitler for a Nazi-dominated government. The timescale was a matter for conjecture but von Schuschnigg was sufficiently concerned to agree to a meeting with Hitler at Berchtesgaden on 12 February, when he intended to raise his concerns about Nazi activity. Nevertheless, von Schuschnigg went to Germany in a mood of some apprehension, reportedly telling his Foreign Minister Guido Schmidt (who turned out to be a Nazi fellow traveller) that 'it would be better for a psychiatrist to undertake this mission instead of me'.[33]

Von Schuschnigg never got the chance to put his concerns to the German dictator. Instead, he was subjected to a tirade of abuse by Hitler, who stationed General Keitel outside the door and forbade von Schuschnigg (a chain smoker) to smoke. Under a threat of invasion, the unfortunate Austrian Chancellor was forced to agree that Seyss-Inquart should be made Minister of the Interior and that there should be an amnesty for the many Austrian Nazis guilty of criminal offences. Austrian independence was being effectively undermined.

In Britain, there was a widespread feeling that, despite the ban placed by article 80 of Versailles, *Anschluss* was virtually inevitable. But the government did not wish to do anything that would encourage expansionism on the part of Germany. Neither, on the other, was it committed to the use of force to preserve Austrian independence. But Hitler had interpreted comments made by Lord Halifax on his visit to Germany in November 1937 as meaning that Britain would take no action in the event of *Anschluss*.

The stakes were raised suddenly on 9 March when von Schuschnigg courageously announced that a plebiscite would be held on 13 March to determine whether the Austrian people wanted to remain free and independent, or whether they wanted union with Germany. He had done this despite the fact that soundings with Mussolini had shown that the Duce would deem such a move provocative. At the time Ribbentrop was in London making his farewells as German Ambassador (he would not be missed), and Halifax told him on 10 March about the dangers that would result from reckless action in Central Europe. The British Minister in Vienna, Michael Palairet, thought that von Schuschnigg's action was correct. 'My own view', he telegraphed to Halifax, 'is that the risk is worth taking. The Chancellor would lose his authority if the present atmosphere of alarm and uncertainty were to continue.'[34] Halifax too, it seemed, was prepared to be robust, telling Ribbentrop that 'it seemed a pretty tall order to say that a Head of State could not have a plebiscite if he wanted to'.[35] Hitler was, of course, desperate to prevent the plebiscite taking place lest the vote go against him and remove any justification for the *Anschluss*.

As Ribbentrop was having his farewell lunch with Chamberlain at Chequers, a letter was handed to the new Permanent Under-Secretary at the Foreign Office, Sir Alexander Cadogan, who was also present. He opened the letter and passed it on to Chamberlain, who read of Germany's invasion of Austrian territory during the night of 11–12 March. When taxed about what this meant, Ribbentrop replied that the German troop movements were merely 'spring manoeuvres'. Von Schuschnigg resigned, but the Austrian President, Miklas, resisted for some time before agreeing that Hitler's stooge Seyss-Inquart should be installed as Chancellor. It is possible that Hitler only finally approved the outright annexation, whereby Austria merely became 'Ostland' and a province of the Reich, when he returned in triumph to his home city of Linz. In reality, it mattered little: a Nazified Austria under Seyss-Inquart would have been a German satellite with only the merest illusion of sovereignty.

In London some, like the anti-appeasement MP Harold Nicolson, had rejoiced when von Schuschnigg called for a plebiscite. He recorded in his diary on 10 March how he and other backbenchers (including Churchill's son-in-law, Duncan Sandys) had congratulated the Austrian Minister Franckenstein on 'having declared a plebiscite and having been so brave as to stand up to Hitler'.[36] When Hitler stamped on the last vestiges of Austrian independence, Chamberlain himself found it 'all very disheartening and discouraging', becoming convinced that 'force is the only language which Germany understands'.[37] On 12 March, the Prime Minister told his Cabinet that Hitler's behaviour was 'a typical illustration of power politics'.[38] Two days later, in the House of Commons, Chamberlain again used strong language to condemn German behaviour, though Nicolson thought the statement 'dry' and giving 'little indication of real policy'.[39] Nicolson's personal animus against Chamberlain was clear-cut, for on 9 March he had written in his diary of how 'the soul of the ironmonger [a sneer at Chamberlain's industrial origins] is not one that will save England'. Some would never be prepared to give Chamberlain credit for a rational and well thought out policy.

Yet what in March 1938 was the alternative to the usual, ritual protest against Hitler's illegal behaviour? The Chiefs of Staff in Britain were again adamant that war could not be risked, especially as Mussolini was now clearly in the German camp. And it was obvious that the French would not act on their own or in concert with Britain. In November 1937, the French leaders Chautemps and Delbos had come to London and agreed that Britain should take the initiative in talks with Berlin and Rome. Prime Minister Chautemps thought it likely in February 1938 that 'central and eastern Europe would slip into the hands of Germany without war'.[40] When the move against Austria came, France was in one of its periodic government crises. In 1934 Mussolini had played a crucial role in safeguarding Austrian integrity, but in March 1938 he made it clear that he regarded Austria as a German problem. (Hitler sent him an hysterically grateful message.) Neither Britain nor France could look to Soviet Russia, where Stalin was in the middle of purging both his armed forces and the Communist Party bureaucracy, for assistance. Summing up the dramatic events of 11–12 March, even Minister Palairet in Vienna had changed his tune, observing that von Schuschnigg's tactics 'may have been mistaken'.[41] He did not indicate what other path the cornered Austrian Chancellor could have taken, but that of the British government was laid down by Halifax when von Schuschnigg asked for help when faced by the threat of German aggression (in the event the response was never sent to Vienna because von Schuschnigg's resignation was known to be imminent). According to Halifax's reply:

> His Majesty's Government cannot take the responsibility of advising the Chancellor to take any course of action which might expose his country to dangers against which HM Government are unable to guarantee protection.[42]

A brutally frank response, perhaps, given Austria's peril, but Mussolini's defection was far more significant from von Schuschnigg's viewpoint, as the Austrians had relied on the Duce's government for protection. Britain had no explicit treaty commitment to Austria, save these general ones implicit in the League Covenant, and deemed itself, in the light of possible perils in the Mediterranean and the Far East to be in no position to render assistance to Austria, especially as the *Anschluss* seemed to be accompanied by a wave of pro-Reich hysteria in Austria itself. Von Schuschnigg himself was forced to pay a heavy price for his independent gesture, for after a brief period of imprisonment in the Hotel Metropole in Vienna (where the Gestapo forced him to clean the toilets), he was incarcerated in a concentration camp. British opinion was shocked by the brutal pogrom that accompanied the German arrival in Vienna, but there was a general consensus that nothing could have been done to save Austria. This was a view shared by the professionals in the Foreign Office a month before the *Anschluss*. Orme Sargent, the Deputy Under-Secretary, usually regarded as a supporter of Vansittart (now removed to the irrelevant post of Chief Diplomatic Adviser), had summarised his views on Austria in a memorandum.

> I think [he wrote] we are all convinced that the process of absorption in Austria by Germany has now begun and will continue steadily to its appointed end. Nothing that we can say is going to prevent this process, and any protests by France and ourselves may merely encourage Schuschnigg and his followers in Austria to prolong the agony unnecessarily, while at the same time revealing our impotence to alter or even delay events.[43]

The only weapon that the British had was secrecy. They could merely hope to confuse the Germans about any likely British response, but the evidence is that Hitler had already second-guessed them.

Czechoslovakia was one of the children of the post-war settlement. It was based on an alliance of Czechs and Slovaks (uneasy bedfellows as it proved), but the new state also contained substantial minorities of Magyars, Poles, Ruthenes and, ominously, three and a half million ethnic Germans. Yet those so-called Sudeten Germans, who lived in the border area bounded by the Sudeten mountains, had never been part of the German Reich, although the Bohemian German aristocracy had played a prominent part in the administration of the old Austro-Hungarian Empire. Prague was considered by them to be a German city, though Czech civilisation had a long and distinguished pedigree of its own. Czech culture was both lively and democratic. In 1933, for example, the German Minister protested against the Czech film *The Donkey and the Shadow* which attacked the Nazis.[44] Czechoslovakia was the only real democracy in Central Europe, dominated politically by Tomas Masaryk, the Father of the Nation (a Slovak), and the Czech Edvard Beneš.

For most Britons, Czechoslovakia was remote and of little interest. Backbench Tory MPs were still wanting to talk about 'Czechoslovenia' in 1938, adding geographical confusion to suspicion of a country which had military alliances with both France and the USSR. There was no more than a small group of Czechophiles, including the writer and former intelligence officer R. Bruce-Lockhart and the historian R.W. Seton Watson. For the British Cabinet in 1938, Czechoslovakia was largely unknown territory. The exception was the former Foreign Secretary, Sir Samuel Hoare, who wrote of how, since the First World War, he 'had taken a very close interest in the Czechoslovak movement that led to recognition of the republic, and I had followed with sincere admiration the fortunes of the new state'.[45] Hoare had been head of the military mission to Russia and Italy between 1916 and 1919, at the time when the so-called Czech Legion (made up of escaped Czechoslovak prisoners of war) had played a significant role in the Russian Civil War. During this time, he had come to know both Masaryk and Beneš, who were in exile in London after Seton Watson had made the initial introduction.[46] Czechoslovakia, therefore, had one friend in the British Cabinet (Hoare was now Home Secretary). But, significantly, Hoare noted in his memoirs that, when Czechoslovakia was in the process of creation in 1919–20, Masaryk had told him 'that he had never asked for the inclusion of the Sudeten Germans in the Czech State'.[47] If this is true, and there is no particular reason to doubt Hoare's testimony on the point, Masaryk already had a fear that the Sudeten Germans were a potential fifth column in his new state. According to Hoare, Masaryk planned to make Czechoslovakia into a federation of nationalities, but his death in 1937 saw the presidency fall to the Czech Beneš, who, although 'a brilliant politician and true Czech patriot', had too narrow a mind to embrace Masaryk's more liberal conception of Czechoslovakia.[48]

A much more typical British attitude to Czechoslovakia appears in the memoirs of Earl Winterton, who was sent to represent the British government at Masaryk's funeral in 1937. According to Winterton, the Czechs were 'the most obsequious of Soviet Satellites' and had been described as 'Slavs with most of the German faults and few of their good qualities'.[49] Foreigners, Winterton wrote, 'do not usually find the Czechs irresistibly attractive'.[50] Winterton's experience confirmed the typical view of the British establishment that Czech and Slovak had little love for each other, with the largely Protestant Czechs thinking themselves culturally and economically superior to the Catholic Slovaks. Winterton claimed that Beneš told him that 'he couldn't learn Slovak'.[51] The recently appointed Chancellor of the Duchy of Lancaster did not believe President Beneš's assurances about how happy and contented the Sudeten German minority were.

Anti-Czech prejudice could certainly be found in the Foreign Office as well. The counsellor in Britain's Prague Legation, Robert Hadow, believed that 'Austria and Czechoslovakia had no right to separate existence' and his Minister, Sir Joseph Addison, who was notoriously anti-Czech, disliked Beneš personally.[52] So too did his successor, Basil Newton, who was the man on the spot as the Czechs came under Nazi threat in the summer of 1938. Even Vansittart, the supposed supporter of collective security, had little time for Beneš, despite his fine record as a supporter of the League of Nations. Beneš, Vansittart had minuted in February 1937, was 'a blind little bat who has done a lot of flapping in his night'.[53] The anti-Czech prejudice of his deputy, Orme Sargent, was much sharper. Unlike Vansittart, Sargent was an obsessive critic of the 1935 Czech–Soviet alliance, and saw Czechoslovakia as 'practically ... the aircraft mother ship' of the Bolsheviks in Moscow.[54] The Prague government, Sargent was convinced, was offering aid and comfort to the Comintern, and Vansittart agreed with Sargent that, when he took up his post in Prague, Basil Newton should investigate what the Soviets were up to.[55] Meantime his predecessor, Joseph Addison, had been bombarding the Foreign Office with diatribes against the Czechs and Slavs in general. 'Order, method, punctuality, honesty in dealing with one's fellow human beings', wrote Addison, 'are as alien to the Slav character as water to a cat.'[56] For his part, Beneš regarded Addison as a 'thick-headed ignoramus'. His Minister in London, Jan Masaryk, also detected what he thought to be British prejudice against the Czechs. 'The English dislike us intensely', he wrote. 'We are a dead-weight for them and they curse the day on which we were founded.'[57]

Masaryk put his finger on an ambiguity of attitudes amongst the British where Czechoslovakia was concerned. British diplomats could not quite adjust themselves to the disappearance of the old Austro-Hungarian Empire, which had been such a reassuring, if dilapidated, presence in Central and Eastern Europe for centuries. Neither could their political masters in London. Austria's existence, after all, might preclude any reason for the British to meddle in the murky waters of Central Europe and the Balkans. But Eden, like Hoare, could recognise some positive Czech qualities. When subjected by Addison to yet another diatribe in a telegram, Eden minuted: 'Whatever the faults of the Czechs they are tough and have a good fighting record'.[58] And Masaryk, unlike his President, was very popular in London.[59] But all of this must be put into an historical context in which Britishers often disdained foreigners. Rumbold, for example, although an excellent reporter on the iniquities of Nazism, disliked *all* foreigners on principle (he was known to refer to the French as 'cads' and 'apes'). What dominated British policy towards Czechoslovakia was a mixture of morality and the application of national interest. But it is significant that a man like Sargent, traditionally portrayed as a doughty anti-appeaser, allowed prejudice against the Czechs to override the potential advantages of Czechoslovakia's alliances with France and the USSR. His bias against the USSR, like that of many of his contemporaries inside and outside Parliament, was even more pronounced.

Eden, at least, was perceptive enough to dismiss the crassness of the Hadow–Addison analysis, and to recognise that the evidence available to the Foreign Office in February 1937 showed that 'the German Government's policy is directed towards the disintegration and domination of Czechoslovakia'.[60] He told Newton, when he had taken up his post, that the British government would not make 'any definite statement in regard to whatever negotiations with Germany the Czechoslovak Government may have in mind to take'.[61] It would be wrong, in Eden's view, to discourage Beneš from talking to Germany about the problem of the Sudetenland, where the Sudeten Deutsch Party under Konrad Henlein was complaining bitterly about Czech discrimination. But, on the other hand, Eden was convinced that the British government should not involved itself in 'any sort of mediation ... either in Berlin or Prague to bring about a settlement of difficulties between Germany and Czechoslovakia'.[62] By the summer of 1938, this policy of magisterial detachment on Czechoslovak matters had clearly been abandoned. The reasons why it was abandoned reflect the story of Britain's increasing involvement in the Czech crisis in 1938.

It is wise at this point, however, to focus on the questions which sucked an unwilling British government into direct involvement with the Sudetenland crisis. In deciding how far the British government was duped in its attempts to defuse the growing crisis in the summer of 1938, it is important to judge how genuine the Sudeten German grievances against the Prague government were. It is foolish to deny that there were severe tensions between the Sudeten Germans and the dominant Czechoslovak majority (in practice, given the distribution of the minority German population, the problem was really one of Czech–German relations). For if it is true that the Sudeten Germans had difficulty in adjusting themselves to their new position in an independent Czechoslovakia, it is also the case that the Czechs saw an opportunity to settle old scores in 1919. There were a series of petty discriminatory acts by the Czech authorities which seemed designed to ruffle German sensitivities. Thus official reports on the debates in the national parliament in Prague were only available in Czech, and on the new republic's banknotes German wording was placed third behind that of Ruthene, although there were three and a half million ethnic Germans in Czechoslovakia and only half a million Ruthenes. Salt was rubbed into German wounds when the Mayor of Prague prohibited shop signs in German, although all other minorities could use their own languages and 50,000 Germans lived in Prague.

Thereafter, Czech–German relations improved somewhat but a dissident core of extreme German nationalists remained. By 1928, eight Nazi deputies had been elected to the Prague Parliament to represent the Sudeten minority (though other German deputies seemed prepared to work with the new Czech democracy). But the coming of the global depression after 1929 affected the Sudeten Germans areas more severely than the Czech areas, probably because Czech industry was more orientated towards the home market. The resultant unemployment and economic distress sharpened the appeal of nationalistic sports organisations like the Volksport, whose members wore Brown uniforms like the SA in Germany. In 1931, the Czech authorities banned the Volksport organisation and put seven of its members on trial for conspiracy against Czech democracy. The seven only received light sentences but Sudeten German feeling was inflamed.

It was out of the ranks of the Volksport, effectively the sporting wing of the Sudeten Nazi Party, that Konrad Henlein came, and he was to be a major player in the events of 1938 in Czechoslovakia. Henlein was a mediocre ex-Austrian army officer and bank clerk who had a certain populist touch and a capacity for convincing British officials what a stout fellow he was. He was, like Hitler, a Pan-German who ultimately wanted to unite his fellow Sudeten German with the Fatherland, although before 1935 his aspirations were vaguely expressed. In 1931, however, an article by Henlein was clear in its anti-Czech sentiment, referring to 'un-German parliamentarism, an un-German party system, which divides our people into organic parts, will and must break down some time'.[63] Yet Henlein and his acolytes proved to be adept at manipulating the very democracy they effected to despise. In the 1935 Czechoslovak elections, Henlein's newly-constituted Sudeten Deutsch Party won the largest share of the popular vote and was the second largest party in Parliament. It was assisted by the chauvinistic and repressive attitudes of Czech police and civil servants in the Sudetenland. These facts were known to the British government although a considerable gloss was put upon them by Addison and Hadow in Prague. But the Czechs claimed that their treatment of national minorities was fair. And they, too, complained in July 1933 about the treatment of their own citizens inside Nazi Germany. Masaryk and Beneš could already see that the new regime in Germany represented a serious threat to Czechoslovakia.[64] But Beneš did not expect the British to be of much help in normalising relations with Berlin, or dealing with the problem of the Sudetenland. In December 1937, he told the German Minister in Prague that Britain and France were 'too far away to understand things'.[65]

Nevertheless, the British government was becoming concerned about the possible threat of a war over the Sudetenland in the wake of the *Anschluss* (not being reassured by an assurance from Göring that Czechoslovakia was under no threat from Germany). On 18 March 1938, Lord Halifax set out his views on the Czechoslovak problem to the Foreign Policy Committee of the Cabinet, using a paper prepared by William Strang of the Foreign Office Central Department. Halifax thought that Germany would object to British meddling in the Sudeten question and that the best policy would be to keep Hitler 'guessing' about British intentions. Thus the possibility of British intervention would exist if France were obliged to honour its treaty obligations if Germany attacked Czechoslovakia. But this attempt to deter Germany would coexist with British pressure on France, to coerce the Czechs, and on the Czechs themselves to make concessions to the Sudeten Germans about their status and treatment within the republic. Halifax was anxious, however, that Germany should not be provoked. 'The more closely we associated ourselves with France and Russia,' he warned, 'the more we produced in German minds the impression that we were plotting to encircle Germany'[66]

In the general discussion that followed Halifax's remarks, Cabinet colleagues endorsed the Foreign Secretary's pessimism. Malcolm MacDonald, son of the now retired Prime Minister and Secretary of State for the Dominions, warned that neither South Africa nor Canada would support a war over the Sudetenland. Sir Thomas Inskip (Minister for the Coordination of Defence) merely passed on the pessimistic assessments of the Chiefs of Staff about Czechoslovakia's chances of survival in the event of war with Germany. Inskip was a competent administrator and former Attorney General whose appointment by Baldwin in 1936 had been ridiculed by Churchill as the worst appointment since the Roman Emperor Caligula made his horse a consul.[67] Alone of the Ministers present on 18 March (who included Chamberlain and the Chancellor Sir John Simon), Hoare took a different line, saying that a new British commitment to France might give a greater feeling of urgency about the need for rearmament in the country. Chamberlain supported Halifax, making his own view about the Sudeten problem clear in one of his regular letters to his sister Ida on 20 March. He did not think Czechoslovakia defensible, surrounded as it was by German territory on three sides after the *Anschluss*. Given this reality, Chamberlain thought the best approach was to ask Hitler what he wanted 'for your Sudeten Germans. If it is reasonable, we will urge the Czechs to accept and if they do, you must give assurances that you will let them alone in the future'.[68] Built into Chamberlain's policy, therefore, was the requirement that Germany recognise Czech territorial integrity if Beneš conceded what Hitler demanded. The burning question at the time, in late March, was what exactly Henlein and the Sudeten German Party wanted.

This began to emerge on 29 March as Henlein, acting under instructions from Berlin, demanded autonomy for the Sudetenland. Hitler had instructed Henlein to make demands which would be 'unacceptable to the Czechs'.[69] This position was endorsed in Henlein's speech at Karlsbad on 24 April. Henlein made eight demands which included one for regional autonomy, but the last one seriously undermined the sovereignty of the Czechoslovak Republic by referring to 'full freedom to profess German nationality and the German political philosophy'.[70]

Meanwhile in Prague the British Minister Basil Newton, whose role in the events of 1938 has been underplayed by historians, was proving no friend of the Czechs. On 15 March he had reported to Halifax his view that 'Czechoslovakia's present position is not permanently tenable' and that, because of this, 'it will be no kindness in the long run to try and maintain her in it'.[71] Yet such bluntness did encapsulate the Czech dilemma. Whatever assurances they may have given, the French had no intention of fighting for the Sudetenland; and, if they did not, Stalin (who had purged his armed forces in devastating fashion in 1937) had a technical opt out from his 1935 treaty obligation. The British government wanted to ensure that France's commitment did not prove to be a snare, which might oblige it to go to war on France's behalf rather than for Czechoslovakia. Newton's influence can be detected in what Halifax said on 18 March when he said that His Majesty's Government had the right 'to decline the risk of involving Great Britain in a fresh war to shore up the present position which seems to us fundamentally untenable'.[72]

The other point exercising British minds was that the Sudeten Germans did seem to have a case, indeed Henderson reported from Berlin that his Czech colleague, Mastny, had admitted to him that, despite what the constitution of the republic said about minority rights, in practice such rights were 'often disregarded'.[73] In Henderson's view, the British position based on the Wilsonian principle of ethnic self-determination had to be 'morally copper bottomed'.[74] And as always the fear of military catastrophe in a war with Germany influenced the policy-makers. The Permanent Under-Secretary at the Foreign Office Cadogan noted that 'we must not precipitate a conflict now – we shall be smashed'.[75] An assumption of military inferiority, especially in the air, was pivotal in the formulation of British policy during the Czech crisis. This may have been erroneous, but it was an intelligence failure in the first instance. Equally striking is the fact that one option was never seriously considered by the British government in the spring and summer of 1938. This was one of complete disengagement giving the French *carte blanche* to honour their commitment to Czechoslovakia if they so wished. Instead Britain became intimately involved in a Central European crisis in a way which it had never done before 1914. Appeasement in the last analysis was not about ignoring the fate of a faraway country, but about ensuring for it a substantial territorial entity which would still acknowledge the national rights of the Sudeten minority. This, after all, was what Versailles and its associated treaties was supposed to have been about, and it was hard for Britain as a drafter of the treaty to ignore claims based on the ethnic principle.

The military factor reasserted itself at a meeting of the full British Cabinet on 22 March. Before them the Cabinet had a Chiefs of Staff report which said that Germany would conquer Czechoslovakia within days, or at most weeks, and that there was nothing that Britain could do about it. Britain and France in the Chief of Staff's opinion would only be able to liberate Czechoslovakia in a long and attritional war, and the situation might, in any case, be complicated by Japanese and Italian intervention in a general war. Halifax told his colleagues that he and Chamberlain had looked at the option of guaranteeing Czechoslovakia, or guaranteeing military support to France if it honoured its 1935 treaty obligations. Halifax claimed that they had looked at the issue 'with some sympathy' but had decided not to follow such a course of action.'[76] When Chamberlain spoke in the House of Commons, he reiterated this view and refused to offer a guarantee of assistance to the Czechs, although he did say that rearmament must be stepped up. With devastating logic, he explained the position to his sister Ida on the same day:

> The Austrian frontier is practically open; the great Skoda munitions works are within easy bombing distance of German aerodromes; the railways all pass through German territory, Russia is a hundred miles away. Therefore we could not help Czechoslovakia.[77]

In fact, the Czechs shared the British assessment of their own peril, and frantically tried to extend their impressive line of fortifications to cover the former Austrian border as well (the existing line only masked the frontier with Germany). Meantime, Hitler made threatening speeches on 20 February and 28 March about what would happen if Sudeten German grievances were not addressed.

Chamberlain and Halifax were concerned about the French. Neither were enthusiastic about the return to power of the Socialist Prime Minister, Léon Blum. They were even more nervous about his Foreign Minister, Paul-Boncour, who not only reasserted French pledges to Czechoslovakia but even talked of assisting the Spanish republicans in their struggle against Franco. Fortunately for British peace of mind, Blum's government fell on 8 April and the British Ambassador Phipps (now a faithful ally of the appeasement policy) intervened to persuade the incoming Prime Minister, Eduard Daladier, misleadingly nicknamed the 'Bull of Vaucluse' by his supporters, to replace Boncour with the pliant Georges Bonnet. On 28–29 April, the two new French leaders were invited to 10 Downing Street to discuss the Sudeten problem with Chamberlain and Halifax. Chamberlain told the French, when Daladier stressed the importance of doing everything possible to check Hitler's attempts to establish hegemony in Europe, that the British Government could not 'contemplate going any further in the way of commitments than had been indicated in the Prime Minister's speech in the House of Commons on the 24th March'. Chamberlain also reminded Daladier and Bonnet that he would have to take into account the attitude of the British Dominions overseas (known to be unsympathetic to the Czechs) when formulating policy.

Bonnet wriggled on the hook of France's commitment to Czechoslovakia. What would Britain's position be, he asked, if Beneš was willing to make concessions which the British government regarded as reasonable. Would Britain stand by France if Hitler rejected the concessions and threatened to attack Czechoslovakia? Would it defend Czechoslovakia against German aggression? Halifax had his answer ready. It 'would be impossible,' he said, 'to accept such a commitment'. Instead it was agreed that the British would make a démarche in Berlin and tell the German government that they were 'doing their best' to find a solution to the Sudeten problem. As the Franco-British were simultaneously making an approach to the Beneš government about the need to make maximum concessions, Hitler would be told that there was no need for the

German government to take action itself. If the Germans then resorted to force, the meeting agreed,

> they would be doing so in the full knowledge of the dangers of which they were aware, namely, that France would be compelled to intervene by virtue of her obligations, and that His Majesty's Government could not guarantee that they would not do the same.[78]

This was as far as Chamberlain and Halifax would go. Their policy was fully endorsed by Tory backbenchers such as Alan Lennox-Boyd. Chamberlain's new Parliamentary Private Secretary, 'Chips' Channon, wrote in his diary, 'it would be utter folly to make new commitments'. Channon also confessed to being 'nuts about Chamberlain'. He was disgusted in early May when Churchill opposed the renunciation of the British government's rights to the so-called 'Treaty Ports' in Ireland (Queenstown, Berehaven and Lough Swilly) and extended appeasement to the Irish Free State, where Prime Minister De Valera was a supporter of Chamberlain's policy towards Germany.

> Is Winston [Channon fulminated] that fat, brilliant, unbalanced, illogical orator more than just that? Or is he perhaps right, banging his head against an uncomprehending country and an unsympathetic government)...?[79]

Chamberlain did not share his subordinate's doubts. Winston would remain outside the government fold.

Another diarist reflected the government's concern about the German air threat. On 29 March, Harold Nicolson met Malcolm MacDonald, the Dominions Secretary, who told him that:

> We are not really strong enough to risk a war. It would mean the massacre of women and children in the streets of London. No Government could possibly risk war when our anti-aircraft defences are in so farcical a condition.[80]

On the political left, the Editor of the *New Statesman*, Kingsley Martin, told Hugh Dalton that 'People were terrified by the combined brutality and efficiency of the Germans' and that if 'there was a war we should lose it'.[81] There was a consensus about the potency of the German air threat, while Churchill railed against the alleged inadequacies of the rearmament programme. He had little support in the House of Commons.

The Sudeten crisis dragged on into the month of May with Ambassador Henderson reporting on 19 May that Hitler was not ready for war because 'Austria is not yet digested, the German army is not ready for all eventualities and [the] Four Year Plan far from its maximum development'.[82] Within days, however, Henderson's optimism received a nasty jolt. This arose from the bizarre set of circumstances behind what historians have come to know as 'the May Scare'. The facts are these. Over the weekend of 20–21 May 1938, the Czech government had information which suggested that Hitler was about to attack. It ordered a partial mobilisation and Czech units entered their fortifications in the Sudetenland. At the same time, France reasserted its commitment to Czechoslovakia, as did the Soviet Union. Halifax used the usual British formula to keep Hitler guessing. The British government, Henderson was instructed to tell Ribbentrop, 'could not foresee the results if force were resorted to and there could be no guarantee that Britain would stand aside'.[83] The British press crowed about how Hitler had been forced to back down.

The irony was that Hitler was not intending to attack Czechoslovakia in May 1938. He was infuriated by the suggestion that he had been, and had been forced to climb down. In Berlin, Henderson rightly recognised that an error had been made because he could find no convincing evidence to support the Czech claim. He had sent his two military attachés, Colonel Noel Mason-MacFarlane (a colourful character who was known to everyone as 'Mason-Mac', and actually volunteered on one occasion to shoot Hitler – the offer was declined!) and Major Kenneth Strong, into Saxony and Silesia on a spying mission.[84] They had found no significant German military activity.

More confusion was added by the episode of the British Embassy's diplomatic train when Henderson hired an extra carriage to accommodate some of his staff who wanted to go on last minute leave. This was perfectly normal but, in the tense atmosphere that weekend, it sparked off a story that the British Embassy was evacuating its staff because war was about to break out. Henderson's colleague François Ponçet, the French Ambassador, was one of those taken in, and arrived on Henderson's Embassy doorstep asking about the story.

The bigger mystery was where the Czechs got their information from, and this remained a matter or controversy for many years. The most likely explanation, recently propounded, is that Soviet intelligence was responsible for the 'scare'. It would be in the Soviet interest to precipitate Anglo-French intervention on the side of the Czechs, allowing the USSR to 'sit, wait, watch, deliberate, and join at the right moment on the right side'.[85] A war would prevent any prospect of a rapprochement between the Western democracies and Germany, something which Stalin feared.

If this was Stalin's motive, he was partly vindicated by Hitler's reaction to the 'May Scare'. On 21 May Hitler had told General Keitel that 'it is not my intention to smash Czechoslovakia by military action in the near future'.[86] But by 30 May he was telling his entourage that it was his 'unalterable decision to smash Czechoslovakia by military means in the near future'.[87] The date 1 October was set for a solution of the Sudeten problem before Hitler resorted to force. Chamberlain, however, saw the events of 20–21 May as a victory for Anglo-French toughness as his Cabinet colleague, Duff Cooper, the First Lord of the Admiralty, noted. He wrote in his diary on 22 May that 'everybody believes here that [Hitler's alleged setback] was entirely due to the firmness of the British Government'.[88] This, said Duff Cooper, was 'a complete misapprehension'. Chamberlain and Halifax thought that, in the short run, moderate advice (perhaps Göring's) had been triumphant in Berlin.

Nevile Henderson knew the truth of the matter, like Duff Cooper. He feared that a repetition of the 21 May warning might drive Hitler into the arms of his 'extremists'. As the summer wore on into autumn, Henderson also began to fear that Hitler might have 'crossed the border-line of insanity'. It was wisest, therefore, not to provoke him by issuing any more 21 May-style warnings. Halifax agreed with this analysis, as did the Prime Minister once he had abandoned the belief (briefly held after the 'May Scare') that threats might work. The 'May Scare' came to be seen as a narrow squeak rather than a victory for collective security.

After 21 May, Chamberlain preferred to work on the French to persuade Beneš to concede more, while also using the sidelined Vansittart's links with the Sudeten Germans to bring them to the negotiating table. When Konrad Henlein came to London on 18 May, and had a meeting with Vansittart, the former Permanent Under-Secretary believed (wrongly) that 'Dr Henlein had no instructions from Berlin'.[89] This offered the hope that Beneš could get an agreement with the Sudetens if he acted quickly. It was surprising that Sir Robert was taken in so readily by Henlein. In contrast, Henderson believed that Hitler's position was 'equivocal in that he takes credit for leaving Herr Henlein free to negotiate with the Czechs at the same time allowing his Party to instigate Sudeten to put forward far-reaching demands'.[90] This was much nearer to the truth as events were to demonstrate.

For Chamberlain the policy of putting pressure on Paris and Prague had to be relentlessly pursued, while Hitler was to be kept guessing about British intentions if he dared resort to force. Only when that eventuality really began to threaten did Chamberlain adopt a more interventionist strategy which involved mediation by surrogate, and ultimately in person.

7

Munich

One of the surviving myths from the seventeenth century is that, following the execution of King Charles I in 1649, Oliver Cromwell came to view the corpse of the dead monarch and was heard to remark, 'Cruel Necessity'. Much the same might be said about the 1938 Munich Agreement which gave the Czech Sudetenland to Germany without a shot being fired. But Munich has remained on the conscience of Britain and France ever since, and it is not difficult to understand why. Everyone has an instinctive sympathy for the little man who is menaced by a bully, and can understand the Czech sense of betrayal about what happened. A contemporary Czech poem written by Frantisek Halas runs:

> The bell of treason is tolling
> Whose hand made it swing?
> Sweet France
> Proud Albion
> And we loved them.

This was not just a matter of treason and Anglo-French insensitivity. Profound military and foreign policy issues were involved, and, for Britain in particular, a guarantee of assistance to Czechoslovakia would have meant the abandonment of an ancient tradition of non-involvement in the affairs of Central and Eastern Europe. This was something that Prime Minister Chamberlain was not prepared to undertake, although he did give the matter serious consideration. He did also intervene in an unprecedented way in the domestic affairs of the Czechoslovak state.

As Hitler's language grew more intemperate in the summer of 1938, so Chamberlain became more concerned about the threat of war. By early June, he and the Foreign Office were actively considering whether to send a British envoy on a fact-finding mission to the Sudetenland. On 8 June, Lord Halifax was minuting about the need 'to act alone – to try and resolve the deadlock'.[1] The French would be told after a British mediator was chosen. Meanwhile, the question was who was to be selected for this delicate task. Some names were speedily ruled out, including the notoriously anti-Czech former Minister to Prague, Sir Joseph Addison, who had his supporters in the Foreign Office.[2] Halifax initially favoured

Lord Lothian (whom Vansittart detested), but he was rejected. By 22 June, the Foreign Office had come up with five potential candidates: Sir Walter Runciman, a former Cabinet Minister; H.A.L. Fisher, a noted historian and ex-Minister; Lord Macmillan (a distinguished judge); and Lord Riverdale and Sir Norman Raeburn, who were both noted industrialists.[3]

Chamberlain's *éminence grise* and chief diplomatic adviser, Sir Horace Wilson (described by Churchill as a 'slithy tove') played a key role in selecting Runciman, who had been in government office in the days of Asquith. Wilson described Runciman as an 'ex-Cabinet Minister of wide and varied experience' who would be capable of 'a crispness which might turn out to be what was needed'.[4] Only a year before, Runciman had been created First Viscount Runciman of Doxford for his service to the Baldwin Cabinet as President of the Board of Trade. But Chamberlain had failed to reappoint him to his old post and Runciman, who had expected to be made Chancellor of the Exchequer (the post went instead to John Simon), turned down the job of Lord Privy Seal as being a demotion. This episode was a bone of contention between the two men.[5]

In June 1938, Runciman was a sixty-eight-year-old industrialist whose political career had been prematurely ended (in his own eyes at least). He was very cautious about accepting Chamberlain and Halifax's brief. He rejected Halifax's offer twice and only ultimately accepted it after insisting that he should be known as a 'mediator' not 'arbitrator'. Runciman's appointment was announced in Parliament over 26/27 July by Chamberlain and Halifax. President Beneš was unenthusiastic about the Runciman mission when informed about it by the British Minister, Basil Newton, and initially refused to accept the idea. But, within the hour, he then changed his mind (realising the importance perhaps of British influence on his ally France) and accepted the mission.[6] Formal Czech acceptance of the Runciman mission was given on 23 July.

Lord and Lady Runciman arrived in Prague on 3 August. They were met at the station by Newton and (significantly) two Sudeten German leaders. Lady Runciman was heard to declaim about 'Bolshevik influence' in Czechoslovakia. She also appeared to be enjoying the attention centred on the couple more than her husband. The presence of the two Sudeten leaders, Kundt and Sebekowsky, has been perceived as ominous and raises the issue of Runciman's subsequent impartiality, although he announced to a press conference that he had 'come as a friend of all and enemy of none'.[7] He brought with him Frank Ashton-Gwatkin, an economic expert from the Foreign Office, and Geoffrey Peto, an ex-MP who acted as Runciman's secretary. Three days later, Peto alarmed the Czechs by commenting to a German diplomat that he understood why the Sudeten German Party disliked Jews.

Nevertheless, it is far too easy to dismiss Runciman's mission as being flawed because of pro-Sudeten German partiality. Runciman also met the anti-Nazi

Sudeten German leader, Wenzel Jaksch, and learnt about the violent tactics used by the SDP to obtain votes in the Sudetenland. He also met the leaders of Jewish organisations and heard how they, like Jaksch, wanted the Sudetenland to remain part of the Czech Republic. Runciman was fair-minded but must have been aware of the official expectation in London that he would apply pressure to the Beneš government to make concessions. Runciman's mission was carried out to a backcloth of increasing Anglo-French diplomatic pressure on Prague.

But there may have been another intriguing element in Runciman's mission, one which involved the United States of America. Traditionally, Chamberlain's disdain for the United States has been emphasised, especially his condescending attitude to American popular culture. His opinion that it was 'always best and safest to count on nothing from the Americans but words' is often cited, and his failure to respond to the so-called 'Roosevelt Initiative' early in 1938 is frequently produced as one of the reasons for Eden's resignation.[8]

Yet this analysis may not be telling the full story. Runciman, unlike Chamberlain, had met Roosevelt in 1937 (while he was still at the Board of Trade) when he was sounding out the Americans about a possible Anglo-US Trade agreement. Unlike Cordell Hull, the Secretary of State, who was fixated by economic issues, Runciman found the President much more concerned about international affairs. 'He is very friendly to us,' Runciman reported on 8 February, 'shudders at the thought of a European war, will not and cannot commit America to action.'[9]

Runciman himself was a strong supporter of an Anglo-American trade deal, and Roosevelt was disappointed when Chamberlain removed him as President of the Board of Trade in May 1937, as he always valued personal contacts in diplomacy. But Chamberlain himself thought that the psychological advantage to be gained from an Anglo-American trade deal would be considerable, and it may be, as has recently been suggested, that the appointment of Runciman to head the Czech mission owed something to a British government desire 'to enlist Roosevelt's support for its policy in Czechoslovakia and for appeasement in general'.[10] The speech made by FDR at Kingston, Ontario, on 18 August 1938 at least raised the possibility of US interest in the Sudeten problem, for he declared that 'We in the Americas are no longer a faraway continent, to which the eddies of controversies beyond the seas could bring no harm or interest'.[11]

The problem from the British perspective was that Hull and the US State Department strongly opposed being drawn into any plan by Chamberlain to solve the Sudeten problem. Chamberlain, though occasionally caustic about the Americans, was at least realistic. Apart from Hull's attitude, FDR also had to contend with Neutrality Acts which inhibited his freedom of action, and the isolationist temper of American public opinion. Churchill's description of Chamberlain's rejection of the Roosevelt initiative in January as the 'loss of the last frail chance to save the world from tyranny' was grandiose but highly inappropriate, given the real situation in the United States.[12] By contrast, the use of Runciman in Czechoslovakia seemed a sensible way of encouraging American interest given that FDR both knew and trusted him. Where Chamberlain is open to criticism, perhaps, is that he himself made no effort to establish a personal rapport with Roosevelt; but, even if he had, the United States would not have intervened meaningfully in the Czech crisis. Chamberlain did not altogether dismiss the relevance of the United States in international affairs, being disappointed that the Americans had failed to be more proactive when Japan continued its aggression in China in 1937. 'If they had,' Chamberlain wrote to his sister Hilda in August 1937, 'there was an off chance of stopping hostilities.'[13] As it was, in August 1938 Chamberlain concentrated his hopes on what Runciman could do in Czechoslovakia.

Runciman has been accused of applying undue pressure on President Beneš as part of an Anglo-French strategy of coercion. In contrast with Henlein, Beneš made himself constantly available to the British delegation, but it did him little good.[14] Runciman's brief had been laid down by Halifax, who was determined that he must not 'take any action that would have the effect of committing this country further than it is already committed, to take action in the event of Germany taking military action'.[15] This arcane formula tied Runciman's hands, even if he had been more sympathetic to the Czech cause. But it was a realistic statement of Britain's position. His Majesty's Government was in no position to offer a meaningful military commitment to the Czechs in 1938; all it could do was to disguise this reality from its unscrupulous opponent in Berlin. In the meantime, Runciman's task was to try and cobble together some sort of agreement that would effect a compromise between the memorandum presented to him on arrival by the Czech Government, and the position of the SDP.

On 30 August, President Beneš received the Sudeten German negotiators, Kundt and Sebekowsky, in the Hradčany Castle and told them that he would accept the eight points put forward by Henlein in his Karlsbad speech. This must have come as a shock to Henlein and his colleagues, as their main task, as instructed by Hitler, was to *prevent* an agreement. The next day, Runciman approved a trip to Germany by Henlein and provided the Sudeten leader with a covering letter. This stated Runciman's belief in 'Henlein's genuine desire for peace'. The Führer reciprocated. When Henlein returned to the Sudetenland on 2 September he quoted Hitler's statement, 'I do not want war'.[16] The Sudeten representatives then engaged in an exercise in obfuscation in Prague which gave no clear response to Beneš's proposal of 30 August.

The next day, 3 September, the British Minister Newton warned Beneš that 'it was vital for Czechoslovakia to accept great sacrifices' to avoid war.[17] Under this pressure, and a warning from Runciman that Beneš should not delude himself into believing that Britain would fight for Czechoslovakia, Beneš gave way. When

Kundt and Sebekowsky saw him, on 4 September, he presented them with a blank piece of paper and asked them to write down a complete list of their demands. Shocked by what Beneš had said, the two Sudeten Germans then agreed to dictate their demands to the Czech President. This became known as 'The Fourth Plan' to resolve the Sudeten imbroglio. Karl Hermann Frank, one of the Sudeten German leaders, reportedly remarked on hearing what Beneš had done, 'My God, they have given us everything!'[18] Frank and Henlein rushed off to Germany with the other SDP leaders. Hitler's orders were explicit. Break off the talks with Beneš, and stage 'incidents' throughout Czechoslovakia.

Meanwhile, the Cabinet wished to avail itself of Nevile Henderson's local knowledge. Henderson was recalled to London and sat in on the Cabinet meeting on 30 August (a rare but not unprecedented honour for an Ambassador). Subjected to close questioning by the Cabinet, Henderson said that he did not think Hitler had made up his mind about the use of force. He reiterated his view that pointless threats would encourage 'extremists' like Himmler and Goebbels. When the Chancellor of the Duchy of Lancaster, Winterton, dredged up the old issue of colonial concessions, Henderson told him that Hitler knew that an attack on the Czechs would rule out any such concessions.[19] As ever, the British Cabinet was trying to second guess what Hitler would do.

Chamberlain's own inclination, particularly when episodes of violence broke out in the Sudetenland (on 7 September, a Czech policeman struck an SDP deputy, causing his party to tell Prague that it would boycott any further talks), was to resort to personal diplomacy. He wanted to go and talk to Hitler under what became known as 'Plan Z', but only Halifax and Cadogan were initially taken into his confidence. Chamberlain planned to descend on the Nazi Party rally at Nuremberg, scheduled to start on 5 September and run to 12 September. When Horace Wilson wrote to Henderson on 9 September, referring back to his visit on 30 August, the latter warned against such a visit, saying that it was 'out of the question' in the febrile atmosphere of the party rally.[20] His advice was taken, but Chamberlain was still determined to go to Germany after Nuremberg. He saw Britain as being in the lead position during the crisis by virtue of its special role in world affairs and mission to restore equilibrium and stability in Europe. Earlier in the year, when commenting to his sister Hilda about the unreliability of the French, Chamberlain had told her 'the world looks to us'.[21] Chamberlain believed this sufficiently strongly to engage in personal diplomacy by air (he had never flown before) at the age of sixty-nine.

In Prague, Beneš and his government waited nervously for Hitler's big setpiece speech at Nuremberg on 12 September. Chamberlain convened a Cabinet meeting for that morning. Predictably, Hitler's speech was rude about Beneš and vowed to protect the Sudeten Germans. There were riots in the Sudetenland.

Chamberlain knew that there were one or two dissenters in his Cabinet but was determined to go to Germany. At the Cabinet meeting on 12 September, Duff Cooper accused Henderson of being hysterical, and wanted Hitler to be sent an ultimatum. Chamberlain warned him of the dangers of provoking Hitler at a moment when he still had not made his speech (it was given that afternoon). Very late on the evening of 12 September, the following telegram was sent to Henderson in Berlin:

> In view of increasing critical situation I propose to come over at once to see you with a view to trying to find peaceful solution. I propose to come across by air and am ready to start tomorrow.[22]

Later in the month, Chamberlain was famously to quote Lord Derby saying this was a real 'leap in the dark'. It was, in fact, a courageous and decisive move showing the attributes which made Chamberlain an effective Prime Minister. When he told his old colleague and supporter, Hoare, about Plan Z on 10 September, the former Foreign Minister warned that he was 'taking a great political risk by personally intervening'.[23] Nevertheless, Chamberlain persisted with his plan. His ally 'Chips' Channon described his intention to fly to Germany on 15 September (after Hitler had been sounded out first) as 'one of the finest, most inspiring acts of all history'.[24] On 14 September, the Cabinet endorsed Chamberlain's decision. Henderson secured a minor victory when he succeeded in having his *bête noire*, Ribbentrop, excluded from the meeting between Chamberlain and Hitler at Berchtesgaden.

So it was that the elderly British Prime Minister and the German Führer met for the first time. By the time Chamberlain had been driven up to the Berghof, it was starting to rain and clouds were hiding the Bavarian Alps from view. But Hitler came down the steps to meet the man the Germans had come to call 'Peace Envoy Chamberlain'. After the usual greetings, Hitler and his guests sat around the tea table in a large room with a panoramic view of the Untersberg, one which Lloyd George had so much admired in 1936, where Hitler had also entertained the Duke of Windsor during his ill-judged visit to Germany in 1937.[25]

Chamberlain asked whether Hitler would speak to him alone, which would have been unusual, but Hitler insisted on the presence of his long-standing interpreter, Paul Schmidt. He was not unduly impressed by his protagonist. He described how Hitler wore

> black trousers, such as we wear in the evenings, and black patent-leather lace-up shoes. His hair is brown, not black, his eyes blue, his expression rather disagreeable, especially in repose, and altogether he looks entirely undistinguished. You would never notice him in a crowd and would take him for the house painter [a popular contemporary myth] he once was.[26]

All this contrasted sharply with Lloyd George's hero-worship in 1936.

Chamberlain is open to the criticism that he sold the pass at Berchtesgaden. Much effort had been expended by the British government beforehand in trying to make the Germans wary about likely British reaction if Hitler persisted with his aggressive policy. Yet Chamberlain's own notes of his conversation with Hitler show that he told the German dictator that in his 'personal opinion' there could be no objection in principle to the secession of the Sudetenland. He prefaced his remarks by saying that he could *not* give an assurance on the principle of secession 'on behalf of the British Government who had not authorised me to say anything of the kind'.[27] Yet Chamberlain appeared to undermine his negotiating position by giving Hitler, undoubtedly aware of Chamberlain's dominance over his Cabinet colleagues, a personal opinion which could only encourage the German dictator to raise the stakes from demanding Sudeten autonomy to outright secession. It was a tactical *faux pas*, even allowing for Chamberlain's conviction that the Sudetenland was not a cause worth fighting for. It may be that this indiscretion followed Hitler's alarming threat to go to war if Beneš did not concede what he wanted, and Chamberlain's then complaint that he had been 'wasting my time' coming all the way to Germany. The impact of this comment, which Chamberlain thought had quietened Hitler down, was undermined by the Prime Minister's following remark that he 'didn't care two hoots whether the Sudetens were in the Reich or out of it'.[28] Or was it? A more subtle interpretation is that Chamberlain portrayed himself as a man who understood German aspirations over the Sudetenland, but as one who might have trouble with colleagues, like Duff Cooper, who were more critical. If Hitler was unreasonable, he might put Chamberlain in an impossible domestic position. Public opinion on the Czech problem was volatile. A Mass Observation poll taken on 22 September found only 22 per cent of the sample in support of Chamberlain's policy.[29] Runciman's mission had been called off on 15 September as Chamberlain thought there was nothing more that he could usefully do.

As it was, Hitler agreed at Berchtesgaden that he would allow Chamberlain to consult his colleagues about the cession of the Sudetenland and the negation of the Czech–Soviet alliance which the British had always disliked. Chamberlain also insisted that the French should be consulted over any solution. Critics of the Berchtesgaden trip were predictable in their reaction. Churchill described Chamberlain's trip as 'the stupidest thing that has ever been done'.[30] Eden was ambivalent. He seemed to support Churchill's demand for a 'Grand Alliance' on the one hand, but conceded that 'he might have done the same' as Halifax had he been in a similar position.[31] His lust for office disillusioned those anti-appeasement MPs like Harold Macmillan who looked to him for a lead.

The issue which immediately exercised Chamberlain was what the French would do. Bonnet was desperate to avoid war and Ambassador Phipps warned that 'Daladier always talks bigger than he acts'.[32] The French leadership duly came to London on 18 September, anxious that its air force, which had been allowed to fall into a sad decline since 1919, would be decimated in any war with Germany.

In discussion, Daladier talked tough with Chamberlain and Halifax. France would not abandon its ally, but would also advise Prague against any provocative mobilisation. He then fatally uncovered French anxieties by requesting that Britain find 'some means of preventing France from being forced into war as a result of her obligations'.[33] This was a devastating admission of French dependence on a British lead, and seemed to confirm Inskip's observation on 13 September that everything 'showed that the French didn't want to fight, were not fit to fight and wouldn't fight'.[34] This presumably was why Chamberlain had not bothered to inform the French before Plan Z was implemented. When he, Halifax and Horace Wilson met a Labour Party delegation on 17 September, Chamberlain brutally pointed out that 'the real difficulty is the weakness of France ... Within the last few days French resolution has crumbled'.[35] A stream of pessimistic telegrams from Phipps in Paris strengthened Chamberlain's view of French weakness. Faced with such evidence from the government, it was difficult for a believer in collective security like Dalton to put a convincing case to his Labour colleagues.

All the French secured in London was that, if they accepted the Berchtesgaden proposals, the Czechoslovak state would receive an international guarantee. The Sudetenland would then be handed over to Germany after a reasonable interval had been allowed to pass. A joint Anglo-French telegram would be sent to Beneš to inform him about what Chamberlain and Daladier had decided. France had effectively abandoned its ally, whatever Daladier may have said at the London Conference.

On Monday 19 September, there was another Cabinet meeting at which Chamberlain told his colleagues of the Anglo-French guarantee to a Czechoslovakia without the Sudetenland. Chamberlain then had to sell the plan to Labour, who had always distrusted him. He had told Citrine, Dalton and Morrison, the representatives of the National Council of Labour (which was the joint Party–TUC Committee), about the weakness of the French position and also of the ambiguity in the Soviet position. (Stalin was in the happy position of not needing to honour his pact with the Czechs unless the French did first.)

At the Cabinet meeting even Duff Cooper, one of the doubters, said that he found the prospect of war 'so appalling that he agreed the postponement of the evil day was the right course'.[36] Thus, with his colleagues' assent and also that of the French, Chamberlain only needed to persuade the Czechs to come to terms. Halifax agreed with the Prime Minister's strategy. He told the same Labour delegation of Citrine, Dalton and Morrison on 21 September that the British Ambassador in Moscow and his military attaché had been reporting that the Red Army was seriously weakened by the purges which Stalin had carried out in 1937 (which had removed 40 per cent of the officer corps). When Dalton asked him whether he had sought further clarification of Soviet intentions, Halifax said he had not.[37] Dalton himself thought that Bonnet had lied in early September when he alleged that the Soviet Foreign Minister, Litvinov, had been evasive about Soviet obligations when he, Bonnet, had assured him that France would honour its obligations. Dalton's suspicions may well have been justified, but British concerns about the efficacy of the Red Army as a fighting force, and Stalin's real intentions were entirely legitimate, as future events were to show. In his interview with the Labour delegation, Halifax also stressed that there was no moral case for British intervention on behalf of Czechoslovakia.[38]

The way had been cleared by 21 September for Chamberlain's second flight to Germany. This time he flew to Bad Godesberg on the Rhine, as Hitler had now agreed to leave his mountain fastness to meet the British delegation. The two men met on 22 September, Chamberlain having spent the night at the Hotel Petersburg before driving down to the ferry which took him and his colleagues over the river to the Hotel Dreesen. For those who searched for omens, it was ominous that Hitler had been staying there before the notorious 'Night of the Long Knives', in June 1934, when he had massacred the Brownshirt leadership.

Chamberlain was bringing what he thought to be good news. He told Hitler that his colleagues had agreed in principle to the cession of the Sudetenland to Germany. He then moved on to the technical point about how high the German population percentage would need to be to avoid a plebiscite. Chamberlain thought that, if 80 per cent of those living in a local area were German, there could be a transfer of territory without discussion. If the percentage was only 65, then a plebiscite would be required to secure approval of a transfer to the Reich. But a Czechoslovakia stripped of its fortifications would need an international guarantee. Britain and France would offer this but it would be in place of existing treaties, thus removing the Czech–Soviet agreement of 1935 which the British so disliked. This offer, Chamberlain thought, would be an olive branch to Hitler and reduce Czechoslovakia to neutral status.[39]

Chamberlain then sat back to await some reward for his hectic diplomacy since Berchtesgaden. Hitler's interpreter, Paul Schmidt, later recorded that he had on his face 'an expression of satisfaction, as much as to say, "Haven't I worked splendidly during these five days"'.[40] Hitler's reply, therefore, came like a thunderclap. 'I'm sorry,' Hitler said, 'but that won't do anymore.'[41] He then went on to tell the shocked British Prime Minister that Czechoslovakia was a mongrel state in which a million Magyars and a hundred thousand Poles were also discriminated against. There were also millions of Slovaks who had grievances against the Beneš government. Although the Germans in the Sudetenland were his first concern, Hitler had to accommodate the demands of others (Polish units were already in fact moving on the disputed territory of Teschen with its Polish majority). He was now losing patience, he told Chamberlain, with the whole Sudeten issue which had to be settled by 1 October at the latest, while all Czech troops, police and officials must withdraw from the area at once. Graciously, Hitler agreed that if the Czechs disputed the language line in areas occupied by German troops, he would accept a plebiscite in the presence of an international commission.

Chamberlain was now an angry man, his face flushed with disappointment. Schmidt noticed how 'his kindly eyes could gleam very angrily under their busy brows'.[42] He believed that he had met Hitler's requirements as laid out in Berchtesgaden, and argued that the Führer was putting forward completely new demands. Hitler replied by becoming more and more abusive about Beneš and the Czechs. Chamberlain told him that he was taking his political life in his hands by coming to Germany and that he had actually been booed at Heston Airport on his way there. Yet he was prepared to make one more concession. Would Hitler 'be prepared to abide by a bare majority vote in the plebiscite'? Hitler replied that he would tell the German military not to initiate any military action against the Czechs, but complained that it was hard to rein in the German response while the Czechs were shooting German hostages. He then threw Chamberlain a back-handed compliment by saying that he was surprised the Prime Minister had achieved as much as he had.[43]

At this point, the three-hour discussion stopped, and it was agreed that the two leaders would resume their discussions the next day. Chamberlain by now was in low spirits. He thought it most unlikely that he would be able to persuade Cabinet colleagues to accept the evacuation of the Sudetenland by the Czechs by 1 October as Hitler now demanded. First thing in the morning he sent over a letter to Hitler telling him that:

> I do not think you have realised the impossibility of my agreeing to put forward any plan unless I have reason to suppose that it will be considered by public opinion in my country, in France, and indeed the world generally, as carrying out the principles already agreed upon in an orderly fashion, and free from the threat of force.[44]

Chamberlain spent the morning pacing the balcony of the Hotel Petersburg with Nevile Henderson while he awaited Hitler's reply. None came and at 5 p.m., Chamberlain instructed Sir Horace Wilson and Henderson to see Ribbentrop and suggest to him that Hitler should enshrine his proposals for the occupation of the Sudetenland in an official document. This Hitler did (Henderson credited the German 'moderates' with a victory here), but the document merely reiterated his demands from the day before.

In the meantime, Chamberlain had seen a telegram from Halifax in London saying that he believed that the Czechs should *not* be prevented from mobilising. At 4 p.m. Halifax, with Chamberlain's agreement, told the Czechs that previous advice not to mobilise was withdrawn. But the Foreign Secretary told Newton that he was to tell the Czechs that such action by them could well 'precipitate action by others', and advise them to avoid unnecessary publicity (perhaps he was thinking back to the 'May Scare').[45] Beneš himself was under acute domestic pressure, with crowds in Prague demanding weapons and mobilisation. He showed some resolution in dismissing the incumbent Prime Minister Hodža and replacing him with the one-eyed General Jan Syrový, who had fought with the Czech Legion in Russia. It was a clever move, as Britain and France had already threatened to abandon the Czechs the previous day and Syrový's appointment reflected the obdurate national mood.

The complexity of the crisis was underlined when, at 4 a.m. on 23 September, the USSR government formally warned the Poles that any concentration of forces against Teschen (Těšín in Czech) would create a situation where the Soviet Union would consider itself absolved from the 1932 Soviet–Polish non-aggression agreement.[46] Perhaps Soviet protestations of help for the Czechs were genuine after all.

Back in Bad Godesberg, Ribbentrop had told Chamberlain that the Germans would draw up a memorandum, but it was after dark before Hitler and Chamberlain met again. News of the Czech mobilisation arrived during what was already a highly-charged meeting. After three hours of wrangling, the only concession Chamberlain obtained was when Hitler grudgingly agreed to put back the date for the Czech evacuation of the Sudetenland to 1 October rather than the completion date of 28 September contained in the German memorandum. Hitler had threatened to march against the Czechs when he heard about their mobilisation, but now agreed to hold his hand while Chamberlain went back to London for further consultations. When he got back to his hotel at two o'clock in the morning, someone asked him, 'Is the position hopeless, Sir?' Chamberlain replied, 'I would not like to say that. It is up to the Czechs now'.[47]

Chamberlain flew back to London on Saturday 24 September, having ensured that an English translation of the Godesberg Memorandum was sent to the Beneš government. It duly arrived at six o'clock. At the same time, and rather oddly, the British Military Attaché in Berlin, Mason-MacFarlane, volunteered to drive to Prague carrying the new map of the Sudetenland (German style) and the accompanying German language memorandum. It was perhaps typical of 'Mason Mac', a man who had volunteered to shoot Hitler, to undertake such a hazardous mission in a time of acute border tension. He avoided being shot by either German or Czech frontier guards, but was not impressed by the morale of the Czech military he came into contact with before his arrival in Prague just before midnight on 24 September.[48] When he reported his observations to London, Mason-MacFarlane got a sharp response from the Foreign Office. R. Speaght of the Central Department minuted that it was

> surprising that Colonel Mason-MacFarlane should find Czech morale poor. This is certainly contrary to information from Mr Newton, to the view of the French General Staff ... and to reports of reliable special correspondents.[49]

MacFarlane's colleague in Prague, Lieutenant-Colonel Stronge, did not share his assessment of the Czech army, which was based, after all, on the most fleeting of visits. Nevertheless, the Chiefs of Staffs' assumption was that, if war came, the Czechs could only hold out (at best) for a few weeks. Meanwhile Beneš was asked by the British to transmit any reply to the Godesberg Memorandum through them, and to consider sending an envoy to London if that would help.

Chamberlain was now more concerned about the attitude of his Cabinet colleagues than whether the Czechs would accept the Godesberg terms. First of all, he spoke to his 'Inner Cabinet' of Halifax, Simon and Hoare and found them generally compliant, although the latter had some reservations about Godesberg. Then a meeting of the full Cabinet was convened at 5.30 p.m. Chamberlain (who must have been feeling the effects of his journey from Bad Godesberg, his meeting with Hitler had only ended at 1.45 a.m. that day) spoke first. He told his colleagues that Hitler

> has a narrow mind and was violently prejudiced on certain subjects, but he would not deliberately deceive a man whom he respected and with whom he had been in negotiation, and he was sure Herr Hitler now felt some respect for him ...[50]

These comments have frequently been held up to ridicule as an example of Chamberlain's hubris, but he had been told after Berchtesgaden that Hitler regarded him as 'a man' and the Führer had acknowledged at Bad Godesberg that Chamberlain's intervention had achieved more than he expected. As a negotiator, and despite Hitler's previous record, Chamberlain had to proceed on the basis that Hitler intended to keep his word. If he did not, he would destroy his own credibility as a trustworthy international leader.

Chamberlain recognised at the Cabinet meeting that the crucial issue was whether Hitler was telling the truth about the Sudeten issue. He believed he was. He also recognised the weakness of Britain's air defences, which meant that war was a risky proposition in September 1938. If war came later Britain would be in a stronger position to fight. This was hardly the language of a man who had been hopelessly gulled by the German dictator. The possibility that Hitler might be guilty of bad faith was fully recognised, as it had to be.

Nevertheless, on that September evening, Duff Cooper, the First Lord of the Admiralty, remained unconvinced, and told Chamberlain that in his view: 'No confidence could be placed in Hitler's promise ... our right course was to order a general mobilisation forthwith. He was sure the Czechs would fight.' Duff Cooper also foresaw a situation where 'the boot of public opinion' would force the government into war.[51] This statement represented a complete turnabout from the position Duff Cooper had taken in Cabinet on 18 September, and was one reason why Chamberlain regarded him as an unreliable colleague. But Duff Cooper was supported in Cabinet by Winterton, de la Warr and Stanley. Recognising that there was some dissent amongst his colleagues, Chamberlain adjourned the Cabinet meeting until 10.30 a.m. on Sunday 25 September. Oliver Harvey, Halifax's Private Secretary, noted that 'the only decision which emerged was an invitation to Daladier and Bonnet to come over here and hear PM's report tomorrow'.[52] France's subsidiary status in the crisis was thus underlined.

Chamberlain and his colleagues duly reconvened on the Sunday morning, and were told by Inskip, the Minister for Defence Co-ordination, that intelligence from the Chiefs of Staff showed that the Germans would only leave nine divisions manning the western Siegfried Line if they attacked Czechoslovakia. Inskip was sure that the French would fight, but his opinion was directly contradicted by Colonel Fraser, the British military attaché in Paris, who was informed that they would not (his source being the French military). Chamberlain, by contrast, defended the Godesberg memorandum and stressed the importance of the Sudetenland being left intact and not deliberately laid waste by the retreating Czechs.

Then Halifax spoke. It was a seminal moment. He had been the most loyal of Chamberlain's lieutenants and, in many ways, he represented the conscience of the Tory Party. On India, he had stood for good sense and reconciliation when Churchill had merely echoed the nostrums of nineteenth-century imperialism. As a fox-hunting High Anglican, he also appealed to Tory traditionalism in a way Chamberlain could not. Conservative MPs could warm to the Master of the Garrowby Hunt where they might be suspicious of the intellectual power which had won Halifax a Fellowship at All Souls.

When Halifax spoke, however, he said things which shook Chamberlain to his innermost core. For Halifax had spent a sleepless night made restless by the strictures of his Permanent Under-Secretary, Alex Cadogan. In his deep sonorous voice, with its slight speech impediment, Halifax said that Hitler was now 'dictating terms, just as though he had won a war ... he did not feel that it would be right to put pressure on Czechoslovakia to accept'. The Godesberg terms should be placed before the Czechs, Halifax argued, but if they were rejected in Prague and France felt obliged to stand by the Czechs, 'we should join with them'.[53]

Chamberlain sent a note to Halifax which reflected his dismay. 'Your complete change of view since I saw you last night is a horrible blow to me, but of course you must form your opinions for yourself.' Chamberlain went on to say that if the French went to war 'thereby dragging us in, I do not think I could accept responsibility for that decision'.[54] Chamberlain thus appeared ready to resign, but he also hoped that the French would get him off the hook by indicating their unwillingness to fight.

This was far from certain as, on that same day, the French Council of Ministers had voted against acceptance of the Godesberg terms. Then to add to Chamberlain's difficulties, at 5 p.m., while the British Cabinet was still in session, the Czech Minister in London, Jan Masaryk, brought his government's reply to the German terms. They represented, the Czechs pointed out indignantly, 'a de facto ultimatum of the sort usually presented to a vanquished nation and not a proposition to a sovereign state'. The terms deprived Czechoslovakia of every vestige of security and they were 'absolutely and unconditionally unacceptable'. The Czech response concluded, 'The nation of St Wenceslas, John Hus and Thomas Masaryk will not be a nation of slaves'.[55] In Prague, the Soviet Minister Alexandrovsky found Beneš to be 'full of fighting spirit' when he visited him in the Hradčany Castle after the rejection of the German ultimatum.[56] He had a gas mask on his desk.

In reality, the resolution of the crisis lay in Chamberlain's hands unless the Czechs were willing to fight Hitler alone without allies, and there is little indication that Beneš ever thought in those terms. Chamberlain therefore continued the dialogue with the French. Daladier and Bonnet flew over for a further meeting that began at 9.25 a.m. on Sunday 26 September. The session started with Chamberlain's outline of what had happened during his two meetings with Hitler at Godesberg. Daladier told the British delegation (made up of the Inner Cabinet plus Cadogan, Vansittart and Wilson) that the French Council of Ministers had already rejected the Godesberg terms earlier in the day.

Chamberlain then let loose the keen forensic legal mind of Sir John Simon, whose brief was to undermine French confidence in the viability of the Czech army as a fighting force. If this was done, the French would surely be unwilling to fight and Chamberlain would be able to convince the waverers in his own Cabinet. But Daladier, for once, lived up to his self-cultivated image as a tough guy, and insisted that France would launch an offensive against the Siegfried Line if forced to go to war. He also claimed that France would bomb German military centres and installations. When Chamberlain countered by saying that the French air force was weak (a perfectly fair point), Daladier conceded this, but still claimed that it would be effective in wartime. In any case, he argued, the USSR had five thousand modern aircraft which would support France, refuting Chamberlain's effort to play up Soviet unreliability.

Daladier remained obdurate, singling out some British sensitivities by saying that, if not stopped, Hitler would turn against France, take Boulogne and Calais, and even embarrass Chamberlain's admirer Mr De Valera by landing in Ireland.[57] The meeting ended in deadlock, but it was agreed that the French Commander-in-Chief, Gamelin, would speak to the Defence Ministers and the Chiefs of Staff the next day about France's war preparations. Meanwhile, a British Cabinet meeting was arranged for midnight, the Anglo-French conversations having only concluded at 11.40 p.m. It confirmed that Chamberlain was still in a minority in his own Cabinet. His attempts to suggest that Daladier and Bonnet had been evasive about France's military plans did not shift the considerable number of doubters, which now included Hailsham, Hore-Belisha and Stanley as well as Duff Cooper, de la Warr and Winterton. Chamberlain thought it significant that Daladier and Bonnet had failed to ask 'if we go to war with Germany, will you come in too?' His colleagues did not, and Halifax still failed to give the Prime Minister the endorsement he hoped for.[58]

Particularly significant now were the attitudes of Hailsham, Chamberlain's oldest Conservative friend and colleague (who had supported Halifax in Cabinet on 25 September) and Oliver Stanley – Stanley was the youngest son of the Earl of Derby, the same 'Eddie' Derby whose services Baldwin and MacDonald had called upon to try and push through Hoare's 1935 India Bill in the teeth of Churchill's opposition. Young Stanley, like his father, represented the landed interest in Lancashire ('cotton and land go hand in hand' was the local slogan) and was popular with the Tory rank and file. Chamberlain could not afford to see such men resign from his Cabinet.

Well organised as ever, Chamberlain had an alternative plan if he failed to shift his colleagues on the issue of French evasiveness. He now proposed to send Sir Horace Wilson as his personal envoy to Berlin. Wilson would carry a personal letter to the Führer appealing for some concession, or derogation, from the Godesberg terms to ease Chamberlain's task as a mediator. Hitler would then be offered an international commission, with German and Czech representatives, to speed forward the transfer of population. If he failed to concede anything, Wilson was to be authorised to warn Hitler that, if he attacked the Czechs and triggered French intervention, Britain, too, would go to war. Duff Cooper disliked this idea and wanted the warning written into the letter to Hitler. He could 'hardly believe' his ears when he heard Chamberlain's proposal, but his own position had lacked consistency throughout the Czech crisis.[59]

Chamberlain persisted with his personal diplomacy, short-circuiting the Foreign Office. Henderson was instructed by Wilson to tell the Germans to disregard any statements emanating from London which did not originate in 10 Downing Street. Such behaviour may appear reprehensible and egotistical until the propensity of Prime Ministers from Lloyd George to Blair to try and run their own foreign policies is recalled. Henderson, of course, was delighted to act as the personal envoy of the Prime Minister. He saw Göring on 26 September, who tried to intimidate the British by saying that, if the USSR came into a war over Czechoslovakia, Japan would come in on Germany's side (the Foreign Office did not believe this). Göring's Luftwaffe aide Bodenschatz also told Henderson that his beloved Yugoslavia (Henderson had been Minister there) would also side with Germany. Again the evidence for this assertion was flimsy. Henderson told Halifax in his latest telegram that, if Britain did not advise the Czechs to make the best terms on offer, 'we shall be exposing Czechoslovakia to the same fate as Abyssinia'.[60]

Meanwhile, Wilson flew to Germany on 26 September and sought an interview with Hitler that evening. Hitler was told of Britain's intention to persist with its mediation. Wilson had experienced, he said, a 'very violent hour' with Hitler, who had been guilty of 'insane interruptions' while he was reading out Chamberlain's message.[61] Nevertheless the zealous civil servant went back to see Hitler again at midday on 27 September and delivered the verbal warning, although, in view of Hitler's tantrums the previous day, he had advised Chamberlain to abandon the idea altogether. Chamberlain told him that Britain must honour its undertaking to Daladier that the warning would be given.

At the meeting on 27 September, Hitler demanded that his demands be met by 2 p.m. the next day, at which point Wilson delivered the verbal warning about the consequences of attacking the Czechs. Hitler, his interpreter noted later, was in such a violent mood that 'it was quite impossible to talk to [him] reasonably'.[62] He shouted at Wilson that, if France and Britain wanted war, it was 'a matter of complete indifference to me. I am prepared for all eventualities'.[63] When the news of Hitler's stormy interview with Wilson reached London, a meeting of Ministers and the Chiefs of Staff was called. War now seemed a real danger and the meeting authorised the calling up of Royal Navy reservists. Chamberlain wanted this to be done secretly, but Duff Cooper expected him to refer to the mobilisation when he broadcast to the nation at 8 p.m. that day. When he did not, Duff Cooper 'was furious' and, according to the First Lord's diary account, was supported by Churchill, who rang him up afterwards and 'was most indignant'.[64]

Those who thought like Duff Cooper (at least in his most recent incarnation) would have been encouraged by what General Gamelin had said earlier that day. Gamelin had assured the British Chiefs of Staff and Inskip that, if war came, he would launch an offensive against the Siegfried Line. France had one hundred divisions available on mobilisation and sixty of those would face the Germans in the west. Germany would also be bombed. Altogether Gamelin gave an impression of serene, imperturbable confidence. This was misleading, for Gamelin had in fact always dismissed the Czech army's capacity for resistance (while championing that of the less-prepared Poles), and told the credulous Daladier that launching a French attack into Germany would only result in 'a modernised battle of the Somme' (such a comment was likely to worry a veteran of the Great

War like Daladier).[65] The evidence suggests that, had war come, Gamelin would merely have launched a 'squib' offensive against the Siegfried Line, occupying a few villages before retiring behind the Maginot Line. He hinted, in fact, at this form of action in his talk to the Chiefs of Staff, and this was precisely what he did do when eventually war came in September 1939. The dapper general much preferred to keep the fighting as far away from French soil as possible. It was also true in September 1938 that, despite his brave words in Downing Street, Daladier hedged his bets by approving Chamberlain's decision to send Horace Wilson to Berlin. Thus, although the French appeared ready to honour their commitment to the Czechs, it remained the case that 'the French position was not easy to gauge, not least because they seemed unsure of it themselves'.[66]

Chamberlain and Simon did not believe that the French would fight, but on 27 September the evidence seemed to be against them. Chamberlain had to recognise this in his notorious radio broadcast on that day, in which, as has been seen, he aroused Duff Cooper's ire by failing to mention the call up of naval reservists. At that stage, no orders had yet been given to mobilise the RAF or the army, although gas masks were given to the population and trenches were dug in Hyde Park as part of the air-raid precautions. Anti-aircraft guns also appeared along the Embankment in London, and it seemed that war was indeed inevitable. Even Henderson had given up the ghost in Berlin. War, he telegraphed to Halifax that day was inevitable, 'and there is nothing to be done except prepare for it. It is in any case quite useless to say anything more in Berlin'.[67]

Chamberlain's radio broadcast recognised the desperation of the situation. Britain was prepared to fight, he said, to prevent German militarism from dominating the world, but he found it

> horrible, fantastic, incredible ... that we should be digging trenches and trying on gas masks here because of a quarrel in a faraway country between people of whom we know nothing ... I would not hesitate to pay even a third visit to Germany, if I thought it would do any good.[68]

It is often forgotten that in this same broadcast Chamberlain did show some sensitivity about the Czech position, saying that he could well understand their reaction to the Godesberg terms.

Instead, Chamberlain has been roundly castigated by generations of historians for his use of the phrase 'a faraway country, between people of whom we know nothing', but the point was that in 1938 Chamberlain exactly reflected the British view of the crisis. Czechoslovakia *was* a faraway country for the vast majority of Britons, just as Serbia had been in 1914. Beneš himself recognised this when he told the German Minister in Prague that the British and French were 'too far away to understand things'.[69] Chamberlain had done his best to 'understand things' and had intervened in the Czech crisis in an unprecedented way. His countrymen's bewilderment was demonstrated by a *Daily Express* headline which bluntly asked, 'Where Is Prague?'. It was not unreasonable of Chamberlain to express his perplexity that a local issue which he thought soluble should lead to a war that would engulf the whole of Europe. It was important that Chamberlain's broadcast was widely heard in Germany itself (to the annoyance of the German authorities), in translation. To ensure that it was, all British transmitters, both regional and London-based, were obliged to carry the broadcast to enhance the signal. British listeners were bemused to hear, instead of the scheduled programmes, a talk in German.

The results were unimpressive until the last minute, when it was suggested that a commercial station, Radio Luxembourg, be used. This was done most effectively at 11 a.m. on 28 September when most Germans were listening, and despite the fact that such action broke an international convention on broadcasting which Britain had signed earlier that year. For once, the protest by Goebbels had legality on its side.[70]

In London, Oliver Harvey's diary reflected an aspect of the crisis which must also have played upon Chamberlain's mind. Harvey, as Halifax's Private Secretary in the Foreign Office, would have seen the telegrams coming in from the Dominions. He found them to be 'definitely lukewarm. They see the issue as a purely Czecho–Sudeten question. S. Africa is the worst'.[71] This was hardly surprising as the Afrikaner portion of the population tended to be pro-German. The old appeaser, Smuts, feared that Britain might became embroiled in a war in Central Europe which would not be supported by the Dominions. Britain ought to remember, he believed, that it was not a continental power and should play no role in checking Germany's eastern advance.[72] His loyalty to the British crown was not in question, but as an Empire and Commonwealth elder statesman, his opinion still carried weight.

28 September 1938 seemed likely to be the last day of peace. But Chamberlain who had not given up the struggle, now attempted to enlist the support of Mussolini for a four-power conference to complete the transfer of the Sudetenland. On the morning of 28 September, Mussolini told his Ambassador in Berlin, Attolico, to advise Hitler to postpone mobilisation of his forces for twenty-four hours and accept Chamberlain's invitation to attend a four-power conference. That afternoon Chamberlain was due to make a statement to the House of Commons to tell his colleagues about what was happening.

The scene in the House was dramatic, with MPs spilling into the gangways and distinguished observers like Queen Mary in the galleries. Chamberlain spoke for about an hour, giving his version of recent events. There had still been no indication that Hitler would agree to his proposal and call off his invasion. Then suddenly a sheet of Foreign Office writing paper was handed in by a messenger to one of the Foreign Office staff in the civil servants' box on the government side of the House. The sheet had on it a précis by Halifax of a telegram which had just come in from Berlin (the Foreign Secretary himself was sitting in the Peers Gallery). The Foreign Office official then attracted the attention of Lord Dunglass (later Sir Alec Douglas-Home and then Lord Home), Chamberlain's Parliamentary Private Secretary, who passed it along the government Front Bench to Sir John Simon who sat next to the Prime Minister. He, according to his own account, had to 'choose the moment to interrupt him, in a whisper without upsetting his orderly account of events'.[73] When this moment came, Simon handed the sheet to Chamberlain, who in unbearable tension read out its contents to the House of Commons. Hitler was inviting Chamberlain to attend a conference in Munich to resolve the Sudeten issue. Chamberlain went on: 'Signor Mussolini has accepted, and I have no doubt M. Daladier will also accept. I need not say what my answer would be.'[74]

The result of Chamberlain's announcement was pandemonium. Order papers were flung into the air and someone (possibly 'Chips' Channon) shouted 'Thank God for the Prime Minister!' Simon had seen nothing like it in thirty years in the House, but Channon did not admit to being the cheer-leader. Instead he wrote in his diary about 'the great day in the House of Commons' and how he was 'sick with enthusiasm, longed to clutch him'. Harold Nicolson, who was no admirer of Chamberlain, confessed to having 'an immense sense of physical relief' because no German bombs would fall on London that night. He thought Chamberlain's announcement one of the most dramatic moments he had ever witnessed.[75] A minority refused to rejoice. Amidst all the hysteria, Churchill remained seated and then told Chamberlain, 'I congratulate you on your good fortune. You have been very lucky'. By contrast, Chamberlain's predecessor, Baldwin, joined in the frenzied clapping in the galleries, forgetting in his excitement the rule which prevented such applause in the House.[76] Even the anti-appeasement Harold MacMillan shared in the general relief that war had been avoided.

Up until 28 September, the Czechs had seen the course of events since Godesberg as promising. They had mobilised one and a half million men in a process that had run smoothly, as the US military attaché had noted in Prague. Beneš was not unduly alarmed by Hitler's violent speech at the Berlin Sportspalast on the evening of 27 September, although he was unaware of Wilson's initiative in Berlin. He wryly remarked that to be singled out for a personal dual with Hitler was something of an honour. And British air-raid precautions, together with the fact that French troops were entering the Maginot Line, seemed proof that Czechoslovakia would not be alone.[77]

Yet the very success of the Czech mobilisation uncovered the roots of the crisis. Although 10 per cent of all Czechoslovak citizens were now in uniform, half the Sudeten Germans liable for military service had fled to Germany, many

Hungarians had failed to answer the call, and only a tiny percentage of ethnic Poles arrived at military depots. The mobilisation, therefore, revealed both the steely resolve of Czechs and Slovaks (although they too had reservations about the republic), and the intrinsic weakness of the Czechoslovak state which critics had emphasised. The ethnic minorities were disloyal in the republic's emergency in 1938, which must raise questions about possible security and sabotage in the September crisis. Nevertheless, informed foreigners like the British Military Attaché Stronge thought the Czech army a good one which would fight, a view seemingly endorsed by Gamelin (a secret detractor of this same army) on 26 September. A young British newspaper woman, Shiela Grant Duff, wrote later that the Czech mobilisation 'went like clockwork', and of how Hitler had lost the element of surprise.[78]

The Czechs did not know that their martial qualities were becoming irrelevant because their fate was being decided elsewhere. Britain was now engulfed by a wave of relief that the peace could be saved, a feeling which was reciprocated in France. Members of the Cabinet waved Chamberlain off at Heston Airport and contemporary photographs and newsreel footage fully convey their elation. Most notably Halifax, the Godesberg 'rebel', had fallen back into line and showed his approval of what 'Peace Envoy Chamberlain' was attempting. He arrived in Munich to be met by Ribbentrop, who had been blatantly trying to get Hitler to follow an anti-British line for years, partly as revenge for the humiliation he had suffered as Ambassador in London. At the airport too was Henderson, Ribbentrop's arch-enemy, immaculately turned out as ever with a carnation in his buttonhole.

Hitler himself had gone to meet Mussolini at Kufstein, just across the former Austro-German border. What the British and French did not know was that the Duce had been conspiring with the Wilhelmstrasse to produce a document to steal away the Sudetenland and acknowledge Hungarian and Polish claims to Czech territory.[79] Mussolini was to pose as master of ceremonies at Munich because he alone of the four leaders could speak all the relevant languages (albeit somewhat crudely where German and English were concerned). Hitler was content to allow his florid ally to play this role because he knew where the real power lay. As for Daladier, he was far more ill at ease than the evasive Bonnet, who had always represented the 'doves' in the French Cabinet who wanted to avoid war at any price, and whom Britain's Ambassador Phipps had tried to make representative of all French opinion.

The Munich Conference was a shambles. Even the inkwell was found to be dry when the four leaders came to sign the agreement without any participation in it by the unfortunate Czechs. Their two representatives were obliged to wait in a nearby hotel before learning their fate. The Russians had been told by Halifax that he personally was sorry that they would not be at Munich (this was diplomatic pretence as he was notorious for his anti-Soviet prejudice), but that Hitler would never allow them to attend.

There were three conference sessions on 29 September, punctuated by lunch and dinner breaks at 3 p.m. and 9 p.m. The surroundings were bizarre. There was no conference table and the four leaders merely sat at one end of a large room in armchairs and on sofas. There was neither a formal agenda nor a chairman. Little wonder that the bureaucrat Wilson found the proceedings 'very imperfect', and they must have offended Chamberlain's businesslike habits.[80] When the main session started at 12.45, Hitler was flanked on his right by the interpreter Schmidt, and next to him were Chamberlain and the ever-faithful Wilson. Opposite them to Hitler's left were Mussolini and Ciano, sitting on a sofa, and next to them Daladier and the Secretary-General of the Quai D'Orsay, Alexis Léger (who like his former English counterpart Vansittart had literary talents, being a noted poet under the *nom de plume* St-Jean Perse).

Hitler immediately launched into a violent diatribe against the Czechs, claiming that only his regard for Mussolini had caused him to postpone his general mobilisation for twenty-four hours, and demanding that Czech evacuation of the Sudetenland be accomplished within at the latest ten days. Chamberlain spoke briefly to thank Hitler for his invitation and Mussolini for his mediation. For once, it was Daladier who seized the initiative, saying that, unless Hitler gave an assurance that an independent Czechoslovakia be preserved, 'There is nothing left for me but to return to Paris'.[81] After an intervention by Mussolini, Hitler then claimed that he did 'not want any Czechs!'[82] Daladier seemed to have his assurance.

The leaders then accepted the draft memorandum for the evacuation of the Sudetenland that Hitler and Mussolini had concocted between themselves. There was in fact an improvement on the Godesberg terms. The evacuation of the Sudetenland would now be in five stages and not all at once. The process was to be completed by 10 October with the occupation of predominantly German ethnic areas. These were to be identified by an international commission which the Munich agreement would set up. The Czechs would be represented on this commission, and areas which did not have a clear German majority would require plebiscites by the end of November. In fact, both Chamberlain and Daladier had wanted a Czech representative to be present at the conference, but Hitler vetoed this proposal saying that it would keep the leaders in Munich for a fortnight. Throughout the session with the other three leaders, Hitler had been conspicuously looking at his watch, while knowing that the two Czech representatives whom Beneš had sent to Munich were confined to their rooms with a Gestapo guard. Only at seven o'clock did these men, Mastny (the Czech Minister in Berlin) and Masarik (the *chef de cabinet* of the Czech Foreign Minister), learn anything about the likely fate of their country from the

British representative, Ashton-Gwatwin, the same man who had accompanied Runciman on his fact-finding mission. At 10 p.m., Wilson came and handed the two Czechs a map which marked those areas of Czechoslovakia that were to be evacuated immediately.[83]

Meanwhile, the representatives of the four great powers had accepted Mussolini's memorandum as the basis of a settlement. At Chamberlain's correct insistence, a supplementary declaration was made concerning property, currency and outstanding loans which referred all those matters back to the international commission. Hitler was in a peevish mood. Chamberlain, he said, 'is like a haggling shopkeeper who wrangles over every village and small detail; he is worse than the Czechs themselves. What has he lost in Bohemia? Nothing at all!'[84]

At 2.15 a.m., Chamberlain spoke to Mastny and Masarik fifteen minutes after the Munich terms had been heard by the President's office in Prague on German radio. Eleven thousand square miles of Czech territory were to be transferred and with it 800,000 Czech citizens and much of the country's industry. Yet, despite these devastating losses to the Czech state, Chamberlain reportedly remarked that he himself was pleasantly tired and kept yawning throughout the meeting. Much has been made by some historians of this human frailty, yet it would be surprising if a man of almost seventy years, who had flown over to Germany only that morning, was not tired by his exertions. The agreement itself had only been signed at 2 a.m. on 30 September. Chamberlain may have been guilty of insensitivity, but he was after all the same man who had said that Hitler was 'half mad' and 'the commonest little guttersnipe he had ever met'. History, however, has been unforgiving. Chamberlain himself described that day to his sister Hilda, in a letter dated 2 October (it is truly remarkable how he maintained this family correspondence so regularly when under such a strain), as 'one prolonged nightmare'.[85] His critics have preferred to pounce on a slip of composure in the small hours of a traumatic day.

Chamberlain was undoubtedly buoyed up by the fact that he had been able to secure Hitler's signature to what became known as the 'Anglo-German Declaration'. This had taken place in two phases. First, at 1 a.m., Chamberlain asked Hitler, when they were waiting for the final draft of the agreement, whether 'he would care to see me for another talk'.[86] The Führer stated that he would and the meeting duly took place after breakfast on 30 September, after William Strang, the Assistant Under-Secretary at the Foreign Office, who had also come to Munich, had drafted a statement of three paragraphs on the future of Anglo-German relations.

The two men met in Hitler's Munich flat and Hitler seemed to be more than willing to sign the document, which referred to the desire of the British and German peoples 'never to go to war with one another again'.[87] Hitler asked when Chamberlain wanted the document signed and the latter replied 'immediately'.

Subsequently, Hitler tried to pour scorn on the document, Ribbentrop's aide Spitzy alleging that he had told the Foreign Minister 'Oh, don't take it all so seriously. That piece of paper is of no significance whatsoever'.[88] According to another report, Hitler had actually been infuriated by Chamberlain's whole role from Berchtesgaden onwards, saying that if 'any other swine' tried to mediate like that he would 'kick him downstairs'. Chamberlain had 'spoilt his entry into Prague'.[89]

It was this piece of paper that Chamberlain was waving on his return to Heston that same day. This, according to his vilifiers, was the behaviour of a credulous 'umbrella man', whom Vansittart lampooned in the phrase, 'if at first you don't appease, fly, fly again'. But, according to his Parliamentary Private Secretary, Dunglass, Chamberlain had told him that 'If Hitler signed it and kept the bargain well and good ... if he broke it, he would demonstrate to all the world that he was totally cynical and untrustworthy'.[90] This was important, Chamberlain told Dunglass, because such bad faith would mobilise 'public opinion against him, especially in America'. The point about the United States was also important, for when Chamberlain had received the invitation to Munich, he had also received a telegram from President Roosevelt which consisted of just two words 'Good Man'. This telegram, which accurately reflected US opinion at the time, has slipped from the collective memory of those American historians who have regarded appeasement as a peculiarly European sin.

For the Czechs, of course, Munich was a tragedy. Beneš felt betrayed by the English and French. He made a desperate appeal to Moscow for help just before his 9.30 a.m. appointment with representatives of the parties in his coalition government on 30 September. Would the USSR advise the Czechs to fight or not? Or should Beneš, now bereft of French, let alone British support, accept the Munich diktat? The Soviet legation in Prague was strangely slow in passing on the Czech request, and no substantive reply had been received by noon. At 12.30 p.m. therefore the Czech Foreign Minister, Krofta, told Newton and the French Minister, Lacroix (who had burst into embarrassed tears at an earlier meeting with Beneš), that his country would accept the Munich Agreement. Later that day, the USSR was informed that the Czech government no longer expected a reply to its request.[91] At 5 p.m., the one-eyed Prime Minister General Syrový told his fellow countrymen and women that they were obliged to accept 'the most ruthless and unfair terms ever forced on anybody in history'.[92] Munich was not, of course, worse than Versailles or Brest-Litovsk, but the hyperbole was understandable. German troops began to enter the Sudetenland at 2 p.m. on 1 October 1938.

Meanwhile, Chamberlain flew back to a hero's welcome. He was then accorded the rare privilege (Churchill also received it in 1945), of being allowed to appear on the balcony of Buckingham Palace with King George VI and Queen Elizabeth.

Delirious crowds lined the route to the palace and when Chamberlain then drove back to Downing Street, the route was almost blocked. It was then that Chamberlain was fatally tempted to repeat Disraeli's comments on returning from the Congress of Berlin in 1878, claiming that he had achieved 'Peace with Honour'. Dunglass claimed that Chamberlain had initially rejected a suggestion that he use this phrase but that someone (never identified subsequently) persuaded him to do so. He clearly regretted that he lapsed into such uncharacteristic showmanship. Within the week he attempted to excuse himself in the House of Commons by explaining the lapse as the result of 'a moment of some emotion after a long and exhausting day'.[93] Disraeli was forgiven for saving an Empire which within decades was to be Britain's enemy in wartime. Chamberlain was not so lucky, his repetition of his predecessor's phrase being held up to ridicule as an example of provincial gullibility and stubborn pride. The truth was quite different. Chamberlain was worried by the adulation and told his sister Hilda that it 'seems to assume so much'. War, he told her, remained a distinct possibility.[94] His supporter Henderson in Berlin also appreciated the frail nature of the Munich triumph. 'Millions of mothers', he wrote to Chamberlain, 'will be blessing your name tonight for having saved their sons from the horrors of war. Oceans of ink will flow thereafter in criticism.'[95] Henderson too was to get precious little credit for his prescience.

Chamberlain's critics had their day when Munich was debated on 3 October. Duff Cooper resigned and was caustic about the Anglo-German Declaration, which Chamberlain had signed 'without any reference to his allies, without any communication with the Dominions and without the assistance of any expert diplomatic advisers'; this was not actually true, as Strang of the Foreign Office had provided the original draft. He remained glad though that, despite surrendering his post at the Admiralty, he could 'still walk about the world with my head erect'.[96]

Churchill had lost none of his rhetorical powers. Having congratulated Duff Cooper on 'one of the finest Parliamentary performances I have ever heard', he himself spoke on 5 October (it was a four-day debate). He did not begrudge, he said, 'our loyal, brave people ... the natural outburst of joy when they learned that the hard ordeal would be no longer required of them', but he thought Munich only 'the first sip of a bitter cup which will be proffered to us year by year'. Most tellingly, Churchill reflected on the fate of the Czechs. 'Silent, mournful, abandoned, broken, Czechoslovakia recedes into the darkness', he told a rapt House of Commons before predicting that the rump Czechoslovak state would not survive for long.[97] Chamberlain could not compete with such oratory, but he could refute Churchill's logic, and continued to do so. He would have noted Eden's ineffective speech in the Munich debate and the fact that Churchill abstained rather than voting against the government.

1. Joachim von Ribbentrop in London, 1936. (*Hulton Archive*)

2. Sir Robert Vansittart and Sir Alexander Cadogan, 1939. (*Hulton Archive*)

3. Anthony Eden, 1935. (*Hulton Archive*)

4. Lord and Lady Baldwin, 1937. (*Hulton Archive*)

5. Sir Nevile Henderson and Lord Halifax, 1938. (*Hulton Archive*)

6. Neville Chamberlain with Mussolini, 1939. (*Hulton Archive*)

7. Sir Nevile Henderson with Hermann Göring, 1938. (*Hulton Archive*)

8. Neville Chamberlain with Hitler, 1938. (*Hulton Archive*)

Chamberlain, though irritated by these critics, basked in the approval – indeed the hero-worship – of a nation, although he was level-headed enough to know that peace could not be taken for granted. In the few weeks after Munich, he received 40,000 letters from well-wishers in Britain and from abroad (this compares with the 4000 received by Duff Cooper after his resignation speech). Messages of congratulations came variously from Smuts, the Dutch Prime Minister, the King of Belgium and the Cardinal Archbishop of Westminster. Ordinary members of the public sent Chamberlain gifts ranging from fishing rods to cases of wine (the Prime Minister was known to be a keen fisherman). Such gifts were still coming in by the time Chamberlain reached his seventieth birthday the following March.

The press was equally jubilant about Chamberlain's achievement. The *Times* believed that 'no conqueror returning from a victory on the battlefield had come adorned with nobler laurels'. This was Dawson at his most enthusiastic, and many of his readers wanted a National Fund to be set up in Chamberlain's honour. The rest of the press was equally enthusiastic, with even the Labour Party organ, the *Daily Herald*, giving Munich its seal of approval. Only the *Daily Telegraph* condemned the agreement alongside the long-forgotten *Reynolds's News*.

In France, too, the peacemaker was lauded with *Paris Soir* offering a patch of French land and a stream where the British Premier could come and indulge his passion for fishing.[98] But whereas Chamberlain expected popular rejoicing, his colleague Daladier did not. As his flight was coming into Le Bourget on the return journey from Munich, Daladier reportedly turned up the collar of his coat to ward off the volley of rotten vegetables he expected on arrival. When, to his amazement, he was greeted with cheering crowds, he said, 'The fools, if they knew what they were cheering' or, according to another cruder version, substituted 'cunts' for 'fools'. In contrast, Bonnet rejoiced at the popular approval.[99]

September 1938 was the moment of Chamberlain's greatest triumph and, according to A.J.P. Taylor, Munich was itself 'a triumph for all that was best and most enlightened in British life'.[100] If Chamberlain, like the triumphant Roman generals on their return to the Eternal City, needed a tap on the shoulder to remind him of his mortal frailty, he found this in Baldwin, who wrote on 30 September saying, 'You have everything in your own hands now – for a time – and you can do anything you like. Use that time well, for it won't last'.[101] By December, Chamberlain himself was to be talking of how he was 'forced by circumstances to walk continuously through dark and perilous ways'.[102]

The Munich settlement has some claim to be regarded as the single most controversial agreement in modern European history. It was unquestionably the zenith or nadir of appeasement, depending upon one's viewpoint. Critics argue, not unreasonably, that Munich was wrong because it was immoral, the surrender of a small nation's territory at the point of a gun because its friends dared not risk a war.[103] Furthermore, it was wrong because it offered aid and comfort to Hitler, made the Czech state into an unviable rump, and encouraged Stalin into a ruthless reappraisal of his own foreign policy that culminated in the Nazi–Soviet Pact nearly a year later. Worse, critics argue, it appeared to offer the stamp of approval for totalitarian realpolitik and involved cynical cooperation in the dismantlement of that very peace settlement which Britain and France had laboured to construct in 1919–20.

The argument about morality can be speedily dismissed. The appeasers also argued that they had morality on their side because of the question of the Sudeten Germans' right to self-determination. But Britain's national interest also dictated policy, and even Churchill recognised this. When the Czech journalist Hubert Ripka visited London in June 1938, Churchill told him that, had he been in office, he would have done exactly what Chamberlain was doing. This did not prevent Churchill from attacking government policy in the House of Commons or castigating it in his memoirs, but the comment is a revealing one, unsurprisingly absent in the wave of anti-appeasement books that appeared between the end of the war and the 1960s. It was also in 1938 that Churchill privately cautioned Beneš and his government about the perils of war.[104]

It was true that Czechoslovakia, stripped of its Sudeten defences, was much more vulnerable after Munich than before. But this does not mean that a war over the Sudetenland would ever have been a feasible proposition in September 1938. This was not least because the Dominions had shown no disposition to fight for the Czechs, and as the Second World War was seen to demonstrate Britain was much more dependent on imperial manpower to defend itself and its Empire than vice-versa. There can be no certainty that in 1938, as opposed to 1939, Canada, Australia, New Zealand and South Africa would have fought with Britain and France, had the latter gone to war after Godesberg.[105] The evidence suggests that they would not have done so.

As for the point about offering aid and comfort to Hitler, his own reaction to the Munich settlement indicates that the Führer was far from happy with his gains. German domestic opinion did not share his zest for war, as Hitler learned when he displayed a panzer division in Berlin during the crisis and was dismayed by the indifferent, unwarlike reaction of Berliners. Nor is it by any means certain that ultimately matters would have gone better for Germany had war come in 1938 rather than 1939, as Hitler later claimed. Nor can we be certain that, had Britain gone to war in 1938 and France collapsed as spectacularly as it did in 1940, that British public opinion would have rallied round as it did behind Churchill.[106]

The point about Hitler's position has frequently been linked with the plot against him in the summer and autumn of 1938. Dissident members of the

German military, led by General Ludwig Beck and supported by civilian leaders like Karl Gördeler (a former Lord Mayor of Leipzig), planned to arrest and depose Hitler should Britain and France go to war over the Sudetenland. To this end emissaries were sent to Britain in the summer of 1938, notably von Kleist, who saw Chamberlain on 19 August to encourage a strong Anglo-French line on the Sudeten issue.[107] Even men with viewpoints as different as Vansittart and Henderson recognised the dangers of British involvement in encouraging German nationals to commit treason, however odious the Hitler regime might be.[108]

The problem with people like Gördeler was that their territorial demands were indistinguishable from those of the Nazis (they included both the Polish Corridor and the Sudetenland). The same members of the German military who were supposedly willing to arrest Hitler in 1938 were leading the German armies into Poland in 1939. Neither was it the responsibility of the British and French governments to go to war in September 1938 so that the German opposition could pluck up the courage to remove Hitler.[109] As it was, the opposition dithered until it was certain that Germany would lose the war, with the heroic but lone exception of the Communist workman, Georg Elser, who came within seven minutes of killing Hitler with a bomb in November 1939. The wartime Churchill government shared Chamberlain's scepticism about the reliability of the German opposition, which only finally grasped the nettle with the courageous but tragic 1944 bomb plot.

The attitude of the Soviet Union at the time of Munich has also been the cause of much debate, not least because it has been suggested that Stalin was willing to assist the Czechs, and had even sent three hundred Soviet aircraft to help them. The comment by Marshal Voroshilov in August 1939 that, 'Last Year when Czechoslovakia was threatened we waited for a sign from France. Our troops were ready: the sign was not given', is often cited.[110] The most recent research suggests, however, that there is no convincing evidence at all that Stalin was sincere in his offer of assistance, and that what is more Beneš knew this to be the case. This helps to explain why Beneš did not wait for a Soviet response to his desperate plea on 30 September before capitulating, it was in fact delivered quite pointlessly on 3 October, thirty-six hours after the Czechs had evacuated their Sudeten defences, and sixty hours after the Munich Agreement had been signed. The USSR claimed that it would stand by its obligations to Czechoslovakia under the 1935 Czech–Soviet Treaty when, in fact, this assurance was completely worthless.

The USSR may have been the ghost at the banquet at Munich, but for days before that Beneš had vainly attempted to secure some meaningful answer to his questions about what the USSR would do if France failed to honour its commitment. These questions were detailed and to the point, but when Beneš asked the

Soviet Minister on 25 September about when the Red Army would march, and how many airborne troops would be sent to aid the Czechs, the latter was unable to answer. Beneš told aides that Soviet aid could not be relied upon, and this was also the view of the pro-Soviet Czech Minister in Moscow, Fierlinger. In after years, when Beneš was the head of the Czech government in exile in Britain, and briefly President again between 1945 and 1948, he was extremely bitter about a Soviet betrayal which he regarded as being as bad as the Anglo-French one.

There were, in any case, all sorts of technical problems which would have bedevilled any Soviet intention to help, even if it had been genuine. One single-tracked railway line linked the Soviet Union to the Czech border via Rumania and it was 500 miles long. Otherwise the largely horse-drawn Red Army would have been reliant on Rumanian goodwill for fodder and this, given the tense state of Soviet–Rumanian relations, could not be guaranteed. The Poles were even less likely to agree to the transit of Russian forces, although the distance involved was only 100 miles.

As regards Soviet air support, it has become clear that the three hundred Soviet aircraft allegedly sent to the Czechs were part of a myth invented by the post-war Czech leader, Klement Gottwald, to defend Soviet behaviour in 1938. The USSR did send its new SB2 bomber to Czechoslovakia in limited numbers, but this was part of an agreement signed in April 1937 and nothing to do with the September crisis. Beneš himself was extremely reluctant to accept large-scale Soviet military aid because he knew of Anglo-French suspicions about Soviet influence in Prague. Even had the USSR been willing to mount a massive airlift, it would have found only twelve airfields available in Czechoslovakia, whose runways were mostly too short for Soviet aircraft. Soviet and Czech communication systems were also incompatible, and it is clear that massive preparations would have been needed to make Soviet help in any way effective, and these would have needed a year to organise. The USSR would also have needed to be prepared to breach either Polish or Rumanian neutrality to aid the Czechs, while at the same time facing a war against Japan in the Far East and an ongoing struggle in Spain, where Soviet aid was going to the republic (it ceased after Munich).[111]

While all this moves the focus away from British attitudes and preoccupations, it entirely justifies the policy of the Chamberlain government in 1938. The British knew that 40,000 Red Army officers had been purged by Stalin in 1937 (including the Commander-in-Chief Tukachevsky, who was executed for treason). Their scepticism about Soviet offensive capacity was therefore entirely reasonable, regardless of what Chamberlain or Halifax thought about the nature of the Soviet regime. Subsequent events in Finland justified British scepticism, and even Beneš did not trust his Russian allies. This was crucial because the USSR was much closer geographically to Prague than France and Britain, and its assistance would have been vital were the Czechs to survive.

Yet even if Czechoslovakia did survive, Britain and France had told Beneš that a victorious war would not bring about a return of the Sudetenland to Czechoslovakia. The historical irony was that Germany's repudiation of Munich ended with the forcible expulsion in 1945 of those very Sudeten Germans Hitler had obtained as a result of his bloodless coup in 1938. German names such as Carlsbad and Eger disappeared from the map of Bohemia forever.

In Britain, Chamberlain was also swayed by domestic factors. He believed Britain to be weak in the air, and in 1938 there was no radar and only one squadron of Spitfires. British anti-aircraft defences were also woefully weak, and Chamberlain knew that the French air force had been allowed to decline in drastic fashion since 1919. By contrast, Germany was thought to be vastly superior in the air (although official British information was inaccurate), and part at least of Czechoslovakia's border had been unmasked by the Austrian *Anschluss*. The strength of Czech defences in the Sudetenland has been rightly stressed, but the effect on them of the *Anschluss* is often ignored.

Chamberlain also had to consider the state of public opinion in 1938. At times during the Czech crisis it was volatile (as has been seen, his support plummeted to 22 per cent at the time of Godesberg), but there is no doubt that the Munich settlement evoked heartfelt relief throughout the land. Labour MPs, led by Attlee, disliked Chamberlain on a personal basis but supported his policy at the time of Munich. Before that they had been critical of it and Labour's National Council had urged Chamberlain to 'unite with the French and Soviet governments to resist any attack upon Czechoslovakia' on 8 September.[112] Chamberlain, however, had every reason to be suspicious of Labour, whose foreign policy position had swung wildly from one pole to another in the thirties. Chamberlain and Baldwin had frequently been accused by Labour of being militarists, and in 1935 Labour had voted against the arms estimates in the House of Commons, despite the crises over Abyssinia and Hitler's flouting of Versailles. In 1936 Labour abstained, but only because it thought that arms ought to be made available to the beleaguered Spanish Republic. Labour continued to oppose the rearming of the RAF with Spitfires and Hurricanes before Munich, and was also to oppose the mild measure of conscription which Chamberlain introduced in April 1939.[113] Given the impractical utopianism of the Opposition, Chamberlain deserves credit for not calling a snap election in the autumn of 1938 to take advantage of his overwhelming popularity. He was acute enough to realise that the public mood could rapidly change if Hitler were to be guilty of bad faith.

In the final analysis, those who criticise Munich do so from a Eurocentric position, ignoring the global perspective. Britain had every reason to fear that Japan and Italy might take advantage of a war in Central and Western Europe to attack its vulnerable Empire (the French had similar fears, given Japanese behaviour in 1940 in respect of Indo-China). The aid of the United States could obviously not be relied upon, and both Britain's potential allies in 1938 were of dubious value. France was only too willing to accommodate Hitler, and its military presented a false air of confidence to their British counterparts (excepting the air force Commander-in-Chief, General Vuillemin, who was so terrified by the prospect of war that he thought his force would be destroyed in a fortnight). Everything suggests too that the Soviet Union would have been a weak reed in the Czech crisis and could not be relied upon to render assistance to the Czechs. Indeed there are grounds for thinking that Stalin expected a war between Germany and the Franco-British to create favourable conditions for a social revolution in Europe which would benefit the USSR.[114] This would allow the Soviet Union to stand aside in 1938 while the rival imperialist powers engaged in bloody conflict. Anxieties about Japan in the Far East were another reason for Stalin to avoid war in Europe, his policy being dictated not by any outrage at Anglo-French cynicism but by brutal Soviet national interest.

Chamberlain had laboured long and hard to preserve peace during the Czech crisis. He had intervened in an unprecedented way in the affairs of Central Europe and thought he had safeguarded the future viability of the Czech state. But he was never the gauche elderly bungler of legend, and always operated in a context where domestic constraints were crucial. It has even been argued that it was surprising that there was any serious consideration given to going to war at all in either Britain or France in 1938.[115] Yet the fact remains that the British Government led by Chamberlain *did* go to the brink of war after Godesberg. Chamberlain was fully aware of Hitler's bullying and aggressive tendencies, but ultimately his first loyalty had to be to the people of Britain and its empire. Lord Halifax had it right. He wrote in his memoirs that Munich was 'a horrible and wretched business, but the lesser of two evils'.[116] Nevertheless, its terms were an improvement on what was on offer at Godesberg.[117]

8

The Armed Forces

In July 1940, the famous anti-appeasement polemic *Guilty Men* was published under the pseudonym 'Cato'.[1] It made a ferocious attack on the stewardship of Britain's defences by MacDonald, Baldwin and Chamberlain successively.

> Here is an epitaph [Cato thundered] which should be placed on the grave of every British airman killed in this war, every British civilian killed by Nazi bombers, every little child in this kingdom who may be robbed of life and happiness by high explosive or splintering metal rained down on this island by Marshal Goering's air force.

Cato went on to quote from Baldwin's assurance (which it denounced as false) to the House of Commons in November 1934 that the British government would never allow 'any position of inferiority with regard to what air force may be raised in Germany in the future'.[2]

Cato had already indicted the appeasers for their dereliction of duty where the army and navy were concerned. Thus, the grave peril which the British army had been placed in earlier that summer on the beaches of Dunkirk was the fault of slumbering politicians, so that Dunkirk was 'the story of an Army doomed *before* they took the field'.[3] The German navy became 'the Navy that Sam Built' because of Sir Samuel Hoare's responsibility for the 1935 Anglo-German Naval Treaty.[4] And so it went on. Chamberlain was lampooned as the 'Umbrella Man' and Inskip became 'Caligula's Horse'. So great was Cato's animus that the little book (just 125 pages) ended with a demand that those, like Churchill, 'now repairing the breaches in our walls should not carry along with them those who let the walls fall into ruin'.[5] Between July 1940 and January 1941, *Guilty Men* ran to twenty-eight impressions, and sold in its hundreds of thousands. The nation listened to Cato's message and ensured that Lord Baldwin lived out a disgraced old age. Chamberlain was mercifully soon to die or a similar fate would have befallen him also.

But away from the dramas and the dangers of that fateful summer, the historian has to ask whether Cato's charge was proven, or whether the reputations of the men who had charge of Britain's defences before the Second World War have been traduced. One thing is beyond doubt: Britain faced a growing military peril between 1931 and 1939. What follows in an examination of how successive British administrations attempted to deal with this peril.

It was understandable that after the Allied victory in 1918, there should be a feeling in Britain that its armed forces should be pruned. Germany's mighty military machine was shackled by the provisions of Versailles, and the war had made such colossal demands on Britain's economy that it was a natural dividend of peace that the armed forces' budget should be cut.

This assumption was most famously enshrined in the 'Ten Year Rule' adopted in August 1919, when defence policy was made dependent on the assumption that there would be no major war for ten years. In 1928, when Winston Churchill was Chancellor of the Exchequer, a modification of the Ten Year Rule was made whereby the policy was to be reviewed on a daily basis. Nevertheless, Churchill was a consistent supporter of restricting the military budget, reverting to the belief in 'retrenchment' over defence spending which had caused him to leave the Tory Party at the beginning of the century. It is important that Churchill's (partly self-created) image as an heroic anti-appeasement critic in the thirties is balanced by an awareness of his role in cutting resources for the forces in the twenties. Only in 1932 in the wake of the Manchurian crisis was the Ten Year Rule abandoned, following a recommendation by the Chiefs of Staff.[6] They had warned that 'the whole of our territory in the Far East as well as the coastline of India and the Dominions, and our vast trade and shipping lies open to attack'.[7]

The period before 1932 was, however, also one where international disarmament was under serious consideration, or in other instances involving a recognition that some sort of military balance needed to be struck. An example was the 1922 Washington Naval Treaty with its provision that Britain and the United States could keep five capital war ships in the Pacific for every three maintained by Japan (a source of Japanese grievance as has been seen). The radical solutions favoured by Ramsay MacDonald between 1929 and 1931 did not find favour with the French or the Germans, who argued that before any disarmament could take place, France should disarm down to their level. In practice, they were already secretly flouting the disarmament clauses of Versailles. In September 1932, the German delegation withdrew from the disarmament conference at Geneva, claiming that equality of rights had not been conceded. Then, after a promise that equality of rights would be conceded to Germany by Britain, France and Italy, its delegation returned to the conference in December 1932. Such utopian hopes of international disarmament were shattered by Hitler's final, and predictable, withdrawal from the process, which was the antithesis of everything he believed in. In Britain, in any case, Conservative politicians had always been deeply sceptical about the practicality of the sort of international disarmament which Labour preached. MacDonald tried to blame the French for the failure of his policy to succeed, saying in June 1932 that 'the French are still at war with Germany. They are afraid of its trade unless it is hobbled'.[8] The reality was that Germany, even before Hitler's appointment as Chancellor, was never serious about disarmament. France, though prickly, had good cause to be reluctant about reducing the size of its armed forces.

Britain laboured under some serious disadvantages when it came to rearmament in the thirties. First of all, it was a democracy. This meant that public opinion could act as a constraint in a way which was never possible in Nazi Germany or Fascist Italy. Secondly, it began rearming later than Germany (increased defence expenditure in the wake of the Ten Year Rule was only authorised in 1934). Lastly, it was inferior to Germany with regard to both population and resources, and its democratic politicians could only allocate a smaller proportion of resources to the defence budget. Churchill hammered the appeasers for allegedly underspending on defence, but whether it would have been politically or economically possible to sustain the level of expenditure which he and his supporters demanded, not always very consistently, is highly dubious. Happily for Churchill, he was out of office between 1929 and 1939 and was not responsible for dealing with the problems associated with the shepherding of Britain's defence resources.

That the British government was rather slow in getting off the mark was undeniable. Only in July 1934 did the Cabinet agree to a programme to make up the deficiencies in the armed forces, and only in February 1936 did the Cabinet approve programmes for a possible war which could be implemented over a three to five year period.[9] This was in a context where Germany was producing twice as many machine tools as Britain and had much superior steel production.

There were good, sound economic reasons for the British government's caution where rearmament was concerned. In December 1935, for example, the Defence Requirements Committee, set up the previous year, recommended that Britain should aspire to a two-power standard for the Royal Navy (which meant maintaining parity in capital ships with the United States). This would have created a large enough navy to deal with a Japanese challenge in the Far East, but also any threat in home waters. A partly-mechanised field force was to be created as well to deal with any continental emergency. RAF expenditure was also to be increased, but the projected cost of such a programme, which was to run from 1936 to 1940, would have amounted to £1,037.5 million by the end of the period.[10] This would have involved an increase in defence expenditure of 67 per cent. In the circumstances of the time, with an economy in the process of recovery from depression, it is hardly surprising that the Treasury balked. Neither would it approve the concept of a defence loan in peacetime to minimise the costs to the taxpayer. Chamberlain was joined in his opposition to the scheme by his Permanent Secretary at the Treasury, invariably an ally, Sir Warren Fisher.[11] As Chancellor, Chamberlain wanted to avoid creating a budgetary deficit, or increased taxation, an ideological *bête noire* for Tories which was to survive him by many decades. He was anxious, too, that the rearmament programme, of which he was a firm supporter, should not interfere with ordinary business. It is easy to deride this position as absurdly traditional and inappropriate until it is recalled that J.M. Keynes, supposedly the most radical economist of the day, also still thought in 1936 that rearmament must not interfere with ordinary business. He believed that the depressed areas of the north east and Scotland would act as a reserve of resources in manpower which would make it unnecessary to interfere with normal trade.[12] Only in 1937–38 did Keynes come to be persuaded that more state interference in the economy was necessary to accelerate rearmament.

There was no doubt of the Treasury's commitment to the rearmament programme. It regarded finance as the 'fourth arm of defence'. It believed that a financial war could be waged with Germany, which Britain would win because the Nazis would ultimately run out of raw materials and foreign exchange. The logic of this argument was that Britain and France could also win a long war in which the British could rely on the blockade which had helped to destroy Germany in the First World War.[13]

Chamberlain and the Treasury had their own concept of how Britain's defence budget could be contained at reasonable levels, while also providing adequate defences. This involved reliance on the Royal Air Force as a strike force, and a strong Royal Navy. Initially, Chamberlain believed that a strong bomber force would deter Germany, while the Royal Navy would guard Britain's trade routes and communications. The army was to be given a much reduced role, with only five divisions (one mechanised) available as a continental field force. This was because Chamberlain opposed a 'land army of indefinite size for continental warfare'.[14] Unsurprisingly, this whittled-down army did not please the professionals. Lieutenant-General Pownall was soon to refer in his diary to 'our poor little army'.[15] But Chamberlain perceived the army as being almost solely an instrument for imperial defence. The French army could surely defend its land space and, if necessary, the Low Countries as well. Churchill seemed to give support to this act of faith when crying 'Thank God for the French Army!' in 1934.

It is clear that Neville Chamberlain dominated the debate about defence throughout his Chancellorship. Baldwin was not uninterested, and certainly saw the power of the aerial threat from Germany, but Chamberlain was the driving force behind government policy. In 1937 Chamberlain remarked that 'there is no real *bona fides* in Germany',[16] and he showed his apprehension by allocating £211 million to the defence budget, when the armed services Chiefs had asked for £286 million, not an unreasonable response. He also abandoned his earlier position by authorising a defence loan of £400 million repayable over five years at 3 per cent interest. This had the effect of allowing the forces to obtain the resources they had originally asked for, if by another route. Chamberlain highlighted the delicacy of his task as Prime Minister when he described (in October 1938) how 'in our foreign policy we were doing our best to drive two horses abreast, conciliation and rearmament. It was a very nice art to keep these two steeds in step'.[17] In the end, Chamberlain presided over a level of rearmament which was unprecedented in peacetime Britain and which, by 1939, compared favourably with the level of rearmament in totalitarian Germany.[18]

The problem, therefore, was never about the commitment of Chamberlain (or Baldwin) to rearmament but the pattern of rearmament. In which direction was the thrust of British rearmament to go, given that resources were finite and the rest of the economy demanded attention as well? This was the particular nettle that Chamberlain and his colleagues were obliged to grasp. He came down firmly on the side of a reduced army role, as has been seen. In an ideal world, the army wanted five regular divisions and twelve territorial divisions fully equipped for continental warfare. In 1936, Duff Cooper circulated a paper about the need for a seventeen division force when he was Secretary of State for War, but Chamberlain replied that such a demand would stretch Britain's industrial capacity to the limit and was only prepared to equip the five regular divisions. He was in no doubt that he was right to do so, telling his regular correspondent Ida (who must have learnt a lot about military technicalities at home in Birmingham) in February 1937 that he was determined that the Regular Army would 'be armed *cap-à-pie* with the most modern equipment, and it is ready to go anywhere anytime. But we are not committed to sending it anywhere anywhen'.[19]

In practice, Chamberlain was only able to offer two divisions to the French at the time of the Czech crisis in 1938. The French wanted Britain to provide a mobile tank-based field force, but the War Office had conceptual problems with this. The great British tank expert Major General J.F.C. Fuller (whose writings were assiduously studied by the Germans) had given up on the War Office in 1933, observing that it was not interested in anything that could not shit or eat hay. Matters did not improve much in the years that followed. By 1939, it was true that of the planned British Expeditionary Force forty-three battalions consisted of infantry and only one of tanks. This was supplemented by two regiments of light tanks, but the British would not put an armoured division into the field until eight months after war broke out in early September.[20] This contrasted with the ten available to the Germans in May 1940 and the four assembled by the French.

Sometimes Chamberlain's civilian status betrayed itself when he entered the debate about the role and size of the army. In a Cabinet discussion on 16 December 1936, Chamberlain emphasised that his objection to a continental field force was not purely based on finance but also on a theoretical objection.

He himself doubted whether we were right in equipping the territorial force *for the trenches* [my emphasis]. He thought the question had been not considered impartially.

It was always assumed that we must make a contribution to a land war. As one of his colleagues had said, the French might not be satisfied, but it was not for the French to dictate to us the distribution of our forces.[21]

This was true, but if the small British force was committed to battle on the Continent, its fate would be in the hands of the French High Command. Nevertheless, Chamberlain's attitude was shared by his military advisers. Pownall wrote in February 1938 that 'they [the French] want to get us nicely committed and tied by the leg – not merely militarily but politically as well'.[22] This was why the British obstinately resisted having staff conversations with the French until March 1939. Even then the government remained cautious about building up the strength of Britain's continental commitment. When peacetime conscription was finally introduced, in April 1939, something the French had long lobbied for, it was in a modest form. The period of service was only for six months, and, of the extra 200,000 troops, conscription would bring in only 120,000 who would be in front-line combat units. 80,000 men would serve in anti-aircraft units, which reflected the desire the government to beef up the country's aerial defences. The men who were allotted to front-line units were also only to serve abroad when war came, and the first men were not called up until August 1939, so the conscription measure had little impact on the army's numbers before war broke out. Ultimately, only four divisions were sent to France in September, although a decision was taken in February 1939 to create an army of thirty-two divisions within twelve months of the outbreak of hostilities.[23]

It has been argued that the Chamberlain government's neglect of the British army contributed to the disaster of 1940, but Chamberlain's strategy was not ill-considered or rash. He had read the book *Defence of Britain* written by the leading British military theorist Basil Liddell Hart (whose advocacy of armoured warfare was also known to the Germans) published in 1939. This suggested that an attacking force needed a three-to-one superiority in numbers, and appeared to support the idea that a defensively-minded French army would easily be able to secure the French and Belgian borders from German attack. Conversely, if Liddell Hart was right, there was no need to send a seventeen or thirty-two division force to France in the event of war because French resources would be entirely adequate to deal with any threat. Britain's role would be limited to operating a First World War style blockade and an aerial bombardment of Germany's industrial areas. Chamberlain, and indeed the French High Command, were confident that the Anglo-French alliance would win a long drawn out war of attrition with Germany. So, too, were Britain's armed service Chiefs. Thus expert opinion appeared to back up Chamberlain's aversion to an over-commitment in land forces, or the creation of unreasonable French expectations. A 'blue-water' strategy whereby Britain depended on the land forces of its main ally or allies, and a strong navy, now supplemented by a modern effective air force was in the absolute mainstream of British defence philosophy. Baldwin had recognised Britain's novel island vulnerability to air attack but the recreation of the massive land involvement of the First World War stuck in most British craws between the wars. Just as America reverted to its traditional isolationism after 1919, Britain reverted to reliance on naval, and now increasingly, aerial forces.

Its government could also be more prescient than its totalitarian counterpart in Germany. In 1936, the Air Ministry asked for the heavy bomber designs that would allow the RAF to devastate Hamburg, Cologne and Berlin between 1942 and 1945. By contrast, the Germans decided not to build heavy four-engined bombers in 1937, seeing the primary role of the Luftwaffe to be one of cooperation with the Reichswehr. The absence of such machines in 1940–41 prevented the Luftwaffe wreaking equivalent destruction on Britain's cities, grave though the sufferings of its citizens were. It is characteristic of the literature of anti-appeasement that the sins of Hitler and the German military are forgotten or glossed over, whereas those of British politicians and military planners are emphasised. In retrospect, Chamberlain's statement on 5 May 1937, just before he replaced Baldwin as Prime Minister, to the effect that Britain could not or ought not 'to enter a Continental war with the intention of fighting on the same lines as the last', seems an eminently sensible recognition of existing realities.[24] Chamberlain knew what the British public would then stomach, however much it might veer around later, and he had the solid expertise of men like Liddell Hart on his side also. The much derided Inskip outlined Britain's defence priorities succinctly in a paper which was placed before the Cabinet in December 1937. They were, first, the protection of the United Kingdom itself against air attack; secondly, the safety of British trade routes; thirdly, the defence of Britain's overseas territories; and lastly, cooperation in the defence of any wartime allies.[25] This was a correct assessment of British priorities, and also dictated the way in which resources were allocated.

It has accurately been observed that the assessment of front-line air force strengths is more an art than an exact science. The debate which raged in Britain about relative Anglo-German air strengths demonstrate this point only too clearly. For, although Churchill and his small band of supporters in Parliament castigated the government for allowing the RAF to fall seriously behind the front-line strength of the Luftwaffe, their information (which sometimes came from government sources) was frequently seriously flawed. A parallel debate was also going on about the thrust of air rearmament. Should Britain rely on a deterrent bomber force or build up its fighter defences?

At first, Chamberlain preferred the idea of a deterrent bomber force, arguing that it would be 'more effective than a field force which could not be put in the field for two weeks'.[26] He was sensitive to the fact that he might be accused of opting for the cheapest available option, but he argued that Britain's existing industrial capacity would not allow it to accept the full demands of the army, navy and RAF. Thus, by April 1937, Chamberlain, with Baldwin's agreement, earmarked funding for seven new capital ships for the Royal Navy and 1500 front-line aircraft for the RAF. As has been seen, designs for heavy bombers had already been sought by the Air Ministry in 1936.

By the autumn of 1938, in the wake of the Czech crisis, perceptions had changed. The Chiefs of Staff had become alarmed by the prospect of a so-called 'knockout blow' that could devastate London, and after September 1938 there were only four radar stations in operation in southern England. Following a paper written by Ismay of the Committee of Imperial Defence in that month, priorities were changed in respect of air strategy. The Cabinet now agreed to put the emphasis on a defensive strategy, which would boost fighter production rather than rely largely on a massive bomber force which would deter Germany. Resources for anti-aircraft gun production were greatly increased, reflecting the anxieties Chamberlain had felt when he had flown over London's largely defence-less streets on the way to Germany. Thus the plan was to raise aircraft production levels so that 3753 aircraft could be produced between January and July 1939.[27]

All the time the government sustained a battering from the Churchillites both inside and outside the House of Commons. They consisted not just of MPs like Churchill and Brendan Bracken but also of technical experts like Desmond Morton of the Government Industrial Intelligence Centre, and Ralph Wigram of the Central Department of the Foreign Office (primed by the resident expert on German air strength, Michael Cresswell). Another key figure, unsurprisingly, was Robert Vansittart, sidelined as Chief Diplomatic Adviser at the end of 1937, but someone whom Churchill visited in the Foreign Office and who encouraged Wigram to become a source of information for Churchill on respective front-line strengths.[28] The coterie was completed by Wing Commander Torr Anderson who told Churchill about RAF training programmes and personnel levels, and Professor Frederick Lindemann, Churchill's ubiquitous 'Prof', an Oxford academic who became his chief scientific adviser in both peace and wartime.

Having men like Morton, Wigram and Anderson as allies allowed Churchill access to the same information as the Air Ministry and the Foreign Office. So started a relationship which became part of the anti-appeasement campaign so vividly portrayed in the pages of The Gathering Storm. According to Churchill's account, Wigram became a regular visitor to Chartwell (Morton was a near neighbour), while Churchill and his wife Clementine visited the Wigrams in their flat in London. Wigram was prepared, according to Churchill, to smuggle official Foreign Office papers out of the Foreign Office building in King Charles Street and down to Chartwell. In doing so, of course, he broke the Official Secrets

Act, but apparently justified this behaviour to himself by claiming that, as the Senior Privy Counsellor of the realm, Churchill was entitled to this information. The cloak and dagger aspect of the relationship was further sharpened by the inclusion in the operation of Lindemann, who took the documents back to his laboratory in Oxford for primitive photocopying, before returning to hand back the documents to Wigram at Chartwell. The embattled civil servant could then take the train back to London and replace the documents in their relevant Foreign Office (or Air Ministry) pigeon holes.[29] This process appears to have started on 6 April 1935, the day after the Foreign Office had learnt that Germany had more front-line aircraft (690 to 453) than Britain.[30]

Subsequently, Wigram made many visits to Chartwell which he used to pass on memoranda about relative British and German air strengths. Both he and Vansittart were appalled in late April 1935 when the latest government air force expansion plan only appeared to aim at achieving air parity with Germany in 1940. Churchill then used a further Wigram memorandum to support a charge in the House of Commons that the government had misled public opinion about the true strength of the Luftwaffe. Wigram also seems to have been the channel for Vansittart-inspired leaks to the British press, one being in March 1935 to Gordon Lennox of the *Daily Telegraph* about Hitler's claim to achieve air parity with Britain.[31] Quite whether Wigram's relationship with Churchill involved such deeds of daring and extreme secrecy as the latter liked to suggest has been questioned, amongst others, by the late R.A.C. Parker (a source generally friendly to Churchill), who wrote that 'some historians have exaggerated the "secrecy" of what they [Wigram and Vansittart] provided and the furtiveness with which they did it'.[32] Another critic of Churchill's behaviour, John Charmley, has written of his 'almost child-like love of "secret" information'.[33] At the time, the government was baffled about where Churchill got his information from. Morton was interviewed by Chamberlain on the subject, a considerable irony, as he was one of Churchill's sources. Chamberlain's distrust of Vansittart led by the autumn of 1938 to his being followed by MI5 agents.

The struggle between Churchill and the government over the issue of front-line strengths went on through 1935 and 1936. But even Wigram began to have some doubts about its ultimate relevance. Contesting such details, Wigram wrote to Churchill, 'is idle. This discussion of first-line strengths, is therefore not only endless, but also meaningless'.[34] There were also warnings to Churchill from Desmond Morton that exaggerating his case about German air rearmament would be counter-productive, as the government might argue that this strength-ened the case for the appeasement of Germany. Baldwin's Cabinet Secretary, Maurice Hankey, pointed out that it was in fact the *deductions* to be drawn from all the statistics which mattered as much as the statistics themselves.[35]

Part of the problem was that the statistics varied wildly. In November 1935,

Churchill said that the front-line strength of the RAF was 960 aircraft compared to Germany's 1500. Three months later, he used French figures (from the Deuxième Bureau) to put German strength at the ridiculously high figure of 4000 machines, with 2396 of these being front-line or combat-ready.[36] These inconsistencies tended to undermine Churchill's case when the point that he wanted to make was clear enough. German rearmament was outpacing Britain's.

One of Churchill's revisionist critics has deplored his 'dreadful hypocrisy and opportunism' in attacking the government's defence policies, when he himself as Chancellor had presided over swingeing cuts.[37] It is equally pertinent to ask how Churchill would have seen things had he had the responsibility of office between 1935 and 1939. For his desperate desire for office meant that, after 1937 certainly, there was a marked fall in the number of speeches he made and a moderation of the tone of his anti-Government rhetoric.[38] It is significant that at the 1937 Conservative Party Conference Churchill completely endorsed the government's defence policy.

Throughout the years 1935 to 1937, the government sometimes had inaccurate information about German air strength, and this pattern continued into 1938. But Churchill was quite wrong to say in March 1935 that 'practically the whole of the German bombing force can reach London with an effective load', for only in 1940, when it had obtained bases in France and the Low Countries, was the Luftwaffe in a position to bomb London intensively, and then never with the devastating power that Churchill and his followers had predicted. Maurice Hankey showed calmer judgement than Churchill, Vansittart, Wigram or Morton when he wrote in 1934: 'The Cabinet are overrating the imminence of the German peril. The peril is there all right, but will take more than five years to develop in the military and air sense'.[39] By 1939, when the peril was evident enough, Britain was already starting to outpace German air production.

Wigram and Vansittart were civilians and could not perhaps be expected to understand the finer points of aerial strategy, but Churchill too had not grasped that, even allowing for the Luftwaffe's growing strength, its planned role in Germany made it incapable of inflicting the destruction which he painted in such vivid, but alarmist tones. But he shared his misperceptions with the supposed experts in the Air Ministry, who began by underestimating the threat, but after 1937, took the opposite view exaggerating 'both the immediacy of the Luftwaffe menace and the capacity of its bombers to deliver a knock-out blow'.[40] The Air Ministry figures were the very same figures that Wigram was feeding to Churchill, alongside information available in the Foreign Office and from Vansittart's private intelligence sources in Germany.

Any assessment of the relationship between arms and appeasement needs to take into account the devastating events of May and June 1940. They have caused history to be read back to front where the British appeasers are concerned, with the extraordinarily rapid German victory attributed Cato-style to the deficiencies of Britain's political leadership.

The first point to be addressed, therefore, is were Britain's forces as deficient in 1940 as the anti-appeasement lobby has suggested? The record suggests not. Britain had the fastest monoplane fighter, the Spitfire, in 1940, which outperformed its main German rival; a string of radar stations whose presence was to be vital; and even (as it turned out) a tank, the Matilda, whose thick armour came as a disagreeable surprise to the Germans in a sharp action around Arras (causing Rommel to exaggerate the scale of what was actually a small Anglo-French counter-attack).[41] The Matildas also had a powerful two-pounder gun which packed more punch than its German equivalent, the Mark III Panzer. At sea, too, the British did not lack innovation. The launching of the *Ark Royal* in 1937 gave the Royal Navy its first real aircraft carrier and one that was to be used to devastating effect, against the Italian Navy in its supposedly safe anchorage at Taranto in 1940. The suggestion, therefore, in *Guilty Men* that the British forces were in some way doomed to defeat in 1940 is nonsense. But it is nonsense compounded by the fact that the British were not, and could not be, masters of their own fate in the Battle of France.

This meant, of course, that the defeat in France and the Low Countries was an *Allied* defeat for which the French High Command was largely, but not wholly, responsible. And much revision of French history has taken place in recent years to explode the theory that France's own defeat in 1940 was a result of chronic political malaise and in particular of the reluctance of the 1936–37, Popular Front government to rearm. In fact, this left-wing administration presided over the most massive rearmament programme in French history.[42] And the 1939–40 Daladier government followed up its work and presided over a notable recovery in French national mood and a tougher attitude towards both Fascist Italy and Nazi Germany.

The French were also let down by their former Belgian allies, who horrified the French commander when he arrived at their River Dyle Line to find almost no defences prepared against an invader. Even so it took a freakish accident to bring about the evolution of the daring, but highly risky, Manstein Plan. A German plane, carrying the German invasion plan, crash-landed in Belgium in January 1940 near Mechelen, and the plan was passed on to the French. At that stage its emphasis was, as in 1914, on a thrust through Belgium, but, after the Mechelen incident, Hitler completely revised the plan. Instead, he adopted General von Manstein's suggestion that the primary German armoured thrust should be to the south in the thickly-wooded, hilly Ardennes sector at the junction of the Franco-Belgium frontier.

The French generals led by Gamelin continued to assume, however, that the primary threat would be through Belgium, with a possible subsidiary thrust through Holland. To cover this contingency, Gamelin invented the understandable, but ultimately fatal 'Breda Variant', which sent the French Seventh Army and their most mobile units in a rapid dash into Holland. This force, which had formerly made up a mobile reserve, was therefore not available to counter the surprise German thrust when it came through the Ardennes after 10 May 1940. The French further compounded the problem by stationing elderly reservists along the scantily defended River Meuse, alongside too few front-line regular divisions. This battle in 1940 was fought and lost between 10 and 14 May well to the south of the British Expeditionary Force, which played no role in its outcome, but was ultimately forced to arrange its own evacuation from Dunkirk to avoid complete annihilation and capture.

Indeed, as far as the British were concerned, it was a mercy that they did *not* have a seventeen division or even larger force in France and Belgium in 1940, when much of it would have been sucked into the French defeat. It is hard to argue that, given the complete strategic and tactical surprise achieved by Germany, the presence of more British troops would have affected the issue. But it needs to be recognised that the scale of the German victory and its speed surprised even senior German generals.

As it was, the BEF fought doggedly and well, as did the RAF. Its performance showed up the deficiencies of the undersized French air force which Chamberlain and his colleagues had warned about for years, and this allowed highly vulnerable German armoured columns to concentrate in the Ardennes with the minimum of molestation. In the end, although the subject of French complaints about selfishness, the British could not be blamed for refusing to throw all their cherished Spitfires and Hurricanes into a Battle of France which was effectively lost by mid-May. In their worst nightmares neither Chamberlain nor Churchill, by then colleagues in the wartime government, could ever have envisaged the shattering speed of the German advance or of France's defeat. But France's defeat was also a defeat for Holland (whose defences rapidly collapsed), Belgium (whose vaunted fort of Eben-Emael was captured with ease by the Germans) and Britain. The British government had for years relied on the invincible French army. The latter's catastrophic defeat completely undermined British strategy and expectations. Likewise, the French relied overmuch on British aerial strength, and it was RAF bombers which bombed the Ruhr, to little effect.[43] Ultimately, however, the decision to strengthen the fighter component of the RAF, while laying plans for heavy bombers, proved to be justified. In this sense, the appeasers' strategy saved Britain in 1940. And its small army still proved well capable of administering a bloody nose to Mussolini in North Africa later in the year.

The events of 1940 matter because classic anti-appeasement studies have emphasised not the brilliant nature of the German victory, or its almost reckless daring, but the so-called 'Phoney War' of 1939–40, which has been used to stress the unwillingness of Britain (and France) to fight an offensive war.[44] This eight-month period has been used to demonstrate that French sloth in particular, and a parallel collapse in morale, made the land defeat in 1940 inevitable. As far as Britain was concerned, the 'Phoney War' has been regarded as a sort of extension of appeasement by a Prime Minister who lacked the guts for war. In fact, although Churchill may have been frustrated by the lack of action (and it was he who was the instigator of the failed Norway campaign), Chamberlain's strategy dovetailed with that of the French. Germany could and would be defeated in a war of attrition. Should it attempt to attack in the west to break the shackles of a British blockade, Chamberlain had Liddell Hart's assurance that the advantage would lie with the Anglo-French defenders (the latter being, of course, much thicker on the ground). Despite what happened in the summer of 1940, the French generals had been confident of victory. When Gamelin heard of the German offensive, a subordinate recorded he was seen to be 'pacing up and down the corridor of the barracks, humming audibly with a martial air'.[45] This was a confidence which the British political leadership, Churchill included, would have expected at that moment.

The German victory in 1940 was neither inevitable nor expected. Had the Allied superiority in tanks been properly exploited, and their more limited resources in the air been properly applied to bomb the vulnerable columns of panzers in the Ardennes and Meuse sector, the result could have been very different. A German defeat in May 1940 would assuredly have made the assessment of British appeasement policy, and indeed its French twin, quite different. Appeasement is crucially linked, therefore, to military disaster and defeat. But Baldwin and Chamberlain cannot be held responsible for a freak accident like the Mechelen Incident, any more than they were responsible for Gamelin's Breda Variant, which was as risky in its way as the Manstein Plan. Gamelin's gamble failed where Manstein's succeeded. Historians have shredded his reputation as they have those of his political masters, Daladier and Reynaud. Though they were ultimately dependent on French military decisions, the reputations of Baldwin and Chamberlain also sank with the tattered defences of the Meuse bridgeheads in 1940. Their rehabilitation is thus long overdue.

9

The Foreign Office

The key body concerned with the formulation of British policy towards the Fascist dictatorships in the 1930s was, of course, the Foreign Office and its sister organisation, the Diplomatic Service. Although it was common practice for serving diplomats to work in the Foreign Office in London before being posted abroad, many diplomats had little experience of working there thereafter. Sir Nevile Henderson, for example, a key diplomat as Ambassador in Berlin between 1937 and 1939, bemoaned the fact that he was constantly abroad after he entered the Diplomatic Service in 1905 (apart from a brief stint in London in 1915). The result, Henderson wrote in his memoirs, was that:

> A man who lives abroad all his life becomes a stranger in his own country and loses touch with his own people and the personalities in it ... The Foreign Office, moreover, has its own habits, methods and idiosyncrasies and it is better that H.M's representatives abroad should be familiar with them. Otherwise there is friction and misunderstanding and a mutual lack of sympathy which is prejudicial to the best possible results.[1]

The converse was also true. Sir Orme Sargent, the Deputy Under-Secretary at the Foreign Office, and therefore a key figure in policy formulation, never held a major diplomatic post and rarely left London throughout a long career. Thus, while it was possible for an Ambassador to 'go native' in a foreign posting and become too sympathetic to the regime to which he was accredited (an accusation frequently made against Henderson), Foreign Office officials in London lacked the experience which would have made it possible to understand the strains that diplomats might be under. This was especially true of men like Phipps and Henderson (Berlin), Perth and Loraine (Rome) and Chilston and Seeds (Moscow) who were posted to totalitarian states. Only after 1943, as a result of the so-called Eden–Bevin reforms, were the Foreign Office and the Diplomatic Service merged into one service.[2]

Nevertheless, it was the permanent officials in London who, together with their political masters, made policy. This had long been recognised by mature and sophisticated ambassadors, one of whom, Lord Bertie (a former Ambassador to Rome), had famously remarked that an Ambassador was nothing more than 'a d...d marionette' whose strings were pulled in 10 Downing Street.[3] Bertie may have overstated his case, but there is little doubt that the influence of

Ambassadors had declined markedly since the days of someone like Stratford Canning, a man supposed to have almost single-handedly ensured that Britain entered the Crimean War against Tsarist Russia (although even Canning's role has been downplayed recently).

The dominant personalities in the Foreign Office in the thirties were the Permanent Under-Secretaries. These were the men in overall charge of the day-to-day running of the Foreign Office, the appointment of Ambassadors and Ministers, and the process of examining and assessing the value of the mass of information that came to London from Britain's embassies and legations abroad. Equally important was the process of working with, and trying to win over to Foreign Office perceptions, successive Prime Ministers and Foreign Secretaries. Poor personal relationships between politicians and permanent officials at the Foreign Office could create tensions which made an already difficult task even more onerous.

This last point is particularly pertinent because the Foreign Office was dominated for most of the thirties by a particularly powerful personality, Sir Robert Vansittart, commonly known in the corridors of the Office as 'Van'. Vansittart was appointed Permanent Under-Secretary at the Foreign Office in 1929 and remained in post until the end of 1937. He had previously been Private Secretary to both Stanley Baldwin and Ramsay MacDonald, and also had valuable experience in the US Department of the Foreign Office.

In some respects, Vansittart was typical of Foreign Office entrants. He entered the service in 1903, after being educated at Eton and Oxford (one of the criticisms of the Foreign Office over many years was its reliance on public school Oxbridge-educated officials). Thereafter he moved, it seemed, with effortless ease up through the ranks of Foreign Office mandarins.

But this image was misleading. 'Van' was not a typical Foreign Office official, or indeed a typical civil servant. He wrote poetry and plays (several of which were performed in the West End). He even wrote film scripts under a pseudonym, most notably for the *Four Feathers*, a well-known film of the late thirties. In a sense, Vansittart can be seen as a sort of Renaissance man markedly different from his fellow officials in the Foreign Office.

Certainly his temperament was mercurial. He wrote long, rambling memoranda which irritated his colleagues. One of his closest colleagues was to write, 'What a child he is – and suffers from childish complaints like vapours and irritations. Nothing rational about him at all – just silly, uninformed impulse'.[4] This comment by his successor, Sir Alexander Cadogan, also reflected the view of some of Vansittart's political masters, who found him overbearing and too anti-German. Anthony Eden wrote of Vansittart that, amongst all the Foreign Office officials he worked with during the period, he had never known one to compare with Sir Robert as a relentless, not to say ruthless, worker for the views he held strongly himself. The truth is that Vansittart was seldom an official giving cool and disinterested advice based on study and experience. He was himself a sincere, almost fanatical crusader, and much more of a Secretary of State in mentality than a permanent official.[5]

Eden's partiality is clear here, and there were those who thought that his animus was a result of a fear that he, as Foreign Secretary, was being overshadowed by the older man.

In fact Vansittart's reputation for fanatical anti-Germanism is not entirely deserved. In the years immediately after Hitler's coming to power, he worked hard for an understanding with Germany, and complained to his brother-in-law, Sir Eric Phipps (then Ambassador in Berlin) in 1935 that the Nazis were attempting to portray him as a Germanophobe.

> They say [Vansittart wrote] that I am anti-German ... It is of course completely untrue. I am not anti-German in the least. I have always thought that Germany got far too rough usage at Versailles and have always wished to see minimised the imprudences then committed.[6]

But Vansittart's warnings about the rising level of German rearmament were unpalatable to both Baldwin and Chamberlain, who wanted to mend fences with Berlin. He was also perceived to be too pro-French, and it was true that he was sympathetic to French anxieties in the face of the form of rabid German nationalism represented by Hitler. Vansittart's lengthy memoranda to successive Foreign Secretaries and Cabinet members, largely unsympathetic to the appeasement of Nazi Germany, were an irritant, as were his known links with those outside the Foreign Office, like Winston Churchill, who were critical of government foreign policy. His house in Park Street was regarded by the appeasers as a nest for vipers liable to undermine carefully laid plans for accommodation with Germany. As has been noted, Vansittart had his own private intelligence sources which he used to raise the alarm about Nazi intentions. He continued to advertise their findings even when he had lost his power base as Permanent Under-Secretary.

Within the Foreign Office, too, Vansittart had his adherents. Orme Sargent, the Deputy Under-Secretary, was one, although the two men did not agree about everything. Sargent was far more hostile to the Soviet Union than Vansittart.[7] But 'Moley', as Sargent was nicknamed in Whitehall, could be relied upon to endorse Van's anxieties about Germany (the nickname itself acknowledged his work in burrowing away against the appeasers). Others were the Leeper brothers, Allen and Rex, two Australians who were also sceptical about the direction of British policy towards Germany during the thirties. Above all, Ralph Wigram, head of the Foreign Office Central Department on whom Vansittart relied a good deal.

It was Wigram and Sargent who proposed, in November 1935, that there should be a concerted attempt to reach an accommodation with Germany because 'the British public will expect this policy to have been attempted before we proceed to intensive rearmament'.[8] Once the effort had been made, and had been rebuffed as Vansittart, Sargent and Wigram expected the case for rearmament would be overwhelming. Wigram worked himself into an early grave in 1936, lamenting the fact that he had not been able to convince either Parliament or the British public about the growing danger represented by Nazi Germany. He had often 'triggered the inspiration for Van's own thoughts' about the German question,[9] and was, like Vansittart, an ally of Churchill's in his campaign to raise awareness about the need for rearmament. Wigram was devastated by the news that Germany had sent troops into the demilitarised Rhineland in March 1936, and told his wife Ava, 'Wait now for bombs on this little house. All my work these many years has been of no use. I am a failure.'[10] Vansittart, proved right ultimately by events, was to give the same verdict on his Foreign Office career. 'Mine is a story of failure,' he wrote after the war, 'but it throws light on my time which failed too.'[11]

It would be quite wrong, however, to create the impression that the Vansittartites in the Foreign Office were inveterate anti-appeasers. A German Foreign Office official reported in May 1938 (after 'Van' had been sacked as Permanent Under-Secretary) that even Vansittart was not as 'anti-German as he is always said to be'.[12] Neither were he and his allies outright enemies of Italy or Japan. Vansittart, after all, was the author of the secret Hoare–Laval Plan of 1935 which gave Mussolini most of Abyssinia without firing a shot, until it was disowned by the British government and Foreign Secretary Hoare had to resign. Neither was Vansittart averse to appeasement of Japan, recognising as early as 1935 that 'we are in no condition to have trouble with Japan'.[13] He would not go as far as Neville Chamberlain or Warren Fisher (the Permanent Under-Secretary at the Treasury) in seeking a non-aggression pact with Tokyo, but he recognised Germany to be the primary threat and wanted to avoid needlessly provoking the Japanese.

Vansittart had also become somewhat disillusioned with the Americans, whom he, like colleagues, had hoped in the twenties would join Britain in policing the world. Britain had given up its old alliance with Japan (dating from 1902) to appease Washington and had got little back in return. By 1934, Vansittart was writing that 'we have been too tender, not to say subservient, with the US for a long time past. It is we who have made all the advances and received nothing in return'.[14] The lesson was obvious. If the United States could not be relied upon to support Britain in the Far East, then appeasement of Tokyo was logical, despite Japan's invasion of Manchuria in 1931 and the rest of mainland China in 1937. As a leading member of the Defence Requirements Committee, Vansittart was uncomfortably aware of Britain's military deficiencies and a constant advocate of a more vigorous rearmament programme. But in the short run, as Vansittart recognised, Britain was in no position to fight a war against both Germany and Japan.[15]

This fact influenced Vansittart's attitude towards Britain's third potential enemy, Italy. Like many people inside the Foreign Office and outside it, Vansittart saw Mussolini as a possible counterweight to and moderating influence upon Hitler. He was prepared to go a long way to prevent Mussolini from entering the German camp, believing like most that Britain's Mediterranean bases, notably Gibraltar and Malta, were vulnerable to Italian attack in wartime. The nightmare scenario would of course be a war against *three* great powers simultaneously. A war which all the advice that the Foreign Office and successive governments were getting suggested that Britain (and presumably France) had no hope of winning.

Vansittart did not share Anthony Eden's faith in the League of Nations. His attitude towards known Italian aspirations about Abyssinia was, therefore, severely pragmatic. As early as 8 June 1935, months before Mussolini's attack on the African kingdom, Vansittart minuted the then Foreign Secretary, Samuel Hoare, 'Italy will have to be bought off – let us use and face ugly words – in some form or other, or Abyssinia will eventually perish'.[16] The 'some form or other' was the notorious Hoare–Laval Pact, details of which were leaked to the French press and caused uproar in Britain where Mussolini's blatant aggression had outraged public opinion. Hoare was replaced as Foreign Secretary in December 1935 by Eden, who was hostile towards Mussolini (although far more receptive to the concept of accommodation with Germany). The collapse of the Hoare–Laval Pact was a major defeat for Vansittart and the Foreign Office, although it is clear, despite Eden's protestations later, that Hoare had Cabinet approval for what he agreed with Laval. Faint hearts then deserted Hoare, who was made the scapegoat for the fiasco.

The Abyssinian crisis showed that Vansittart could be an appeaser when it suited him. His famous quip, 'if at first you can't appease, fly, fly, again', at Neville Chamberlain's expense (a reference to the Prime Minister's three flights to Germany to try and save the peace over Czechoslovakia), needs to be seen in this context. Vansittart correctly identified Germany as the primary threat to British security, but he was not quite the hero of the anti-appeasers' camp that he was made out to be subsequently.

Even in the German context, Vansittart could be guilty of serious errors of judgement. He persisted in 1937–38 in seeing the Nazi stooge Konrad Henlein, the leader of the Sudeten German minority in Czechoslovakia, as an independent politician when even Henderson, the much maligned Ambassador in Berlin, realised that Henlein was taking orders from Hitler.[17] Neither ultimately did Vansittart have any faith in those German nationalists like Gördeler who opposed the Nazi regime. Their aspirations were ultimately indistinguishable from the territorial ambitions of the Nazis, and recent attempts to portray Van as one of those Britons who would have supported British assistance to the anti-Nazi resistance lack conviction.[18] By the time the war came, the former Permanent Under-Secretary had become a professional anti-German whose subsequent publications, including the notorious *Black Record*, a polemic against German militarism and aggression, became an embarrassment to the government. Relations with the Chamberlain government had already become so poor that, as the government's Chief Diplomatic Adviser (the meaningless 'promotion' given to Vansittart at the start of 1938), he was kept out of the day to day process of policy making.

Vansittart's career as Permanent Under-Secretary showed the problems which could arise when the most senior permanent official at the Foreign Office was at odds with the Prime Minister and Foreign Secretary. Thus Baldwin and Eden had actually tried to remove Vansittart from office in 1936. The idea was to get him to accept the Paris Embassy, an offer that was pushed no less than three times in twelve months. Vansittart had no intention, however, of being sidelined in Paris and declined the offer, using the excuse that his wife's health was too delicate.[19] An extra factor was that the Paris Embassy was already earmarked for his brother-in-law, Eric Phipps, with whom Van's relationship was difficult. Snapping up the Paris prize from in front of his brother-in-law's nose would not have helped matters. As it turned out, Phipps became a notorious defeatist where French resistance to Hitler's ambitions were concerned, and relations became even more tense.

Vansittart had already been removed from his post as Permanent Under-Secretary when Lord Halifax replaced Eden as Foreign Secretary in February 1938. Vansittart had written off Eden as gauche and unoriginal, and had no great opinion of Halifax either. He was also bitter about Eden telling the Labour politician Hugh Dalton that 'he thought of Eden as a man with whom he had often had to go out tiger shooting, and who, in the end, had shot him in the back'.[20] He was probably right in his belief that Eden was jealous of him and sought his removal. Neville Chamberlain was overjoyed at Van's fall, and boasted that he had achieved in a few days what Baldwin had been trying to achieve for years.

But what ultimately did Vansittart's removal mean? To a degree, it was the result of a personality clash as much as of a policy difference, but there were fundamental differences as well. Vansittart did not trust the new German leadership, and neither could he have lived with the way in which Chamberlain was trying to direct foreign policy from Downing Street. But he did not differ greatly from the Cabinet on how to manage relations with Italy and Japan. And as far as rearmament was concerned, the debate, as with Churchill, was about the pace rather than the principle. As it was, his views were increasingly ignored even before his sacking. The Chamberlain Cabinet regarded Vansittart as merely an irritating Cassandra, serving out his time as a public servant. Unless he resigned from the Foreign Office and took his message to the country he could be safely ignored (although the activities of his private intelligence army continued to irritate Chamberlain).

Vansittart's successor as Permanent Under-Secretary was Sir Alexander Cadogan, a former Ambassador to China who had also spent many years in the League of Nations Department of the Foreign Office. Cadogan, like Vansittart, was a product of Eton and Oxford, but there any similarity ended. Where Vansittart was strong-willed and fiery, Cadogan was unobtrusive and diligent. His Private Secretary at the Foreign Office, Gladwyn Jebb (later Lord Gladwyn), has left us with this pen portrait of his chief.

> I knew and liked Alec Cadogan [Gladwyn wrote in his memoirs], who was the antithesis of Vansittart. Careful, cautious, reserved, conventional, clearly shy, clearly repressed emotionally, he was nevertheless a man of quiet charm and native intelligence. He was also usually fair in his judgements about people and sensible in his judgements about things. Everybody trusted and most liked him.[21]

Jebb's comments about Cadogan being emotionally repressed were apt, but former colleagues were shocked by the publication in 1971 of Cadogan's diaries whose language revealed a side of his character hitherto unknown. Pejorative comments about foreigners (the Italians, for example, were commonly referred to as 'Ice Creamers') were combined with swingeing attacks on Foreign Office colleagues. Vansittart was a 'silly creature' but Nevile Henderson was no better.[22] He, too, was described as 'rather excitable and silly',[23] but there was little to choose between them. On 24 February 1939, Cadogan wrote of the two men in his diary: 'I don't know which is the sillier of the two, or which destroys his case more effectively, Van I think.'[24]

Nor did politicians escape castigation. Lord Halifax, whom Cadogan served as Foreign Secretary for over two years, obviously irritated him as well. 'In times of crisis', Cadogan moaned, 'Halifax goes off to Yorkshire on a Friday afternoon. When he's in London, he is at a loose end and doesn't know what to do with himself so ruins everybody else's day.'[25] When Duff Cooper, the First Lord of the Admiralty, resigned in protest over policy towards Czechoslovakia in September 1938, he was witheringly dismissed in the diaries. 'Good riddance of bad rubbish', Cadogan wrote.

It is true, nonetheless, that Cadogan's position as Permanent Under-Secretary would have tried the patience of a saint. For, in addition to the management of the Foreign Office and the Diplomatic Service at a time of extreme peril to Britain, Cadogan was saddled with the continued presence in the office of Vansittart as the Government's Chief Diplomatic Adviser. In practice, Vansittart's post was a meaningless one, for, although the announcement from Downing Street spoke of the need for it to be filled by 'a person of international reputation and authority',[26] he was only consulted after papers had been seen first by Cadogan and the Foreign Secretary. Vansittart's job specification drafted by Gladwyn Jebb (now Cadogan's Private Secretary just as previously he had been Vansittart's), underlined his humiliation. It stated that 'in the event of a paper requiring urgent action, it will be sent by Sir A. Cadogan direct to the Under-Secretary concerned with a slip bearing the words "Sir R. Vansittart after action".'[27] Neither was Vansittart to be involved in the interviewing of foreign ambassadors or other dignitaries.

Nevertheless, Vansittart continued, from Cadogan's standpoint, to be an interfering busybody. His time was being wasted, Cadogan complained bitterly, by Vansittart, who was 'developing the technique of writing minutes on every paper he can lay his hands on and thus trying to become a Super Permanent Under-Secretary'.[28] Underneath the trim, ubiquitous exterior was an increasingly frustrated and angry mandarin. Protests to Halifax failed to secure his rival's sacking. The mystery concerns why Chamberlain and Halifax continued to keep Vansittart in his position. Presumably the reasoning was that in the office Vansittart could be neutralised, outside it he would be a dangerous rogue elephant (although, as suggested earlier, Vansittart's private intelligence sources continued to very active, and it has been argued that, through them, he was more effective in influencing policy after his sacking as Permanent Under-Secretary than before it).[29]

Although Vansittart's continued presence was an irritant and, in fact, an unprecedented Foreign Office anomaly, there was no doubt that Cadogan was in line with government thinking about relations with Germany. Chamberlain believed that Cadogan was a 'sane slow man', whereas Van had the effect of 'multiplying the extent of Anthony's natural vibrations and I am afraid his instincts were all against my policy'.[30] Out in the field in Berlin, Nevile Henderson expressed his relief that Vansittart was going as Permanent Under-Secretary. 'I shall feel happier', he wrote to Lord Halifax in early January (soon to replace Eden as Foreign Secretary), 'with Alec Cadogan as head of the Foreign Office'.[31] Relations between Henderson, who saw himself as the Prime Minister's appeasing emissary in Germany, and Vansittart had reached an all-time low. The difference between the new Permanent Under-Secretary and his predecessor was immediately evident in Cadogan's assessment of Henderson's work in Berlin. His diary entry for 30 January 1938 read 'Nevile Henderson dined. I think he's very good'.[32] It is only right to add that Cadogan was to change his assessment later.

Others, apart from Chamberlain and Nevile Henderson, admired Cadogan's qualities. Eden's Foreign Office Private Secretary, Oliver Harvey, believed that Cadogan was 'by nature the most retiring and simple of men', who hated all the publicity surrounding Vansittart's 'elevation' and would 'do nothing to enhance his own position'.[33] Nevertheless, Cadogan could fight his corner when the need arose, and he was soon faced by a crisis over Austria which was threatened by Hitler, and actually absorbed into Germany in March 1938. Chamberlain and Halifax had no intention of fighting to preserve Austrian independence and Cadogan agreed with them. He confided to his diary on 15 February his view that 'Personally I almost wish Germany would swallow Austria up and get it over ... I shouldn't mind if Austria were *gleichgeschaltet*'.[34] This may read like callousness, but, unlike Vansittart, Cadogan was convinced that it was pointless to make promises of support to Austria which could not be kept.

The two men had a big row over Austria on 11 March as German troops began to pour across the border.

> I had it out with Van [Cadogan wrote]. I said 'It's easy to be brave in speech: will you fight?' He said, 'No'. I said, 'Then what's it all about? To me it seems a most cowardly thing to urge a small man to fight if you won't help the former'.[35]

In fact, Vansittart's views were ignored during the Austrian crisis, but it is important to note that his ally, Orme Sargent, still in post as Deputy Under-Secretary, had minuted a month earlier in agreement with Cadogan's views.

> I think we are all convinced [Sargent wrote] that the process of absorption of Austria by Germany has now begun and will continue steadily to its appointed end. Nothing that we can say is going to prevent this process ...[36]

Sargent also believed, as did Cadogan, that protests by France and Britain in the interim would merely encourage the Austrian government pointlessly to prolong its death agony. Ultimately, the British government would merely reveal its impotence 'to alter or even delay events'.[37]

Cold-blooded but realistic, given the weakness of Britain's military position, which both Cadogan and Sargent knew all about. Neither did Cadogan dissent from government policy during the summer of 1938 when Czechoslovakia rather than Austria was the main focus of Foreign Office attention in Europe. Chamberlain and Halifax believed that the Czechs should be persuaded to make concessions to Germany over the issue of the Sudetenland. If they would not, then Britain and France should abandon them to their fate. Cadogan had long taken the view that Britain, which had no alliance with the Czechs, unlike the French, could not fight a war for the Sudetenland with its majority of German speakers. In March, he had written that 'We must not precipitate a conflict now – we shall be smashed'.[38] As a former Ambassador to China, Cadogan was particularly aware of the Japanese threat in the Far East; a war in Europe over Czechoslovakia might tempt Tokyo to take advantage. Neither could Mussolini's neutrality be taken for granted. Cadogan therefore fully subscribed to Chamberlain's policy of keeping the Germans guessing about British intentions over the Sudetenland, in lieu of the real military strength needed to deter Hitler.

The crisis for Cadogan came in September after Neville Chamberlain had flown to Germany a second time to try and prevent a war over the Sudetenland. When Chamberlain met Hitler at Godesberg, the German dictator raised the stakes by demanding evacuation of the disputed territory by 1 October 1938. This demand, and Chamberlain's apparent willingness to accept it, was too much even for the apparently taciturn Cadogan. His belligerent streak showed itself in his diaries where he wrote of his horror about the Cabinet meeting of 24 September when Chamberlain was 'quite calmly for total surrender'. Halifax was also apparently willing to capitulate to Hitler's other demands, which included the settlement of Polish and Hungarian claims against the unfortunate Czechs. Cadogan wrote that night that he would 'rather be beat than be dishonoured. How can we look any foreigner in the face after this?'[39] The reserved, immaculately turned out civil servant had been transformed overnight into a bulldog.

It was Halifax Cadogan savaged, giving the gangling Foreign Secretary 'a bit of my mind'. The Godesberg terms, he told Halifax, were unacceptable, and the shock administered by the normally unflappable Cadogan kept the Foreign Secretary awake all night. The next day Halifax sent for Cadogan and said, 'Alec, I'm very angry with you. You gave me a sleepless night. I woke at one and never got to sleep again'.[40] But Halifax was convinced and told a startled Chamberlain that the Godesberg terms were not acceptable, and that his conscience would not allow him to accept the coercion of the Czech government.

Clearly Cadogan and not Halifax was the hero of this particular hour, despite attempts by historians to give the latter the credit for the Godesberg revolt.[41] Sadly for the Czechs, it made little difference in the long run. The Munich settlement, which followed within a week, still gave the Sudetenland to Hitler without a shot being fired. Cadogan convinced himself that Munich was inevitable, a result of Britain and France's failure to make enough concessions to Germany in the 1920s.

Cadogan remained anxious about the situation in the Far East and the Mediterranean, and in mid-October wrote a lengthy memorandum about Britain's perilous global position. The need for more rearmament was stressed and the fact that for 'some time to come, we must be on the defensive'.[42] The alliance with France (although it still lacked any military commitment on paper) must be maintained, and further efforts were needed to get on terms with Mussolini. Shortly before, Cadogan had also minuted his concerns over Japan and Britain's fundamental dilemma, 'Are we to fight Japan now, and prevent her possible accession of strength, or wait for a possible war later?'[43] This, as Cadogan fully realised, had been precisely the problem confronting the British government over Czechoslovakia in the European theatre. Fears about the situation in Europe also meant that the British government was reluctant to station a fleet permanently in Singapore. Less excitable than his predecessor, Cadogan must still have pondered these questions in the watches of the night.

In the winter of 1938–39, Cadogan, like his political masters, was bombarded by warnings about possible attacks. Between mid-December and mid-April, there were no less than twenty warnings from different sources about German or Italian aggression. The most alarming were scare stories about a surprise German air attack on London which started in December, and lingered on into the New Year. Other inaccurate intelligence suggested that the Germans might make surprise attacks on Holland and Switzerland. Nevile Henderson was inclined to blame SIS for such misleading reports but Cadogan took the Ambassador to task over this. It was the Foreign Office's job to sift through the intelligence it received and decide on its reliability, Cadogan told Henderson.

> In that we may fail [he wrote] and if so, it is our fault but I do not think that it is fair to blame the SIS. Moreover, it is true to say that the recent scares have not originated principally with the SIS agents in Germany, but have come to us from other sources.[44]

These last comments were undoubtedly a sideswipe at Vansittart, whose sources included a motley collection of journalists, diplomats and German oppositionists. And valiant though Cadogan's defence of SIS had been, there is no doubt that both he and Halifax were sceptical about their reports too. The official government line remained that Hitler's intentions were pacific, and that he would honour his misleading promise at Munich that he had no further territorial ambitions in Europe.

All such illusions were shattered on 15 March 1939 when German troops entered Bohemia and Moravia. As German troops entered Prague, Cadogan admitted that 'It is turning out – at present – as Van predicted and as I never believed it would. If we want to stem the German expansion, I believe that we must try to build now'.[45] Cadogan now became a supporter of the policy of collective security which included giving a guarantee of assistance to the Poles, obviously in danger of being Hitler's next victims. This guarantee was given on 29 March, and Cadogan thought that its main objective was to 'deter Germany from any further acts of aggression'.[46] He did not believe, like Henderson and some others, that giving such a guarantee effectively put the control of British foreign policy in Polish hands. Neither could he see that the Polish alliance (which became a full-blown military pact in August) made any agreement with the Soviet Union less likely. The antipathy between Poles and Russians was ancient, and Cadogan like Chamberlain felt that the price of a Soviet alliance was being pitched too high.

Cadogan was a more natural appeaser than Vansittart, just as he was a more

natural Foreign Office official. He deplored Vansittart's excitable rhetoric, which
he believed ignored the realities of Britain's international situation, and by 1939
his more measured approach had majority support in the Foreign Office. Unlike
Vansittart, also, Cadogan was prepared to support colonial appeasement and
'recognised that Britain could not go on policing Europe and must give first
attention to the Mediterranean'.[47] A career civil servant to his fingertips, it is
hard to imagine Cadogan being guilty of the sort of disloyalty which Vansittart
showed to Halifax and Chamberlain, even when, as over the Godesberg terms,
he fiercely disagreed with government policy.

The foot soldiers of British diplomacy in the thirties were the Ambassadors and
Ministers abroad. Vansittart, Cadogan, Sargent and their colleagues in London
relied on these men's perceptions about the countries to which they were accredited in determining what British policy should be. And their telegrams were
read by successive Foreign Secretaries and, on occasion, circulated to Cabinet
(more rarely ambassadors were invited to sessions of the Cabinet to report).

The crucial embassy was Berlin, where the Diplomatic Service was served
successively by Sir Horace Rumbold, Sir Eric Phipps and Sir Nevile Henderson
in the period after Hitler came to power. The first two diplomats were largely
critical of what they saw in Nazi Germany, while Henderson was accused by his
critics of being too sympathetic to German aspirations.

Horace Rumbold arrived in Berlin in 1928 in the last years of the Weimar
Republic. It was the last posting of a distinguished career which had taken
Rumbold to Tokyo, Constantinople, Warsaw and Berlin (on a previous tour of
duty before the First World War). Rumbold became increasingly dismayed by
what he saw in Berlin, and his last despatches from the German capital were
devastating. The Nazis, he told the Foreign Office, had succeeded in 'bringing to
the surface the worst traits of the German character, i.e. a mean spirit of revenge,
a tendency to brutality and a noisy and irresponsible jingoism'.[48] He had greatly
admired the moderate German Foreign Minister Stresemann, who had worked
for reconciliation with Britain and France, and the contrast between Stresemann
and people like Goebbels, whom he dismissed as 'vulgar, unscrupulous and
irresponsible', distressed him.[49] As for Hitler himself, Sir Horace thought that,
although he was no statesman, 'he is an uncommonly clever and audacious
demagogue'.[50]

Although, as his French colleague François-Poncet noted, Rumbold's appearance was undistinguished, he was shrewd, and the Frenchman was impressed
by his courage and his horror of Nazism.[51] In his final despatch, on 30 June
1933, Sir Horace told the Foreign Office that in his opinion Hitler, Göring and
Goebbels were 'notoriously pathological cases', that the Nazi leadership as a
whole was made up of 'fantastic hooligans and eccentrics', and that there could

be no doubt that 'the persons directing the policy of the Hitler Government are not normal'.[52]

In retirement, Rumbold's message was the same. When Nevile Henderson sent him a copy of his book *Failure of a Mission* in 1940 about his days in Germany, Sir Horace wrote back saying that he thought the title of the book inappropriate 'as nobody could have succeeded in Berlin'. The nature of the Nazi regime made this impossible, went on Rumbold, who thanked his 'lucky stars that I left Berlin before having social intercourse with those ruffians surrounding Hitler'.[53]

The message was not, however, welcome in Whitehall. Rumbold's so-called 'Mein Kampf' despatch (as it was known in the Foreign Office) of April 1933, which analysed Hitler's objectives as stated in his book, was not well received by Ramsay MacDonald and his Cabinet, who were anxious for accommodation with Germany. Rumbold's retirement, therefore, was greeted with relief by the appeasers, who were reluctant to face up to the realities of life in Nazi Germany.

Changing the messenger did not, however, change the message. Rumbold was replaced by another experienced career diplomat, Sir Eric Phipps, married to Vansittart's sister-in-law, who had previously seen service in Madrid, Paris and Vienna. Phipps was 'Latin rather than English in appearance, a man of great charm and wit, shrewd and somewhat cynical'.[54] He was also, in the opinion of another colleague, more suited 'to Paris salons' than to Berlin.[55] Phipps was convinced, not altogether accurately, that Vansittart had it in for him. In a letter to Sir Maurice Hankey in 1940, Phipps complained bitterly about 'constant stabs in the back from my relative at the FO'.[56] There was scant evidence of this treachery, however, while Sir Eric was in Berlin, between 1933 and 1937, when the two men were in accord about Germany.

In his less bluff style, Phipps was equally scathing about the Nazis. When, after the bloodbath on 30 June 1934 (during which Hitler settled scores with Nazi rivals), Göring arrived late at a dinner party apologising that he'd been out shooting, Phipps responded tartly 'Animals *this time* I hope'. Like Rumbold, he had a low opinion of the Nazi leaders, describing the Ribbentrops, for example, as 'interfering busybodies'.[57]

After his first interview with Hitler in 1933, Phipps still had some hopes, reporting back to the Foreign Office that Hitler 'may possibly respond to some rather theatrical personal appeal to his emotions'.[58] But he was soon disillusioned. Personal relations with the Führer rapidly worsened (by contrast, François-Poncet was Hitler's favourite Ambassador), and Phipps came to see Hitler as 'a fanatic who would be satisfied with nothing less than the dominance of Europe'.[59]

Such hostility worried Phipps's political masters back in London, where a 'whispering campaign' began against the Ambassador in 1936. In December 1936 Stanley Baldwin's close adviser, Tom Jones, advised the Prime Minister that Phipps ought to be recalled. A month later, he repeated the advice, telling Baldwin that 'Phipps, our Ambassador, "has no telephone line to Hitler who despises him"'.[60] While the Foreign Secretary, Anthony Eden, had tried to reassure Baldwin about Phipps's alleged anti-Nazism, he also advised him that members of the Diplomatic Service 'should be posted to best advantage'.[61] This was merely code for what Baldwin and Eden wanted. It was time for Phipps to be moved on and for a more emollient approach in Berlin. Sir Eric was duly moved to Paris where, by some irony, he became a much more palatable diplomat as far as the appeasers were concerned. He constantly sided with the French appeasers, such as Bonnet, rather than with the *bellicistes* (hawks) like Georges Mandel. Phipps remained in Paris until 1939, when he retired from the Diplomatic Service.

The man representing the new emollient approach in Berlin after Phipps was Sir Nevile Henderson, an appeaser who has attracted more historical abuse than even Neville Chamberlain. Henderson has variously been described as 'our Nazi ambassador in Berlin', 'the Beau Brummel of diplomacy' and '*un homme néfaste*' (an ill-starred man).[62] There have been few dissenters from the view that Henderson was an unmitigated disaster in Berlin.[63]

Henderson, like Rumbold and Phipps before him, was an experienced career diplomat who had served in Paris, Constantinople, Cairo, Belgrade and Buenos Aires before coming to Berlin. His appointment became controversial in retrospect, but he was Vansittart's choice at the time. 'Van' admired the way Henderson had dealt with the authoritarian King Alexander in Yugoslavia and thought he should be given a chance in the diplomatic 'First Eleven'. Eden had never met Sir Nevile at the time he was appointed early in 1937, but Baldwin believed him to be 'a man and a good shot' (Henderson had met Göring at King Alexander's funeral in 1934 and they were already shooting partners).[64] These strange qualifications were balanced by the fact that Henderson was thought to be a safe pair of hands. Vansittart had rejected suggestions that Halifax or Willingdon, both former Viceroys of India, should be sent to Berlin instead. Experience of dealing with the saintly Gandhi might not have been the best experience for dealing with Adolf Hitler, but Vansittart's real concern was to avoid the appointment of a non-diplomat, an outsider who might be a nuisance.[65] The irony was that Henderson was to prove Vansittart's *bête noire* in the few months left to him as Permanent Under-Secretary.

The problem was that Henderson tended to take a messianic view of his role as ambassador. He believed that he had been 'specially selected by Providence for the definite mission of, as I trusted, helping to preserve the peace of the world'.[66] Worse, from the Foreign Office point of view, Henderson regarded himself as Neville Chamberlain's personal emissary rather than the representative of the Diplomatic Service. This notion seems to have been the result of an interview he had with Chamberlain, then still Chancellor of the Exchequer, in April 1937 (although no document about the interview survives). Henderson claimed that, throughout his time in Berlin, he 'followed the general line he [Chamberlain] set me',[67] one which he totally believed in himself. The whole purpose of Henderson's diplomacy was to bring an end to the acrimony which had been a feature of both Rumbold's and Phipps's time in Berlin.

His different approach soon brought him into conflict with Vansittart, who rapidly came to believe that Henderson was exceeding his brief, giving aid and comfort to the Nazis. Within months of Henderson's arrival in Berlin, the two men were at loggerheads over Henderson's planned visit to the annual Nazi Party rally at Nuremberg (which Phipps had boycotted). This was done without consulting the Foreign Office first, and Vansittart minuted furiously that it was extraordinary that Sir Nevile should 'not only (a) take an important decision like this off his own bat without giving us a chance of consultation ... but also (b) announce it to a foreign colleague as a decision' (Henderson had told François-Poncet about his intention to go to Nuremberg).[68] Vansittart ought to have remembered, and he knew Henderson well, that the Ambassador was an unorthodox diplomat who did not always adhere to the rule-book.

More seriously, the two men disagreed about the whole issue of managing Anglo-German relations. In a notorious memorandum dated 10 May 1937, Henderson had stated that Britain should be able to accept 'without too great discomfort ... the surge and swell of restless Pan-Germanism'.[69] This, together with an apparent acceptance of German economic and even political predominance in Eastern Europe, infuriated Vansittart, who soon came to regret his role in Henderson's appointment. Nevertheless, it was Henderson, not Vansittart, who was more in accord with Chamberlain's policy.

In fact, Henderson was not pro-Nazi, and he did not approve of Hitler's annexation of Austria in 1938, but, like many of his generation, he believed that Germany had been deeply wronged by the Versailles Treaty. He also suffered from the illusion that there were moderates in the Nazi leadership (notably Göring, with whom he got on well) who could be used to restrain Hitler. As Göring himself acknowledged, however, Hitler, and Hitler alone, was the ultimate decision-maker.

On occasion, Henderson's role in carrying out government policy was important, notably in September 1938 when he persuaded Cadogan and Halifax not to send an ultimatum to Hitler over the Sudetenland right in the middle of the annual party rally. But he did not make policy, and did not deserve the abuse heaped upon him by generations of historians after his death in 1942. He did himself few favours by regaling the Foreign Office with tales about how he had met the fanatically pro-Nazi, Unity Mitford, and forgot his usual response to the mandatory *Heil Hitler!* which was 'Rule Britannia!' In so doing, he made himself look ludicrous, and his relationship with Göring appalled his critics. One was the Labour MP, Josiah Wedgwood, who lamented the fact that Henderson 'smiled, fraternised with evil, and did not stand apart with nose in the air'.[70] Yet Henderson was not alone. Lloyd George met Hitler in 1936 and was most enthusiastic about the Führer.

Such criticism ignores the reason why Henderson was sent to Berlin in the first place, which was to try and build bridges. Also largely forgotten is the fact that Hitler could not abide Henderson. Tall and well-dressed, the elegant Ambassador was for Hitler 'the man with the carnation' (that flower being an essential part of Henderson's diplomatic veneer), who represented everything about upper-class Englishmen that irritated him. Relations with Foreign Minister, Ribbentrop, were even worse. The two men loathed each other, and Henderson wrote to King George VI about how the Foreign Minister was 'eaten up with conceit'.[71] King George would doubtless have remembered Ribbentrop's oafish behaviour when he was Ambassador in London (one among many gaffes was to give the monarch the Hitler salute, hence his nickname in London of 'von Brickendrop'). Henderson's critics have never quite explained how a man who was so disliked by both Hitler and Ribbentrop could have influenced their perception of Britain as much as he has been accused of doing.

Ultimately, Henderson's greatest sin was that he did not repent. His memoir, *Failure of a Mission*, published in 1940, defended the appeasement policy of Baldwin and Chamberlain, while those colleagues who survived into the postwar period in the Foreign Office (like Gladwyn Jebb) developed a convenient amnesia about their role in the 1930s. Henderson was safely dead, and he, like Chamberlain, became a target for those who at the time were not conspicuously at odds with government policy. There was nothing essentially ignoble about Henderson's obsession with avoiding a war with Germany.[72]

Henderson's conduct in Berlin is linked to another aspect of the Foreign Office's relationship with Nazi Germany. This concerned the anti-Nazi opposition, which Henderson was accused of ignoring. Certainly his advice to Chamberlain and Halifax was that it was not to be taken seriously, for which he has been castigated.[73] Even Vansittart, however, initially sympathetic to the anti-Nazi cause, became sceptical when anti-Nazis like Gördeler made exactly the same territorial demands as Hitler, including the return of the Polish Corridor and the absorption of Austria by Germany. Two factors were involved as far as the Foreign Office was concerned. Should Britain be involved in subverting a legitimate, albeit odious regime? Was it appropriate for the British government in 1938 to do the anti-Nazis' job for them by threatening war over the Sudetenland (the idea was that if Britain and France fought, this would provide the German opposition with the opportunity to depose Hitler)?

The answer to both these questions was no. Vansittart told an emissary from the German opposition in August 1938 that what he was suggesting was treason, precisely the same sort of language that Henderson had used. Chamberlain himself found that the opposition reminded him of the Jacobites at the time of William of Orange, and believed that what they said should be treated with caution.

The passage of time found the Foreign Office actively hostile to the opposition. Orme Sargent reflected its animosity in a brutal minute in April 1939, when Britain was seemingly doing its best to create an anti-Nazi bloc in Europe.

> Last year [Sargent wrote] we were reportedly told that moderate opinion was disap-pointed and discouraged because HMG was not standing up to Hitler. Now that HMG are standing up to Hitler, we hear this same moderate opinion is disgusted with us and can't understand why HMG are standing up to Hitler.[74]

Attempts to blame the Foreign Office for the failures of resolution and planning inside the *Widerstand* (the German opposition) do not convince. Throughout the Hitler period, the dissidents inside the German armed forces had the means to remove Hitler but showed a lack of will until it was too late.

The Foreign Office finally reflected the prejudices and dogmas of its time. There was a degree of sympathy for German grievances against Versailles, as there was prejudice against the Soviet Union. Indeed prejudice against Slavs was a characteristic of many in the Foreign Office and the Diplomatic Service. A classic example is provided by the case of Joseph Addison, the British Minister in Prague from 1930 to 1936.[75] When a young *Observer* foreign correspondent asked Addison if he had any Czech friends, he was dismissive, saying, 'Friends ... They eat in their kitchens!'[76] Small wonder that the Czech case often went by default in Britain in 1938, or that ignorant backbenchers still spoke of 'Czechoslovenia'.

More disturbing to the modern eye was the amount of open anti-Semitism in the Foreign Office, although again this reflected upper-class British prejudice. Addison, unsurprisingly, was an open anti-Semite, making blatantly anti-Jewish comments in his London club, while R.H. Hadow, the Counsellor in the Prague legation in Addison's time, made an insulting reference to Hore-Belisha's Jewish origins (Hore-Belisha was then Secretary of State for War) in a letter to Henderson. Even Horace Rumbold, though sympathetic to Jewish sufferings under the Nazis, reflected this general suspicion of Jews in the service. On arriv-ing in Berlin in 1928, Rumbold wrote to the then Permanent Under-Secretary about how he was 'appalled by the number of Jews in this place. One cannot get away from them'.[77] In Rumbold's case, it is only fair to record that he was consist-ently suspicious of *all* foreigners or non-Britishers, including Jews and Germans, but, in such a climate the infamous wartime reference to 'whingeing Jews' hardly comes as a surprise (this was a Foreign Office reaction to early information about the Holocaust from Poland).

It can, of course, be argued that such prejudices, though disturbing, merely reflected the attitudes of a bygone age. The past is a foreign country and its ways are not our ways. Nevertheless, it remains true that people like Addison and Hadow were far more disposed to make allowances for Germans, both having served a stint in the Berlin Embassy before going to Prague. By contrast, anti-Soviet paranoia was widespread, although Vansittart and Laurence Collier, head of the Northern Department in the late thirties, tried to encourage a more balanced view. Only in 1939 did the Foreign Office view of the USSR shift away from the belief that Anglo-Soviet relations must be based 'on a mutual and inevitable antipathy'.[78] Although often assumed to be pro-French, the Foreign Office frequently showed itself to be more understanding of German aspirations. This policy, the professionals might well have argued, was dictated by the realities of the international situation.

The divisions which separated Vansittart from Cadogan were, if anything, even more sharply defined in the Foreign Office's policy towards the Far East. Here Britain's Ambassador in Tokyo, Sir Robert Craigie, formed an alliance with Chamberlain and Warren Fisher. Their belief was that a closer relationship with Japan would be beneficial; ideally, it should incorporate a non-aggression pact. Vansittart did not wish to go that far when he was Permanent Under-Secretary, but was prepared to encourage the tensions which existed between Tokyo and Moscow along the common Far Eastern border. War, Vansittart and his supporters believed, would be dangerous because a victory for either the Russians or the Japanese might fatally alter the balance of power in the Far East to Britain's disadvantage.[79] Preserving the balance was Britain's task, although Soviet and Japanese cooperation in avoiding war could hardly be relied upon.

Craigie was in an unenviable position in Tokyo. Like Henderson in Berlin, he was an ally of the Prime Minister rather than the Foreign Office, which had a strong pro-Chinese orientation. Indeed it has been observed that the attitude of the Foreign Office to Japan was undermined by prejudice against the Japanese, and persistent underestimates of their military strength which derived from entrenched belief in white supremacy.[80] Craigie, by contrast, hoped to work with those pro-British moderates in Japan who favoured an accommodation.

The Foreign Office fought tooth and nail against such a policy line. The Head of the Far Eastern Department, Charles Orde, believed that a proactive policy towards Japan would 'weaken Russia in the Far East ... and might lead to further Japanese aggression in south-east Asia'.[81] Orde and the influential commercial attaché in the Tokyo Embassy, Sir George Sansom, also warned that such a policy would endanger Britain's considerable trading interests in China and result, Orde said, in 'violent Chinese resentment against us'.[82] The diplomatic and military backcloth to this debate was that, between 1931 and 1938, Japan was engaged in trying to conquer China. Orde and Sansom also pointed out that any Anglo-Japanese pact might endanger the relationship with the United States, which was sympathetic towards China and suspicious of Japanese intentions in the region.

The result was bitter political in-fighting in Whitehall, especially when Sansom finished his tour of duty in Tokyo and returned to the Foreign Office, where he was regarded as the fount of all wisdom on matters Far Eastern. Craigie was criticised within the Foreign Office, but his ally, Sir Warren Fisher at the Treasury, thought Orde a 'pedantic ass, admirably suited to join the eclectic brotherhood of Oxford or Cambridge'.[83] Sansom was equally negative about Craigie, who, isolated in Tokyo, despaired about the Far Eastern Department's 'Bourbon-like inability to learn from past events'.[84] Successive Ambassadors in Peking followed the Foreign Office line of admiration for the regime of the authoritarian Chiang Kai-chek. Cadogan was one of them (the Japanese machine-gunned his successor's car in 1937, forcing Sir Hugh Knatchbull-Hugessen, or 'Snatch' as he was affectionately known, to come home early), and the highly thought of Sir Archie Clark-Kerr, later Lord Inverchapel, another. All preached the gospel of sympathy for China and a cold shoulder for Japan. By contrast, Craigie, a personal friend of Warren Fisher, shared Chamberlain's distrust of the Americans.

Ultimately, policy towards Japan and China was driven by the Foreign Office in a way which policy towards Germany was not. Halifax listened to the advice from the Far Eastern Department, even though the pro-China lobby made an agreement with Tokyo unlikely. In this instance, Chamberlain was unable to prevent the Foreign Office perception of Japan from dominating policy. He appreciated Craigie's qualities (just as he fully supported Nevile Henderson), writing to his sister of Craigie's ability to 'preserve his calm and never get rattled ... Only the anti-Japanese bias of the Foreign Office in the past has never given him a chance'.[85]

Ultimately, the odd thing about the Foreign Office's Far Eastern Department was that it seemed to ignore the undoubted dangers of provoking Japan in the interests of protecting Chiang Kai-shek. Vansittart identified Japan as a major threat, if a lesser one than Germany, in 1934, and Britain could not risk a war with all three authoritarian powers at once. Craigie's policy of trying to postpone a conflict with Japan therefore made sense, given the real likelihood of a war in Europe in 1938–39. Mussolini, on whom the British lavished much attention, was, at best, a doubtful quality and, as events proved, not to be trusted when Nazi Germany won cheap successes. Nevertheless, the task facing the Foreign Office in getting the balance right in the full knowledge of Britain's finite resources and global commitments was a daunting one. It was also unique. Never before in its history had Britain faced such a potentially fearsome coalition.

10

Poland

Peace was to last less than a year in Europe following the Munich Agreement. War when it came seemed, to the critics of appeasement, an inevitable consequence of government misjudgement in Britain and France as much as it was the result of Hitler's aggressive foreign policy. Yet the war began over one of those territorial flaws in the Treaty of Versailles which the appeasers had warned about since 1919. Territorial revision before Hitler's advent to power in 1933 might perhaps have avoided hostilities, but there was no real chance that a Poland in nationalist mood would give up territory in the so-called Polish Corridor which it deemed essential to its national integrity; or that Hitler would moderate his demands.

One thing became clear by March 1939, and that was that Hitler's word was not to be trusted. Any dealings with him would have to be backed by the real threat of force if he transgressed again. For he had done so, despite his promises at Munich that he desired no territory inhabited by non-Germans, by destroy-ing the Czech rump state and allowing Slovakia an illusory independence as a German satellite. The 15 March 1939 was the 'Ides of March' for British foreign policy as it was for an independent Czechoslovak state. Now Chamberlain had to decide what price Britain would have to pay to deter Hitler, making it clear to the German dictator that he could not risk another adventure without provoking a real danger of British intervention and with it a general war in Europe. Thus, all the evidence suggests, Hitler did not want war in the autumn of 1939 but could he be persuaded that Chamberlain and Daladier, the 'little worms' he had seen at Munich, would protect Polish independence if it came under threat? The British government, the Foreign Office and the Diplomatic Service laboured to ensure that he was so persuaded, but, in the case of such a mercurial yet ideologically driven leader, the outcome could never be certain. After Munich the likelihood of a war in which Britain would be involved increased month by month.

The winter of 1938–39 was a time of alarms and excursions as far as the Chamberlain government was concerned. The alarms concerned a series of disturbing warnings about a surprise German air attack on Britain, and espe-cially London. Between mid-December 1938 and mid-April 1939, no less than twenty warnings were received by the Britain government about likely German and Italian moves from a variety of sources. As early as 11 December, Ivonne

Kirkpatrick, the First Secretary in the Berlin Embassy, warned that the Germans had broken the British ciphers (the quoted source was 'a high German official') and that Hitler had given orders for a surprise air attack on London in three weeks' time. The Cabinet took Kirkpatrick's warning very seriously and such fears about a sudden 'knockout blow' which could paralyse the centre of Britain's government lingered on into January 1939.[1]

A new scare emerged in mid-January via Vansittart's secret intelligence sources which were working in parallel to the Secret Intelligence Service. The story was the same, that the Luftwaffe would launch a surprise attack on London. A few days later, the Secret Intelligence Service reported that Hitler and his advisers thought London could be destroyed in a few days from the air (a complete delusion if the rumour were true). More misleading intelligence suggested variously that the Germans would make a surprise attack on Holland or even on Switzerland. One consequence of these rumours, which may have been planted by the *éminence grise* of the German Abwehr, Admiral Wilhelm Canaris (a secret opponent of the Nazis) was that, at the Cabinet meeting on 1 February, Chamberlain and his colleagues accepted the principle of a bigger continental commitment, which the Prime Minister, in particular, had fought against for so long. But the corollary of all these scares was that Chamberlain and Halifax, at least before 15 March, became increasingly sceptical about the trustworthiness of their intelligence. More reliable an indicator was the unscrupulous German behaviour on the international commission supposed to realign the Czech German frontier after Munich. The Germans persisted in demanding plebiscites beyond the 1910 census line in the Sudetenland and, although the Czechs protested, Britain, France and Italy accepted German demands in the first instance before ultimately standing up to them. German tactics disgusted the Foreign Office but it was ultimately unable to prevent the transfer of a further forty thousand people, mostly Czechs, to the Reich on 14 November 1938. No Czech protest was allowed against the change. Roger Makins of the Foreign Office, who had been sent out to observe the workings of the international commission, complained to William Strang that 'the proceedings have been apt to degenerate into a shouting match, four or five people frequently shouting at once'.[2]

Even more shocking was German behaviour at the time of the so-called *Kristallnacht* on 9–10 November 1938. Following the assassination of a German diplomat in Paris by a young Polish Jew, Grynzspan, a national pogrom in Germany was unleashed by Goebbels. Jewish synagogues were burned down and Jewish businesses wrecked, while at least twenty thousand Jews were taken to concentration camps. In Berlin, the Chargé d'Affaires, Ogilvie-Forbes, was trenchant in his criticism of Nazi behaviour (he was standing in for Henderson, who was on sick leave). And at home, too, opinion was shocked. The Chamberlain loyalist Channon wrote in his diary on 15 November: 'The pogroms in Germany and the persecutions there have roused much indignation everywhere. I must say Hitler never helps, and always makes Chamberlain's task more difficult.'[3]

The Prime Minister himself wrote to his sister Hilda about the 'barbarities' being committed in Germany while the press and the House of Commons reiterated British distaste for Nazi thuggery and racial persecution.[4] Halifax sent an angry note to the German government which received the curtest acknowledgement from Goebbels. He himself admitted to having been 'always rather anti-Semitic' in the mode of the inter-war British upper class.[5] But he was genuinely outraged by the events of the *Kristallnacht*, although the Foreign Office was not instructed to withdraw British diplomatic representation in the way that the US State Department had done with their American counterpart. Amongst the anti-appeasers Harold MacMillan gave refuge to some Czech Jews who had fled the Sudetenland (he had been so angry about Munich that he and his wife Dorothy burnt an effigy of Chamberlain on Guy Fawkes Night).[6]

Halifax was sufficiently exercised about *Kristallnacht* to convene a special meeting of the Foreign Affairs Committee of the Cabinet. He told colleagues that 'The happenings in Germany of the last few days following on the sequence of events since Munich had made the position very difficult'. A memorandum had also been produced by Gladwyn Jebb of the Foreign Office which stated that Germany was close to bankruptcy (this thesis about the vulnerability of the Nazi economy was becoming central to British thinking), and likely to follow a bold, but desperate, programme of expansion which would include the Black Sea area, Turkey and even India. These dire predictions seem to have come from the same confidential sources inside Germany which were later to feed the 'knockout blow' scares.[7] Such evidence also suggested that Hitler, egged on by the anglophobe von Ribbentrop, now regarded Britain as his primary opponent.

The Anglo-German Naval Treaty of 1935 had been at the heart of appeasement strategy since the days of Baldwin, just as Britain had vainly sought to get Hitler to sign an air pact in the mid-thirties. Thus Hitler's announcement in December 1938 that he would exercise Germany's right under that treaty to increase its submarine strength up to that of Britain's was ominous, as was the increasingly vitriolic tone of the German press.

In these circumstances, Chamberlain and Halifax fell back on the well-tried strategy of trying to conciliate Mussolini in the hope that he could bring some influence to bear on Hitler. They left for an excursion to Rome on 10 January, despite the winter 'scares', and Chamberlain felt that the visit, which included an audience with the Pope, had been a success. Chamberlain found Mussolini to be 'straightforward and considerate' and believed that the trip to Rome 'had definitely strengthened the chances of peace'. Mussolini was rather alarmed by Chamberlain's apparent popularity in Italy (he always found the unwarlike tendencies of his people frustrating), but in reality, the trip achieved nothing of real substance.[8] The gulf between the two sides was demonstrated by the negative diary entry by Mussolini's son-in-law, Ciano, on 11 January. 'Effective contact has not been made. How far apart we are from these people! It is another world.'[9]

Chamberlain was perhaps guilty of wishful thinking where Mussolini was concerned. But the situation was complicated by Mussolini's aggressive claims to territory in French North Africa. On 30 November 1938, there had been a noisy demonstration in the Italian Parliament against France and cries of 'Nice, Corsica, Tunis', but the French had robustly rejected Italian demands. Neither would Daladier listen to British requests to adopt a more conciliatory attitude to Fascist Italy. This was the exact reversal of earlier Anglo-French policy towards Italy, as the French were now more robust because Mussolini directly threatened their colonial empire, and indeed metropolitan France in the cases of Corsica and Nice.

Ultimately for the British, there could be no real choice. They had to stand by France, which was increasingly confident about its ability to face down the Italians. By March, Daladier was telling the British Ambassador, Sir Eric Phipps, that the Italians were 'gangsters'. Another French Minister reportedly remarked that 'They [the Italians] can have a pier, but no more'.[10] In one sense, this new French toughness was welcome news for the Chamberlain government, which often despaired about its French ally, but it was also evident by January 1939 that Mussolini had thrown in his lot with the Germans to such a degree that he could play no useful role as a mediator with Berlin. He was happy to flirt with the British, if only to demonstrate some illusory independence from his German ally, but the Rome visit never went beyond flirtation. Chamberlain would have to deal with Germany on a bilateral basis, without any assistance from the Italians. Neither could he afford to show any undue sympathy for Italy's campaign for territorial aggrandisement in North Africa. A further danger was that France itself might be lured into some sort of accommodation with Germany. Ribbentrop visited Paris in December, but, in their new tougher post-Munich mood, the French would not abandon their close relationship with London. Privately, Daladier could be damning about the British, describing Chamberlain as 'a desiccated stick' and George VI as 'a moron', but the Entente with Britain remained the linchpin of French strategy.[11] The Germans claimed that the slippery Bonnet had said that France had no interest in Eastern Europe, which it recognised to be a German sphere of influence. This was unlikely. The French were making renewed efforts to strengthen their traditional financial and economic influence in the area, and the accusation was strongly denied both by Bonnet and Léger, the Secretary-General of the Quai d'Orsay. The obtuse Ribbentrop may merely have deceived himself about French attitudes before returning to Berlin.[12]

Chamberlain continued to hope that an accommodation could be reached with Germany. On 28 January 1939, despite the alarms of that winter, Chamberlain spoke in his beloved Birmingham and offered Hitler an olive branch. In the speech, he emphasised the defensive nature of British rearmament and asked that other states should now make a contribution to the achievement of international peace. The text of the speech was sent over to Germany before Chamberlain began to speak. Hitler responded on 30 January and referred to the desirability of a 'long peace', although he also made a ferocious threat against international Jewry, whom he made responsible for the threat of war. Chamberlain was encouraged, believing that Hitler had made a last-minute alteration to his speech to make it sound more pacific (the British Embassy in Berlin had told him this).

Chamberlain's colleague backed his peace offensive. On 10 March, the Home Secretary Sir Samuel Hoare spoke about the coming of a new 'golden age of peace', and on 13 March Halifax told Henderson (now returned from sick leave) that 'in the last few weeks there has been a negative improvement in the situation, in that rumours and scares had died down, and it is not plain that the German Government are planning mischief in any particular quarter'.[13] Sceptical no doubt as a result of false intelligence in the preceding weeks, Halifax could hardly have been more wrong. But the place Hitler chose to act was not in the west as SIS reports had seemed to indicate, but in the Czechoslovak rump state.

On Saturday 11 March, the German press reported that the Slovak leader, Monseigneur Tiso, a Catholic cleric, was asking for German help against alleged Czech intimidation. Then, as the Slovak Cabinet met, using the greater autonomy conceded by Prague after Munich, their meeting was interrupted by the appearance of the Austrian Nazi Seyss-Inquart and five German generals. Seyss-Inquart 'encouraged' the Slovak leadership to declare their independence from Prague, while Tiso himself was summoned to attend a meeting with Hitler in Berlin. On 14 March, the Slovak Diet voted, not with much enthusiasm, for independence. Hungary had already been approached by Hitler offering it the prospect of gobbling up what was left of Czech Ruthenia, and at 3 p.m. on 14 March a Hungarian ultimatum was received in Prague demanding Czech withdrawal from Ruthenia. The pretext given was 'intolerable' incidents on the Czech-Hungarian frontier.

What followed was all too reminiscent of the fate of von Schuschnigg in 1938, it was just that the chronology of abuse was accelerated. Two Czech delegates, President Hácha and Chvalkovský, volunteered to go to Berlin in an optimistic effort to reason with Hitler. When they arrived the two men were taken before Hitler, Göring and Keitel at 1.15 a.m on 15 March. Also present was Hitler's interpreter Schmidt, who watched as the elderly Hácha tried to make a tribute to Hitler's greatness and say how grateful he was to have 'the destiny of Czechoslovakia ... in safekeeping'.[14] It did Hácha little good. He was silenced by the same sort of tirade which had been unleashed upon von Schuschnigg just over a year before. It was, reported Schmidt later, 'one long accusation against the Czechs by Hitler'; nothing had changed, according to the Führer, since the days of Beneš.[15] Hácha was told that nothing could prevent the descent of the German army on Prague. Having ordered Hácha to ring Prague and order his forces to offer no resistance, Hitler curtly terminated the interview.

In this gangsterlike atmosphere technology failed just as the inkwells had run dry at Munich. The lines to Prague were out of order and, when they were reopened, the unfortunate Hácha fainted clean away. He had to be revived by Hitler's quack physician, Professor Morell, with an injection. He and Chvalkovský then spoke to Prague, to the obvious relief of Göring, who had feared that the elderly Czech President might die in the Reich Chancellery. Schmidt then prepared a communiqué which stated that the Czech President had laid 'the fate of the Czech people and country in the hands of the Führer of the German Reich'.[16] This time, to paraphrase Churchill, the Czech provinces of Bohemia and Moravia *were* about to recede into the darkness. And with their demise came a rapid re-evaluation of British foreign policy. In the meantime, there was nothing Britain and France could do to save the weeping and desperate citizens of Prague from the fate that awaited them.

There is no doubt that Hitler's Czech coup represented a real body blow for Chamberlain. Some, like Harold Nicolson, doubted whether he could survive. 'The feeling in the lobbies', he wrote on 17 March, 'is that Chamberlain will either have to go or completely reverse his policy.'[17] Chamberlain's local acolyte, Channon, was outraged by Hitler's duplicity when he heard the news. 'No balder, bolder departure from the written bond had ever been committed in history', he recorded in his diary.[18] On the Labour side, Dalton wrote of how Hitler had swooped on Prague like 'a bird of prey'.[19]

What would the Prime Minister do in this new situation? On 15 March, as the news came in from Prague, Chamberlain's disappointment was reflected in his speech in the House of Commons. He told the House that he did not think 'that anything of the kind which has now taken place was contemplated by any of the signatories of the Munich Agreement at the time of its signature'.[20] Chamberlain also cancelled a visit by his colleagues Oliver Stanley and Robert Hudson to Berlin, and the Foreign Office showed its displeasure by withdrawing Nevile Henderson from his post in Berlin. He did not return until 24 April.

Chamberlain's critics thought his response too bland. But they underestimated their man. On 17 March, Chamberlain was due to speak in his old family fiefdom of Birmingham, and this time his anger shone through. 'Is this', Chamberlain asked his audience about Hitler's latest piece of aggrandisement, 'the end of an old adventure, or the beginning of a new?' Or was it, the Prime Minister went on, 'a step in the direction of an attempt to dominate the world by force?'[21] Chamberlain continued in this vein by saying that Britain would consult with

France, the Commonwealth countries and states in south-eastern Europe which might now feel themselves to be under threat. Nevertheless, a caveat was entered, Britain would not make 'any new unspecified commitment', Chamberlain said, but he finished by warning that no one should imagine that 'this nation has so lost its fibre that it will not take part to the utmost of its power in resisting such a challenge'.[22]

The speech was powerful and effective, but it left a question in the air. What would or could Britain do to deter Hitler, who had now shown himself be utterly untrustworthy? And how could such a policy of deterrence avoid making some new commitment to action in Europe? Events conspired to force Chamberlain into action more speedily than he may have originally envisaged.

It took little imagination to see after 15 March that Poland might be Hitler's next victim. It, too, like Czechoslovakia, contained a large ethnic German minority and, more pertinently, Poland held territory that had formed part of the old German Reich. This had not been true of the Czech Sudetenland.

Ethnic minorities were Poland's Achilles heel to an even greater degree than had been true of Czechoslovakia. In the Poland that emerged in 1919–20, only 69 per cent of the population were ethnic Poles, leaving Ukrainians and Ruthenians to make up 14 per cent, Belorussians almost 4 per cent and Germans well over 3 per cent. Poland also had the largest Jewish minority in Europe, at 7.8 per cent, and smaller minorities of Czechs, Russians and Lithuanians.[23]

Poland started its new independent life (after more than a century under Russian, Austrian and Prussian domination) as a democracy, but it did not flourish, beset as it was by economic and social problems. The constitution was almost absurdly democratic, with a proportional representation system which allowed thirty-two political parties representation in the *Sejm* or Parliament. Those who were concerned about the stability of the new Polish state would have remembered the notorious unanimity rule in the country's eighteenth-century assembly which helped to deliver it to its foreign enemies via a series of territorial partitions.

The dominant figure in the new Poland was Marshal Pilsudski, who had commanded a force of Polish legionnaires which was integrated into the old Austro-Hungarian army. In 1917, however, Pilsudski had refused to fight for the Germans and had been imprisoned by them until the end of the war. Thereafter he had been prominent in the defence of Poland against the Bolshevik Russian invasion of 1920, which almost reached the gates of Warsaw. Many thought, however, that Pilsudski had provoked the Russian invasion by his reckless plunge into the Ukraine beforehand, which had infuriated Lloyd George in particular. The Poles survived the emergency, but the Treaty of Riga in 1921 left them with large tracts of territory in eastern Galicia and Belorussia, dangerously east of the so-called 'Curzon Line' suggested by the then British Foreign Secretary during the peace talks in Paris in 1919.[24] Surrounded as Poland was by two powerful and potentially hostile neighbours, this acquisition of extra Russian territory was offering a hostage to fortune.

Polish behaviour in 1920–21, therefore, had irritated British Ministers, who had otherwise been sympathetic to the creation of a Polish state, albeit not one that should be part of any French strategy to hem in and neutralise Weimar Germany. Poland's transformation into an authoritarian dictatorship after Pilsudski's *coup d'état* of May 1926 (which cost five hundred lives) was also not viewed with favour in London.

Meanwhile Poland underwent something of an economic revival, and the construction of the port of Gydnia gave it another outlet to the Baltic to supplement the German-majority part of the city of Danzig whose port facilities were presented to Poland in the post-war peace settlement, although the League of Nations administered it as a free city.

The system which ran Poland after May 1926 was known as the *Sanacja* (or 'Cleansing'), but its chief characteristic was the way it favoured Pilsudski's ex-legionnaires. One of them, Jósef Beck, became the Foreign Minister in 1932 and ran the so-called policy of 'two enemies', whereby Poland would pursue an independent course between Germany and the USSR. Good relations would be maintained, but Poland would avoid alliance with either power. This doctrine still allowed Poland to make non-aggression pacts with the USSR in 1932 and Germany in 1934. The unlikely agreement with Germany had at least the advantage of dampening down tensions over Danzig and the Corridor, although its long-term prospects in a context of Hitlerite *Lebensraum* could hardly be deemed good.

Pilsudski was contemptuous of Polish democracy, describing the *Sejm* as 'a sterile jabbering thing'.[25] In 1935, the year he died, the parliamentary elections were boycotted by the Opposition parties, meaning that less than half the Polish electorate voted. After Pilsudski's death, the 'Regime of the Colonels', as it came to be known, attempted to set up a national movement of its own under the Inspector-General of the army, Smygly-Rydz. The regime was strongly anti-Semitic and ultra nationalist but, given its military ethos, failed spectacularly to shore up Poland's defences. The army was never mechanised to meet the external threat, and the air force consisted largely of obsolete planes.

Beck's foreign policy was self-seeking. Poland won few admirers by treacherously seizing Teschen from the Czechs at the time of Munich, even if the action could be defended by pointing out that the Czechs had seized the area with its large Polish population in the midst of Poland's emergency in 1920. Beck has been described as 'devious and two-faced'.[26] It is not an inaccurate description, as the British were to discover.

At the time of the Teschen episode, Commander Stephen King, the editor of the famous *British Newsletter* and normally an enemy of Nazism, wrote that 'If Hitler were to march into Poland, I would say *Sieg Heil*', and this expressed common revulsion about Polish diplomacy.[27] But not long afterwards, Neville Chamberlain would be calling the Poles 'that great virile race', which demonstrates to a degree British ambiguity about Poland.

That doughty diplomat Sir Horace Rumbold was a typical example of this syndrome. Rumbold had a healthy British scepticism about all foreigners and would occasionally burst out into outright animosity. But he was puzzled by the Poles. Arriving in Poland in 1919, he found its inhabitants 'thoroughly corrupt' and wondered 'if they will ever make anything of their country'. Yet Rumbold was well able to sympathise with Poland's unhappy historical experience and geographical vulnerability, remarking on how the Poles had 'been heavily handicapped at the start and need and deserve encouragement'.[28]

They did not get much at the time. While serving in Warsaw as Minister in 1919–20, Rumbold tried to secure a three million pound loan for the Poles, but the Treasury refused to agree. It was to prove niggardly again in 1939. And Lloyd George's anger about Pilsudski's Ukraine adventure had underlined his reservations about the Polish settlement. In 1919, when the shape of the new state was being hammered out in Paris, he had asked, 'Was it necessary to assign so much German territory, together with the port of Dantzig [sic]'. Neither did Lloyd George have a very high opinion of Polish administrative capacities.[29]

There were exceptions among the British political class, if not many. One was Hugh Dalton, the future Labour Under-Secretary of State at the Foreign Office. Dalton's partiality towards the Poles was mixed with a strong streak of anti-Germanism (he described Germans as 'fat, ugly and badly got up'), but he thought it wrongheaded to suggest that a revision of Poland's frontier with Germany was essential to secure European peace.[30] Neither did he have any sympathy with those who campaigned on behalf of Poland's national minorities. This he called 'the cult of pet lambs'.[31] Much more typical of British attitudes, however, was Vansittart, who attacked Pilsudski's regime in his memoirs. Its failings, Vansittart claimed, 'antagonised not only their neighbours' but also the 'few British politicians who knew anything of Poland'.[32] Ignorance about, and suspicion of, Slavs remained axiomatic in the British political establishment, but Pilsudski and Beck did the Poles few favours with their foreign policy.

On the very day that Chamberlain gave his Birmingham speech, his hand was seemingly forced by the intervention of the Rumanian Minister in London, Viorel Virgil Tilea. Early that morning, Tilea received a telephone call from Paris which put the forty-three-year-old diplomat into a panic. He had already set alarm bells ringing to a degree in Whitehall by advising that the Stanley–Hudson visit should be cancelled on 14 March. Now he went to see Lord Halifax at the Foreign Office, asking for British support and claiming that the Rumanians had received an ultimatum from Berlin which threatened them with invasion.[33] Having alarmed the usually placid Lord Halifax, Tilea then sped round to see Alexander Cadogan, the Permanent Under-Secretary, with his news before spreading it throughout the entire diplomatic corps in London. Tilea's press attaché then got the story into the newspaper headlines for 18 March alongside reports of Chamberlain's Birmingham speech. Cadogan's diary entry for 17 March reports Tilea's visit to him, and also the Foreign Office response, which was to send telegrams to 'threatened' states in south-eastern Europe about the alleged threat to Rumania, and what they proposed to do about it if the threat proved to be genuine.[34]

There has been much controversy about Tilea's source of information in Bucharest but two possible sources have been identified. One was a Rumanian industrialist, Max Aušnit, the other an unknown senior official at the court of King Carol of Rumania. But it is clear that Tilea was not acting under direct instructions from the Rumanian Foreign Office, because the next day (18 March) the British Minister in Bucharest, Sir Reginald Hoare, telephoned London to say that the Rumanian Foreign Minister, Gafencu, had denied the existence of any such ultimatum.

What is known is that the Rumanians felt under pressure from Germany in economic talks which began in Bucharest on 23 February. German demands included one that Rumania's oil production should be adapted to meet German requirements, and that a joint German–Rumanian petroleum industry be created.[35] This was a crucial matter for Germany, which had no indigenous oil supplies. It would therefore be reliant in wartime on Rumanian oilfields at Ploesti. The Rumanians seem to have been sufficiently alarmed by the tone of German demands to mobilise five army corps on 16 March in the expectation of a joint German–Hungarian invasion (the Hungarians had long-standing claims to Rumanian Transylvania and were regarded as hostile). Events in Prague on 15 March could hardly have steadied Rumanian nerves, and a sixth Rumanian army corps was mobilised on 19 March. Hungary then mobilised its forces in response.

All this meant that Tilea had some reason to feel anxious by 17 March, but the Tilea affair was also notable for its unusual involvement of parts of the British political establishment. The Channon diary for 18 March reports that the Liberal MP Robert Bernays first alerted the Foreign Office about the alleged German ultimatum, his source supposedly being the Rumanian Princess Marthe Bibescu, who was related by marriage to the Asquith family. Yet in 1971 Princess Bibescu strongly denied Channon's version of events, which implied that she had told Bernays that King Carol 'had had an ultimatum from the German Government, saying they would invade Rumania'.[36] According to Channon, Bernays then rushed to a call-box and phoned the Conservative Minister Walter Elliot, who then rang Oliver Stanley at the Foreign Office. To add to the confusion, Tilea, who died in 1972 before being able to publish his own account of events, disputed Cadogan's version, whereby the Permanent Under-Secretary claimed in his diary entry for 18 March that he 'confronted' Tilea with Gafencu's denial that the ultimatum had been received.[37] In contrast, the Foreign Office files show Tilea sticking to his story, which he attributed to 'the general manager of a big Roumanian industrialist [Aušnit?]' who had come to Paris especially to pass on the news to him.[38] Tilea was adamant that the story about the ultimatum, or at least some form of German warning, was true.

More significant in every way than the debate about what Tilea said, and who his source was, is the impact that the Rumanian Minister's intervention on 17 March had on the evolution of British foreign policy. According to the latest study, Tilea cannot be charged with unilateral intervention and neither (as has been suggested) was he acting in concert with Vansittart, whose unofficial intelligence activities continued to irritate the government.[39] But his impact on the volte-face which took place in British foreign policy after 15 March cannot be denied.[40]

This is because Chamberlain's response to the Prague coup and Tilea's 'scare' was to seek out a 'declaration of intent' by Britain, France, the USSR and Poland about possible common action in the event of further German action against threatened states such as Rumania, Greece and even Turkey. Chamberlain preferred this to the suggestion from the Soviet Foreign Minister, Litvinov, that an international conference be convened to discuss possible further German aggression. His last experience of an international conference at Munich had not after all been a very happy one. Neither had the responses (Turkey apart) from the so-called threatened states to the Foreign Office overtures on 17 March been especially positive.

Even then the response from France, the USSR and Poland was not very positive. The USSR was distinctly frosty, preferring Litvinov's option, while the French Foreign Minister Bonnet claimed that negotiations with the USSR would upset Mussolini.[41] Jósef Beck responded by saying that Poland was unwilling to make any move that might provoke Germany, trying as ever to balance his country between Moscow and Berlin. All the Poles would agree to was some sort of bilateral agreement with Britain, which was not what Chamberlain and Halifax had in mind. They would not coordinate military strategy with Rumania, which felt obliged to sign an economic agreement with Germany on 23 March. The German representative in Bucharest, Dr Wohltat, had every reason to be pleased with his work, in the agricultural, mineral, oil and financial spheres, which he believed would soon 'secure Germany the dominant position in south-east Europe'.[42]

Before that, however, Hitler had further demonstrated his bad faith by annexing the German majority city of Memel in Lithuania. This followed an effective ultimatum from Ribbentrop to the Lithuanian Foreign Minister on 20 March in Berlin. On his return home, he was further harassed by phone calls from the supposed moderate State Secretary, von Weizsäcker, in the German Foreign Ministry.[43] Such bullying had its desired effect. Early on 23 March, Lithuanian representatives signed away Memel in Berlin. Ribbentrop was able to pass on the news of this latest triumph to Hitler, who was feeling decidedly seasick on the pocket battleship *Deutschland* prior to entry into Germany's latest acquisition.

In a week Hitler had, therefore, annexed Bohemia and Moravia, reduced Slovakia to an impotent client status and also secured German sovereignty over Memel. Tilea's information may not have been entirely accurate, but the British Government was now convinced of the reality of the threat in south-eastern Europe. Halifax had talked to Bonnet in London on 21–22 March and both agreed that it was essential to bring Poland into some sort of security system.[44] Unusually Bonnet, whom Daladier distrusted and who was not renowned for his political backbone, now talked of cajoling the Poles 'even to the extent of threats'. This urgency was partly based on an overestimate of Polish military strength by the British, and an assumption (prompted by despatches from the Military Attaché, Colonel Firebrace, in Moscow) that the Red Army had only defensive, not offensive, capacity.

The British attitude was undergoing a perceptible change even before the Memel coup. At the Cabinet meeting on 18 March, Halifax told his colleagues that:

> The attitude of the German Government was either bluff in which cause it would be stopped by a public declaration on our part; or it was not bluff, in which case it was necessary that we should all unite to meet it, and the sooner we united the better.[45]

Leslie Hore-Belisha, the Secretary of State for War, was bolder still, wanting Britain to make open alliances with the Poles and the USSR. But only Walter Elliott, the Health Minister, supported this line.

Chamberlain was still apprehensive about any alliance with the USSR. For him, at a follow-up meeting on 19 March, 'Poland was very likely the key to the situation', and he tried to exclude the Russians from the conversation.[46] He even resurrected the idea of using Mussolini as a mediator in Berlin, despite the fact that the January Rome visit had offered no hope that this would be a useful strategy to pursue. But, he told his sister that same day, he wanted to write to the Duce as a way of making plain Britain's anxiety about Hitler. This, he hoped, would be a way of restraining Mussolini. In fact (had Chamberlain but known it), the occupation of Prague had driven Mussolini into one of his occasional fits of anti-German exasperation. 'Every time Hitler occupies a country,' Mussolini told Ciano, 'he sends me a message.'[47] Prickly Italian pride had been wounded by the failure of their allies to inform them about the forthcoming destruction of Czechoslovakia. The problem with Mussolini was that these emotional wobbles could not be relied upon to make Italy a reliable or useful partner, as events were soon to show.

British Ministers were still concerned about relations with the USA and the Far East, which needed to be kept stable in the light of the volatile situation in Europe. Chamberlain thought it would be useful to ask the US administration to send a fleet to Honolulu.[48] This might deter the Japanese from openly aligning themselves with the Axis powers. He knew he could count on the absolute support of the US Ambassador in London, Joseph P. Kennedy, who had been a friend of President Roosevelt (though relations had cooled). On 22 March, Roosevelt himself agreed to resume secret Anglo-American naval talks in Washington. These developments show that the accusation that Chamberlain discounted or ignored the Americans is a palpable exaggeration.

In his statement at the Cabinet meeting on 20 March, Chamberlain also showed that he had Hitler's measure.

> The real issue [he told colleagues] was that if Germany showed signs that she intended to proceed with her march for world domination, we must take steps to stop her by attacking her on two fronts. We should attack Germany, not to save a particular victim, but to pull down the bully.[49]

The question now exercising Chamberlain and his colleagues was how to find the most effective mechanism for pulling down 'the bully'. Chamberlain had long been sceptical about Churchill's pet 'Grand Alliance', because of his aversion to the Soviet Union. But could Hitler be deterred without Soviet participation in an anti-Nazi bloc?

Chamberlain wanted to avoid such a scenario and the option he now favoured was some sort of Rumanian–Polish mutual assistance pact underwritten by the British and French. This would push the USSR into the background and show an understanding of Polish anxieties about the Russians, which Chamberlain well understood. He also shared with the Poles a disposition not to abandon all hope of accommodation with Berlin, although his Cabinet comment on 20 March about a possible German march to 'world domination' showed that the Prime Minister was not naive about what could be expected from the Germans. In the meantime, it made sense to construct some sort of eastern front to deter Hitler. The USSR was not to be involved in this, in part because, as Chamberlain told his sister in one of his numerous epistles, he had 'the most profound distrust of Russia';[50] but also because he knew that neither Poland nor Rumania would be associated with any bloc or agreement binding them to the Soviet Union. Both these states feared that any such association would provoke Hitler. The Memel coup did not shift Polish and Rumanian attitudes, even though it had provocatively been staged in the Soviet Union's backyard. It had long been predicted in London, and the need now was to prevent Poland or Rumania going the same way. Neither did the British government pay much heed to Litvinov's agreement on 23 March to sign the declaration of intent once France and Poland had agreed to do so. More important were German complaints about the treatment of their minority in Poland (a familiar reprise of the tactics used in the Sudeten crisis), and the Polish partial mobilisation that followed to head off any threat of a Nazi coup in Danzig.

Churchill responded to this growing tension by tabling a motion in the House of Commons on 28 March with thirty-three others (one of whom unusually was Eden). It demanded that a National Government should be formed with emergency powers. In theory, of course, it was already in existence, but Chamberlain's administration was effectively a Conservative one with a National Liberal and National Labour rump which preserved an illusion of unity. The motion was lost, as it was bound to be, given Chamberlain's huge majority.

On 29 March, Cadogan had an interview with the somewhat over-enthusiastic correspondent of the *News Chronicle* in Berlin, Ian Colvin. Colvin, who was distrusted by people like Cadogan in the Foreign Office as an alarmist, was, in fact, one of Vansittart's private intelligence circle. But, on this occasion, the threatening situation in Poland overrode Cadogan's scepticism when Colvin came to see him. So he took young Colvin to see first Halifax and then Chamberlain himself. Colvin told them that the Germans were about to attack Poland, citing as evidence the build up of rations for military purposes on the German–Polish border. Worse still, Colvin reported, Hitler intended to occupy much of Poland, leaving only a German puppet state akin to Slovakia between the expanded Reich and the USSR. Colvin dressed up his information by predicting that a German attack on Poland might come within twelve hours.[51]

Cadogan was still doubtful about Colvin's story but Halifax seemed inclined to take it at face value. The upshot was that Chamberlain agreed that the best way to deal with this apparent German threat was 'an immediate declaration of support' for Poland. To the Tilea scare was added the Colvin scare. The combined effect of these alarms was to drive the British government beyond a declaration of intent to a full-bodied guarantee of assistance to the Poles. The irony was that there was not a shred of evidence to back up Colvin's accusation. Colvin had a bad record of spreading alarmist rumours, but he was believed.[52] The fact was that he reflected the change of atmosphere in the government after 15 March. But the government, and Chamberlain in particular, had to face the fact that the attempt to create a deterrent front amongst the countries of south-eastern Europe had failed. The Prime Minister may have felt that the Poles were the key to the situation, but by the end of March they were the only part of the diplomatic-military jigsaw left in place.

So it was that Chamberlain, having accepted the argument for a Polish guarantee, rose to speak in the House of Commons at 2.52 p.m. on 31 March. He told the House that if there was any action which 'clearly threatened Polish independence', and which the Poles thought it 'vital to resist', they would have the support of the British government.[53] The former Labour Foreign Secretary, Arthur Henderson, said that Chamberlain had made 'as momentous a statement as has been made in this House for a quarter of a century'.[54] But the statement importantly did not commit Britain to defend the existing Polish frontiers, which Chamberlain thought should be open to revision. Rather it promised British support if Polish independence should be endangered, a crucial distinction.

Chamberlain then sat down to await the response to his announcement. Surprisingly, perhaps, he sent a note to his old foe Lloyd George, who signalled his assent to a private meeting about the announcement with a nod of the head. When they met in the Prime Minister's room at the Commons, Lloyd George told the Soviet Ambassador Maisky that he had laughed when Chamberlain had said that Hitler would not risk a war on two fronts, if the second front was provided by the Poles. Lloyd George told him that 'your statement of today is an irresponsible game of chance which can end up very badly'.[55] But Lloyd George did not understand the purpose of the guarantee. Chamberlain knew from military advice that Polish resistance in the east might not last long, but took the view that it would still have deterrent value because of Germany's internal weaknesses. SIS was continuing to report that Germany was not ready for a general war, and this view was supported by Henderson and Kirkpatrick in the Berlin Embassy. The purpose of the guarantee was therefore to constrain Hitler, not to save the Poles from aggression.

Chamberlain made his statement on the Friday. On Monday 3 April, Churchill replied in the debate. He said that he found himself 'in the most complete agreement with the Prime Minister' and was going to give him 'my full support'. More surprising perhaps, coming from the advocate of the 'Grand Alliance' (with its emphasis on a Soviet alliance), was Churchill's conciliatory tone about the feelings of the Poles, the Rumanians and the Baltic States in relation to Russia. Britain, he said, must be 'largely guided at this juncture by the feelings of those states'.[56] And Chamberlain had been, which was why his 31 March statement had limited itself to a guarantee of Polish independence, and this had been cleared with Warsaw beforehand (according to one account, Beck accepted the guarantee between 'two flicks of a cigarette'). Ironically, Lloyd George, who had laughed at Chamberlain's second front on 31 March, showed more realism about likely Polish attitudes to a Soviet alliance with Britain when he spoke next.[57]

Nevertheless, however pragmatic British policy towards Poland was, the

31 March statement marked a major turnabout in British policy if not the end of appeasement. Britain was, against the canon of traditional British foreign policy, making a commitment to preserve the integrity of an Eastern European state. It was doing so, moreover, in the absence of any specific warning from the Chiefs of Staff, who offered no advice to the Cabinet when it met on 30 March and 31 March. In this instance, it was the politicians primed by Colvin's alarmist report who decided that action was necessary, although on 31 March the War Office had passed on information to the Foreign Office about the threatening German posture in Danzig.[58] The Foreign Office concluded that Germany was trying to force Poland to accept a compromise over the city, but none of this directly influenced the tone of Chamberlain's statement.

Where the British military were involved was in considering the possible implications of an Anglo-French guarantee to Poland. The Committee of Imperial Defence presented a paper on this subject to the Chiefs of Staff Sub-Committee on 3 April. The paper assumed that the USSR would adopt a posture of benevolent neutrality if Germany attacked Poland (an optimistic assessment as it turned out). This was the first military assessment of the potential consequences of a British guarantee to Poland, but it overrated the strength of the Polish army which it thought (contrary to the evidence available), to have good equipment and high morale (the latter at least was true). Nevertheless, the final conclusion was bleak, 'it would only be a matter of time ... before Poland was eliminated from the war'.[59] Chamberlain may have been misled by assessments of Polish military strength, but this was irrelevant. The guarantee did not depend for its efficacy on the Polish capacity to resist. Conversely, Beck did not see the existence of the guarantee as any sort of inhibition to Polish efforts to reach an accommodation with Berlin about Danzig and the Corridor. He opposed its extension to Rumania, because he feared that such a move would antagonise the Hungarians.

Chamberlain, who continued to hope for an accommodation with Hitler, had now hedged himself in with a commitment to the Poles. Any surviving hopes about Mussolini's usefulness as a mediator were dealt another blow when the Duce, with cavalier disregard for the religious susceptibilities of his Catholic nation, attacked tiny Albania on Good Friday, 7 April 1939. Traditionally this invasion was seen by historians as Mussolini's answer to Hitler's Prague coup in mid-March, but in fact the seizure of Albania had been advocated by Italian naval staff since at least 1935 as a means of securing Italian control of the Adriatic.[60] There was certainly a degree of pique with Hitler for treating the Italians in so offhand a manner, but Mussolini had his own expansionist agenda.

His aggression provoked consternation in London, where the resident clerk at the Foreign Office learnt at 5.30 a.m. that King Zog (who had splendid credentials as a bandit chief), his wife and their two-year-old son had fled to Greece. A disillusioned Channon wrote in his diary,

'Et tu Benito?' for Mussolini had only recently assured us that he had no territorial claims whatsoever on Albania, and her invasion, or really annexation, is a complete violation of the Anglo-Italian Agreement.[61]

Chamberlain himself remarked that any 'faith as I ever had in the assurances of dictators is rapidly being whittled away'.[62] Oliver Harvey, Halifax's Private Secretary, recorded a strange visit by a Mr Solomon who wanted to send the Foreign Secretary a message that 'we had just thirty-six hours to unite Christendom and the Moslems against Italy if we acted at once – as they were both so enraged at Mussolini's behaviour in Albania'.[63] Halifax's reaction to this bizarre messenger is unrecorded, but he did not press Chamberlain to take action against the Duce.

Earlier that day at two o'clock, Harvey had seen off Colonel Beck at Victoria Station after a visit which had begun on 4 April. On an earlier visit, Beck had disgraced himself by his drunken antics (he certainly had a drink problem), but this time he seemed to be on his best behaviour. But he was characteristically obdurate about any agreement with the USSR, which he said would cause a crisis in Polish–German relations.[64] The flaw in Churchill's 'Grand Alliance' scheme was thus further demonstrated. How could Poland and the Soviet Union be brought into a collective security pact simultaneously?

Nevertheless, there was still disappointment in London about Beck's attitude. Chamberlain told his Cabinet colleagues on 5 April that Britain had been offered not 'even a Three Power Pact, but a Two Power Pact, and every attempt which we made to suggest that other Powers should be brought into the arrangements had been quietly, but firmly resisted by Colonel Beck'.[65] The key factor was Beck's continuing belief that Poland could reach an accommodation with Berlin, and must retain its freedom of action to do so.

Although Rumania was now deemed by the British government to be of far lesser importance, Chamberlain allowed himself to be persuaded by the French to offer a guarantee of assistance to Bucharest on 13 April, and to Greece and Turkey as well. Thus a government which had been unwilling to guarantee the Czechs, six months earlier, was now guaranteeing states as far off as Turkey. But the extent to which the Poles had blown a hole in Chamberlain's attempt to reinvent collective security was demonstrated by their statement on that same day that they disassociated themselves from British attempts to guarantee the Greeks and Rumanians. Meantime, Channon noted in his diary that where the Foreign Office was concerned Chamberlain 'saw eye to eye' with R.A. Butler, the Under-Secretary of State, more than anyone else.[66] Channon was surprised that Rumania had been included in the guarantee alongside Greece, but knew that 'it was a last minute decision taken after luncheon at the urgent request of the French'.[67] Chamberlain announced the guarantees to the House of Commons on the afternoon of 13 April.

Chamberlain has been accused of being 'thoroughly truculent' about the need for an alliance with the USSR, but he did recognise the necessity of a measure of conscription in the United Kingdom, something the French had been lobbying him about for years.[68] This was duly introduced on 26 April, but it was a modest measure which limited the number who could be called up, restricting their deployment outside the United Kingdom to wartime. It made a large number of the conscripted young men only available for service with anti-aircraft batteries (although this was a recognition that Britain's aerial defences needed to be beefed up).

The perils associated with Beck's policy were underlined, however, a couple of days later on 28 April. Hitler made a speech in the Reichstag in which he said that the Anglo-Polish Declaration broke the spirit of the 1934 Polish-German Non-Aggression Pact. He also took the opportunity to repudiate the Anglo-German Naval Treaty, which had been at the very core of British appeasement policy. Beck, however, continued to believe that Polish-German rapprochement was possible. For Chamberlain, the denunciation of the Treaty meant that Britain might have to take on board the unwelcome prospect of a military alliance with the USSR.

By early April 1939, the British Chiefs of Staff had already reached the conclusion that Anglo-French guarantees to the small states of south-eastern Europe would be worthless without Soviet involvement. On 3 April, they considered a report from the Joint Sub-Committee on Imperial Defence which said that neither Britain nor France could supply Poland or Rumania with armaments, so that they would 'have to depend for assistance in this respect solely upon the USSR'.[69]

On the Soviet side, there was an awareness of their advantage. Already in March, Stalin had made his famous 'chestnuts' speech to the party congress when he had warned unspecified powers (obviously Britain and France) not to rely on the USSR to come to their aid in the event of war with Nazi Germany. And on 4 April the Soviet Foreign Minister Litvinov, who was closely associated with attempts to form an anti-Nazi bloc, wrote to a diplomatic colleague, 'We know very well that to hold back and stop aggression in Europe without us is impossible and that the later they [the Anglo-French] appeal for our help, the higher our price will be'.[70]

In the Foreign Office and the Government there was a reluctance to meet the price even now. The Foreign Office refused to consider a suggestion from the Soviet Ambassador, Ivan Maisky, that Litvinov should make a visit to London ahead of Anglo-Soviet talks. Sargent and Cadogan were strongly opposed, and Halifax unenthusiastic. Where the USSR was concerned, he minuted on 19 April, 'we want if we can – without making a disproportionate amount of mischief – to keep them in with us'.[71] It is significant that R.A. Butler's post-war memoir has nothing at all to say about the important subject of Anglo-Soviet relations during this period.[72]

When all due acknowledgement is made of British reluctance to consider a Soviet alliance, the context of Anglo-Soviet relations has to be recalled. Ever since 1917, there had been severe tensions, partly at least caused by Comintern activity. More pertinently, the British government had good reason to be dubious both about Soviet intentions and Soviet military capacity. Stalin's purges of his armed forces in 1937–38 had seen all eight admirals in the Red Navy perish, three out of five Red Army Marshals (including the Commander-in-Chief), sixty out of sixty-seven Corps Commanders, 136 out of 199 Divisional Commanders, and 221 out of 397 Brigade Commanders. It is likely also that between forty and fifty per cent of the entire Red Army officer corps had been either shot or imprisoned.[73] Doubts about the USSR, therefore, were not just a matter of ideology but also about how meaningful such assistance as it might render could be. The problem was that, without Soviet participation, British and French capacity to assist the Poles and the Rumanians, let alone the Greeks and the Turks, would be minimal. Eventually Stalin would, in his own phrase, have 'two suitors'. Germany, too, had begun to flirt with the USSR via low-level contacts in the winter of 1938–39. But months would pass before the rough wooing involved would commence. In the meantime, even the French with their 1935 security pact with the USSR were reluctant to strengthen ties with Moscow. The French Chargé d'Affaires in Moscow, Payart, was trying to stir his government out of its lethargy on 2 April by warning Paris that the USSR might retreat into an isolationist policy.[74]

On 19 April, the USSR appeared to reaffirm its interest in collective security by proposing a triple alliance between Britain, France and the Soviet Union, which would be supplemented by a military convention. Each power would be obliged to assist the others in the event of aggression. The Russians also wanted a specific British pledge that their Polish guarantee applied only to German aggression, and an Anglo-French one that neither power would make a separate peace without consulting the USSR first after war had broken out.[75]

Chamberlain did not wish to make such pledges for fear of alienating Germany, and in the Foreign Office Alexander Cadogan was equally exercised about offending Portugal, Spain, Yugoslavia, Rumania and Poland. Cadogan thought that the main reason for considering a Soviet alliance was the need to placate what he called 'the left wing' at home (Churchill and his supporters hardly came into this category). But then Cadogan had an awkward final thought. Might there not be a danger of the USSR and Germany coming to terms? The same thought had also occurred to Nevile Henderson in Berlin, who 'felt intuitively that Germans are getting at Stalin'.[76] The danger in the British position was the assumption that Soviet-Nazi animosity was likely to be permanent and that therefore a Soviet alliance could easily be had at Britain's convenience. Chamberlain fell into this trap, confidently telling the sympathetic US Ambassador, Joseph Kennedy, that he could 'make a deal with Russia at any time now, but is delaying until he definitely gets the Balkan situation straightened away'.[77]

Cadogan's thoughts on the subject were put in a paper presented to the Foreign Policy Committee of the Cabinet on 19 April. Halifax was absent, but Chamberlain enlisted the support of R.A. Butler to ensure that his colleagues rejected the Soviet proposal. Instead, Britain would tell France that it planned to try to persuade the Soviet Union to make a declaration of intent without any preconditions. This would demonstrate Soviet willingness to assist any Eastern European state that asked for help. The French liked the idea of a triple alliance but had their own scheme for one which Georges Bonnet put to the Kremlin.

All this assumed a continuity in Soviet foreign policy. But this seemed to be threatened by the surprising news, printed in the Soviet press on 4 May, that Litvinov had been dismissed. The previous morning, Litvinov had discussed the Anglo-Polish guarantee in his usual fluent fashion with the British Ambassador, Sir William Seeds. Seeds was therefore dumbfounded to hear the news, although he lived in the same diplomatic fog about Soviet intentions as his predecessor Viscount Chilston. Litvinov's successor was V. M. Molotov, an unknown quantity as far as the Foreign Office and the Diplomatic Service were concerned.

The reasons for Litvinov's dismissal remain controversial. It is possible that his removal shows that Stalin was not serious about his attempt to secure an Anglo-French alliance, because Litvinov was a man of Geneva closely associated both with the League of Nations, which had finally admitted the USSR in 1934, and the attempt to make security pacts with the West. Conversely, if Stalin wanted agreement with Germany, Litvinov, a Jew who was so closely associated with the attempt to create an anti-Hitler bloc, was hardly the man to secure it.[78]

Whatever the cause of Litvinov's dismissal was (perhaps Stalin was tired of Anglo-French caution?), it caused alarm in London. The US Ambassador in Paris, Bullitt, happened to be visiting London at the time and paid a courtesy call on Vansittart whom he found 'intensely apprehensive' and fearful that Soviet isolationism would destroy all hope of anti-Nazi resistance in Europe.[79] In the House of Commons, Harold Nicolson had a chat with Lloyd George's son Gwilym (a future Tory Home Secretary), who told him about a conversation he had had with Maisky. The Soviet Ambassador had been unable to 'make the Litvinov business out'. Nicolson noted in his diary that left-wing people were 'very upset' at the news because 'they are not at all sure that Russia may not make a neutrality pact with Germany'. Nicolson added, 'I fear this terribly'.[80] Two days before on 2 May, Nicolson had received an interesting insight into mainstream Conservative attitudes from Commander R.T. Bower, the MP for Cleveland, who had overheard a conversation between two Tory MPs. The first had asked, 'I suppose we shall be able to get out of this beastly guarantee business?' His colleague had replied,

'Oh, of course. Thank God we have Neville'.[81] The government did not share this cynical view of the Polish guarantee, but neither was it disposed to be hurried into a further commitment by Stalin and Molotov. The latter was soon trying to extract a promise from the British that they would support the Soviet Union in any war with Germany.

By late May, the attitude of the British Cabinet was changing, however, and Chamberlain and Butler found themselves in a minority. This was because the Chiefs of Staff, who in April had been pessimistic about the Red Army's effectiveness, had begun to change their tune. The new Minister for Defence Co-ordination, Lord Chatfield, told the Cabinet that the COS now thought that the Red Army had 9000 quality tanks and a navy which could keep the Germans tied down in the Baltic. Ministers decided that it was better to have some sort of pact with Russia even on their terms rather than no pact at all. The bewildering changes in COS assessments must have puzzled them, but Chamberlain had to take account of his colleagues' preference. Chatfield also told his colleagues, after Anglo-French talks on 3 May, that if Germany and Poland went to war Gamelin would remain on the defensive in the west, regardless of French commitments to the Poles. When General Ironside, the Inspector-General of Overseas Forces, told Chamberlain that a Soviet alliance was essential in June, the Prime Minister's reluctance was still evident. 'It was', he told Ironside (oddly nicknamed 'Tiny' despite his great height), 'the only thing we cannot do.'[82] Ironside had overlooked the ongoing problem presented by Polish attitudes towards the USSR. Gamelin's reluctance to abandon a defensive strategy in the west was still manifest, too, and Britain was in little position to complain.

Any remaining hopes that Mussolini would be much of a counterweight to Hitler received another blow in May when the Rome–Berlin Axis became a formal military alliance known as the Pact of Steel. The Duce seemed to swallow German assurances that a Polish war would remain localised (Ciano did not), but he entered a caveat into the new alliance, via the so-called Cavallero Memorandum, to the effect that Italy would not be ready for a major war until 1943.[83] Nevertheless, relations with London were poor when, on 27 May, Mussolini saw the new British Ambassador to Rome, Sir Percy Loraine (whom Churchill later accused of being too soft with Mussolini), he described Chamberlain's policy 'as completely misdirected and pernicious'.[84] He even blamed Polish-German tensions on the British government, which he claimed was trying to encircle the Axis powers with its guarantees. Three days earlier on 24 May Chamberlain had finally grasped the nettle where the USSR was concerned. The Cabinet agreed to try to negotiate an alliance with the Soviet Union. Halifax made it clear that failure to make this overture could result in a Nazi-Soviet pact instead. This decision in its way, after twenty years of animosity and distrust, was as revolutionary a step for Britain to take as had been the Polish guarantee in March.

Stalin and Molotov now pressed home their advantage. Seeds and his French colleague were insulted by Molotov, who resented their attempt to bring the League of Nations into the proposed treaty text. The Soviet Commissar for Foreign Affairs tried to get the treaty extended to cover Finland and the Baltic Republics, which had never asked for Soviet assistance and did not want it. When Seeds complained that this was inappropriate, Molotov countered by refusing to include Switzerland and the Netherlands in any agreement. But in late June Chamberlain and his colleagues were still insisting on the inclusion of these two small neutral states. Chamberlain's remark on 10 July to Ironside quoted above, reflected his irritation at Molotov's tactics. By 19 July, Chamberlain was telling the Cabinet that he could not 'bring himself to believe that a real alliance between Russia and Germany was possible'.[85] A dangerous assumption. On 20 May Molotov had asked the German Ambassador to outline a political basis for Soviet-German economic cooperation. By 17 June, the Ambassador Schulenburg was reporting to his masters in Berlin that Soviet-German relations were on the mend. Meanwhile, Molotov was complaining to Maisky in London that 'the English and French want to conclude a treaty with us which would be advantageous to them and disadvantageous to us'.[86] A miasma of mistrust enveloped the Western attempts to secure an agreement with Stalin.

Soviet–Western wrangling continued into July. On 1 July Molotov saw Seeds and Naggiar, the British and French Ambassadors. He objected, with the stone-faced obduracy which earned him the nickname of 'Mr Niet' years later during the Cold War, to the inclusion of the Netherlands, Luxembourg and Switzerland in the list of states to be defended from aggression. He also haggled about a definition of 'indirect aggression' that the USSR wanted to include in any agreement with Britain and France. This was supposed to cover a Czech-style scenario when Hácha had been bullied into delivering Bohemia and Moravia to Hitler, and Tiso had presided over his countrymen's defection from the Czechoslovak unitary state. This, in Soviet eyes, amounted to nothing less than an internal coup. Two days later, on 3 July, Molotov gave a formal response to the Anglo-French proposed for a tripartite pact. The USSR insisted on the inclusion of a definition of 'indirect aggression' being put into a secret protocol to be attached to any agreement along with the list of states to be defended against German aggression. Furthermore, Molotov demanded that assistance should be rendered automatically to any one of the three great powers which found itself at war because of 'direct or indirect aggression' by a European power.

How was Britain to respond to this latest exercise in semantics by the Commissar for Foreign Affairs? Chamberlain and Halifax wanted to stop the argument, and told the Foreign Policy Committee of the Cabinet that the tripartite pact should contain provisions to allow joint consultations in cases which did not involve a direct German attack on Britain, France or the USSR.

Halifax thought that the proposed pact would stop the USSR from cooperating with Germany. But the leading advocates of a Soviet alliance in the Cabinet, Hoare and Stanley, wanted to push more strongly for agreement. Britain and France, they argued, should give up their insistence on aid for the Netherlands, Luxembourg and Switzerland in return for Stalin and Molotov abandoning their demand for a definition of indirect aggression. Years later, Hoare was to describe the peculiar difficulties which the unfortunate Seeds had to combat in dealing with Molotov (he had already been sent reinforcements in the shape of William Strang, a former Counsellor at the Moscow Embassy). Molotov

> sat upon a throne and frequently left the meeting(s), no doubt to obtain guidance, and whenever the Ambassadors attempted to maintain a sustained argument, he interrupted them by saying that the Soviet Government had given their decision, and demanding that they should pass on to the next item on the agenda.[87]

There were also Anglo-French tensions. When the British Cabinet suggested a fall-back position, where a simple tripartite treaty was negotiated with possible extensions later, Bonnet protested. France wanted an agreement which would include provisions for a Soviet commitment to the defence of Poland and Rumania. This had been the French position since the end of April, and Bonnet, the arch dove over Czechoslovakia in 1938, was now an ardent proponent of a Soviet alliance.[88] The French were considerably more enthusiastic about the prospect of a real military alliance with the USSR than were the British, but the commitment to Poland and Rumania was important for them. Only *in extremis* should the Anglo-French fall back on the limited three-power pact alone.

Meanwhile in Moscow, Seeds and Naggiar continued their war of attrition with Molotov. On 9 July, they spoke to Molotov from 6 p.m. to 8.30 p.m., and on the next day from 6 p.m. to 9 p.m. By now Molotov was insisting on simultaneous signings of political and military agreements. Startlingly, he redefined 'indirect aggression' to mean any situation where a long list of states allowed their territory or their armed forces to be used for aggressive purposes. The British and French were equally alarmed by Molotov's pronouncement that any of these states, which included near Soviet neighbours such as Estonia, Latvia and Finland, might allow this to happen under the threat of force *or*, he added ominously, without any 'such threat'. British and French enthusiasm for a Soviet alliance might vary, but both powers could clearly see that this would give Stalin *carte blanche* for intervention anywhere along his borders if the USSR deemed such action appropriate.[89]

Nevertheless, Chamberlain was still confident enough to tell the Foreign Policy Committee that he thought that 'the Soviet Government is intending to make an Agreement with us'. Puzzlingly, Halifax cited Henderson's opinion that 'it would be quite impossible for Germany and Soviet Russia to come together', which seemed to fly in the face of what the Ambassador had written to Cadogan on 31 May. Halifax rightly objected to any formula which allowed the USSR to intervene in other states when it felt inclined to do so.[90]

In the same Cabinet discussion, Halifax also said that American opinion would also find giving the Russians permission to intervene in small neighbouring states immoral. In doing so, he probably overstated the level of American interest in matters European, for the United States in the 1930s was the country of the isolationist Senator William Borah, just as it was the home of the German-American Bund, the neo-Fascist 'Radio Priest' Father Coughlin and the heroic lone aviator Charles Lindbergh, whose visits to Germany had left him hopelessly seduced by the brash and brutal force of National Socialism.[91] Franklin Roosevelt had not been so seduced, but he waged an unsuccessful struggle to reverse the impact of the 1937 US Neutrality Act. In March 1939 Senator Pittmann, with administration backing, put forward a new Peace Act which would have repealed the arms embargo section of the 1937 legislation and allowed the sale of arms to any belligerent who was able to pay for them. Even so, there were still to be no loans to belligerents (and Britain would certainly be heavily dependent on US financial assistance in wartime, as it had been during the Great War), and no American citizens were to travel on belligerent shipping. Roosevelt himself was to be granted discretionary powers to create combat zones from which all American ships and visitors were to be excluded.

Senator Pittmann's Bill found US opinion hopelessly split. The press was divided, as was the American Labor Movement and the churches. Months of internal wrangling merely produced Pittmann's extraordinary statement on 16 May (with the Pact of Steel already in place) that 'the situation in Europe does not seem to induce any urgent action on neutrality legislation'.[92] Having failed to get anywhere in the Senate, Roosevelt and his Secretary of State for Foreign Affairs, Cordell Hull, then turned to the House of Representatives for assistance, but it unhelpfully decided to adjourn ahead of the planned visit by King George VI and Queen Elizabeth to the United States.

Ironically the visit, which started on 12 June, was a great success. It was the first visit to the United States by a reigning British monarch, albeit a brief one which only lasted four days. The American media were impressed by the informality of the visit and the charm of Queen Elizabeth in particular (a sharp contrast to Daladier's damning comments about her). The King and Queen went to the Roosevelt family home at Hyde Park near New York, but lunched in an appropriately populist spirit on beer and hot dogs rather than champagne and caviar. King George thought that, if war was to come in Europe, President Roosevelt would do everything he could to help Britain and France. The Foreign Office was much pleased by the royal couple's part in the wooing of American opinion, but knew that ultimately only events would sway it towards helpful intervention.[93]

Meanwhile Roosevelt did what he could. He has been criticised, probably rightly, for being a President 'who preferred stealth to openness', and one who did not try hard enough to rally American opinion to the cause of global collective security (his support for Munich has already been noted).[94] Nevertheless, in 1938, he had secured the passage of the Naval Expansion Act, which authorised spending of $1 billion over a ten-year period, and aimed to give the United States a navy equal in size to the combined fleets of Japan, Germany and Italy (critics noticed that this only actually involved a 20 per cent increase in spending on the current US naval programme). And in 1939 Roosevelt obtained an extra appropriation of $525 million, most of it earmarked for the strengthening of American air defences, which had been as porous as Britain's.[95]

So far and no further was the story as far as Roosevelt's attempts to widen American perspectives was concerned. For when the new 1939 Bill was presented to the House of Representatives for approval, a last-minute amendment put in a limited embargo on exports of arms. So Roosevelt's Bill was rendered toothless. When he attempted to renew the pressure in the Senate, its Foreign Relations Committee voted to postpone consideration of neutrality legislation until January 1940 (by which time Britain and France had been at war with Germany for months, and independent Poland had vanished from the map of Europe). The most Roosevelt could do for the British was to tell them (via their Ambassador in Washington, Sir Ronald Lindsay) that, if war did come, he would establish an American naval patrol over the whole of the Western Atlantic up to 500 miles from the US coastline denying the area to Axis warships. Even this suggestion, however, was a characteristically hard-headed and pragmatic one. America's gesture would require British reciprocation in the shape of leases on bases for the US Navy in Trinidad, Tobago, St Lucia and Bermuda. Foreign Office legal advisers were cautious about the legal implications of this move. Churchill was later to encourage Britain's citizens, with the line 'westward look the land is bright', but in the summer of 1939 its lustre was still dim for the British government. The emphasis was still on what America might do, rather than any confident expectation that it would really commit itself to the anti-Fascist cause in Europe. Even Churchill, with his American blood, would not have been able to secure such a commitment had he been Premier in 1939.

Meanwhile, in Europe, the fateful summer months of the dying peace slipped by. Chamberlain continued to hope that Britain's commitment to Poland would deter Germany, while contemplating the unpleasing option of a military and political agreement with the USSR.

11

The Coming of War

In late August 1939, a decisive period in inter-war European diplomacy was reached during which Joseph Stalin was effectively the arbiter of peace or war. If Stalin decided to ally himself to Britain, France and Poland then Hitler might be deterred from starting a war over Danzig and the Polish Corridor. If he did not, and reached an accommodation with Germany, then the likelihood of Hitler risking a Polish adventure was greatly increased. The British assumption had long been that such an accommodation was impossible, on the face of it a reasonable analysis when the history of intense ideological hostility between the Soviet Union and Nazi Germany was taken into consideration. What Chamberlain and his colleagues underestimated, however, was both the residue of suspicion between them and the Kremlin, and Stalin's reaction to the USSR's exclusion from the Czech settlement a year earlier. Stalin may well never have had any intention of coming to the assistance of the Czechs, but he was quite capable (as he had signalled in his March 'chestnuts' speech) of harbouring deep suspicions about the reliability of the Anglo-French imperialists. When Halifax looked forward to military conversations with the Russians which would 'drag on ... In this way, we shall have gained time and made the best of a situation from which we could not now escape', he was tempting fate in the personages of the Soviet dictator and his inscrutable henchman Molotov. Foot-dragging by the British (rather than the much keener French) made the temptation to respond to Nazi wooing all the greater. A positive Soviet response to Hitler's blandishments made war for Danzig almost inevitable, once he was freed from the threat of Soviet intervention.

On 23 July 1939, the British and French Ambassadors in Moscow agreed that their respective governments would sign a military agreement with the USSR before a political one. By now, Anglo-French insistence on guarantees to Holland, Switzerland and Luxembourg had been dropped. In response, Molotov had dropped Soviet conditions for mutual assistance pacts with Poland and Turkey. On 23 July, he indicated that he wanted military talks to start at once, and Sir William Seeds and his French colleague supported his proposal. Miraculously, Molotov was now prepared to see the definition of 'indirect aggression' as a minor issue. At the same time, however, Stalin and Molotov toyed with their 'two suitors', for the Soviet Chargé d'Affaires, Astakov, was dining with a German economic expert, Schnurre, in Berlin on 26 July. The former was surprised to learn that the Germans now believed there to be no fundamental problems in Soviet-German relations.[1]

Chamberlain and his colleagues faced the question of who was to represent them on the military mission to Moscow. There was also the related problem of how the delegation was to reach the Soviet Union. Here mythology has once again replaced fact where the history of British appeasement is concerned, for legend has it that the anti-Soviet Chamberlain and Halifax sent incompetent second-raters to Russia by the slowest available means of transport, compounding an already difficult situation by increasing Soviet suspicions.

The man chosen to head the mission was Admiral Sir Reginald Plunket-Ernle-Erle-Drax, an apparently Blimpish member of the naval hierarchy sent when a general would have been much more appropriate. We are also told that the British Embassy in Moscow was appalled by the low status of the delegation which ought to have been headed by Halifax himself.[2] A Foreign Office official had thought that the mission should be sent in a fleet of fast cruisers to show the Axis powers 'that we really meant business', but Halifax had thought that this would be 'rather provocative' as the ships would have to sail through the Baltic.[3] Instead the British government chose to send the mission in an elderly ship, *The City of Exeter*, which took five days to get to Leningrad, while William Strang of the Foreign Office, who had been preparing the ground for the negotiations, was allowed to fly home. Nothing in the anti-appeasement lexicon is trotted out more regularly (save Chamberlain's 'Peace in Our Time' folly), as an example of the myopia of British Ministers during the thirties. Incompetence is allied to ill-will where the Soviet alliance is concerned.

The true record suggests a completely different story. Drax was no fool to start with. He was a former head of the Royal Naval Staff College, and earlier that year had been involved in a reassessment of British naval strategy in the Mediterranean and the Far East. He went on to render distinguished service at the time of the Dunkirk evacuation. And the fact that Drax was an admiral was in no sense evidence of British bad faith where the Soviet Union was concerned. Britain's most distinguished international historian has pointed out that, although leading generals like Dill and Alanbrooke were available, they would hardly welcome a posting that would find them stranded in Russia if war broke out. This was why an admiral was chosen. The decision to use *The City of Exeter* had a similar motivation. It would have made little sense to put one of the Royal Navy's small number of convoy escort vessels at risk in the Baltic when war threatened, or one of the larger, faster passenger liners with secretly strengthened hulls, which were lined up for convoy duties when six-inch guns had been provided.[4]

There is also an answer to the accusation that it was folly not to send the mission by air. In his memoirs, Hoare points out that serving officers could not be flown across Germany in peacetime in military aeroplanes. Britain's few Sunderland flying boats were out of action and the only civil machines available were slow Hannibals with a range so limited that they would be obliged to land on German territory en route.[5] The other option of travelling by train with top-secret information about Anglo-French military planning was even more dangerous. It is significant that the French, always more anxious to conclude an agreement with the Soviet Union, went along with the British travel arrangements when they could have objected if these arrangements were the inept absurdity that they have sometimes been said to have been. It was unfortunate that the Anglo-French mission took five days to reach Leningrad but it was no more than that. Neither was the appointment of Drax the insult to the Soviet government frequently suggested. The British army was, in any case, represented by Major-General T.G.G. Heywood, a former Military Attaché with experience of dealing with diplomats. So much for legend, including the one that an aeroplane could not be found.[6] Those with an inclination for sympathy with the Soviet cause in 1939 have found it all too easy to substitute bad faith for real technical and personnel problems where the British were concerned. Had an underpowered Hannibal crash-landed in Germany in August 1939, and placed the British military mission in Nazi hands, Chamberlain and Halifax would no doubt have been castigated for that as well.

As it was, the Anglo-French Mission arrived in Leningrad early in the morning of 10 August and moved on to Moscow the next day. The talks with Soviet representatives started on 12 August, a Saturday. Voroshilov demanded to see a letter of authority from Drax and his French counterpart, General Doumenc. The general had a letter from Daladier, but Drax had to ask for written instructions to be airmailed from London (this was indeed an odd oversight by the Foreign Office). But in the third session on that same day, Voroshilov, one of the more subtle of the Red Army marshals and one who had survived the bloodletting of 1937–38, came to the crux of the matter as far as the USSR was concerned. How did the Anglo-French envisage Soviet participation if France, Poland and Rumania were attacked by Germany?

The next day, a further point was raised. Would Poland allow the Red Army on to its soil through the Vilna Corridor if hostilities broke out with Germany? Here was the Achilles heel of the Anglo-French position, for they could give no such undertaking. Worse still, the Soviet delegation then began to demand that Rumania too allow transit rights for the Red Army. Without them, the USSR would not intervene in any war between Germany and its neighbours. The next two weeks saw increasingly desperate Anglo-French attempts to secure such a pledge from the Polish and Rumanian governments. Most of the effort came from the French. Voroshilov pressed them to discover whether the Poles in particular had given such an undertaking. At one point, the French tried to pretend that Beck had given such an undertaking, but he had not. No Polish Foreign Minister would have survived for an hour if he had done so. This encapsulated the Anglo-French dilemma. How could the Poles be prevailed upon to accept Russian help if they saw the solution to the problem as being worse than the problem itself? Beck distrusted Poland's new allies, and the French in particular distrusted him.

All Seeds and Naggiar could do in Moscow was to refer Voroshilov's questions back to London and Paris, but when no clear Anglo-French answer was forthcoming two days later, on 17 August further meetings between the Western and Soviet representatives were put off until 21 August. In London the Deputy Chiefs of Staff now felt that the strongest pressure should be put upon to the Poles and Rumanians to agree to Soviet demands. It was clear that 'without early and effective Russian assistance, the Poles cannot hope to stand up to a German attack ... for more than a limited time'.[7] The Chiefs were right in terms of military reality but they ignored the political factor, and the obvious question that Schnurre had asked Astakov on 26 July, 'What could Britain offer Russia?'[8] Nothing it seemed other than a half-hearted willingness to persuade the Poles and Rumanians to play ball. Yet in a real sense Chamberlain did not need the Russians. The object of his deterrence policy was to make Hitler think again. Soviet military assistance was a useful adjunct to bringing about such a rethink, but it was not essential. And it might carry too high a price. The important point was that Hitler should be brought to the full realisation than an attack on Poland meant war with Britain and France, regardless of the degree of meaningful aid that those two powers were able to render to the Poles. To start a war with Poland, Hitler too would have to pay a price – the war in the west involving a second front for Germany. Had he not vowed in *Mein Kampf* that he would not make the mistake of 1914–18 again? If the Russians could offer a second front against Hitler, this was well and good. If not, the Poles would do for Britain, and it became increasingly likely that they would have to do. This strategy did leave open the possibility, however, that what the British deemed impossible might come to pass: some form of agreement between Germany and the Soviet Union.

While trying to secure a somewhat distasteful deal with Soviet Russia, Chamberlain continued his efforts to prevent Poland and Germany sliding into war over Danzig and the Corridor. In Warsaw, the British Ambassador, Sir Howard Kennard, and his Counsellor, Clifford Norton, were trenchant supporters of the Poles, continually contradicting Henderson's opinion that the guarantee might result in Polish recklessness over Danzig that would suck Britain and France into war. Unusually, Norton actually liked Beck and agreed with his former boss Vansittart's assessment of him as a man who only 'meant to keep both his neighbours out of his country'.[9] Norton went hunting with Beck just as Nevile Henderson went hunting with Göring, and also wined and dined him in secret. When Kennard was away on annual leave, Norton was in urgent consultation with London stressing the dangers of an internal coup in Danzig that might result in the overthrow of the League of Nations administration there. When Chamberlain spoke in the House of Commons on 10 July, he warned that such a coup would 'involve a menace to Poland's independence which we have undertaken to defend'. A reference to the need for the Polish government to approach future talks with Germany 'objectively but with goodwill' was dropped after objections by Beck.[10]

Harold Nicolson was as ever an assiduous mixer in political circles in London. On 20 July he had gone to tea at the Soviet Embassy, where Maisky was still trying to convert people to the Soviet interpretation of 'indirect aggression'; so busily in fact that he forgot to offer his guests the tea they thought they had come for (Nicolson was lucky as he got a private audience in Maisky's study, where he was offered a large plate of sandwiches). Maisky, who was not to know that Molotov would drop his insistence on such a definition a couple of days later, told Nicolson that his belief was that, if Chamberlain got a compromise over Danzig, he would 'allow the Russian negotiations to lapse'. Maisky had a 'definite impression that the government do not really want the negotiations to go through'.[11] Nicolson then bustled round to have dinner with Lord Lothian, who had rejected the appeasement sympathies of the earlier thirties prior to being sent as British Ambassador to Washington. Lothian, Nicolson reported, had promised to behave like an 'affable moron' while in post in Washington.[12] In contrast to Nicolson, Channon's diary for the same period is remarkable for its absence of reference to the issue of a Soviet alliance and the Polish question. Only on 29 June is there the briefest of references to the great events in the wings of Channon's usual hectic social round. 'Hitler is a bandit,' he wrote, 'we are all mad; and Russia is winking slyly – and waiting.' This comment at least showed a degree of prescience, but otherwise Channon contented himself with assaults on critics of the Prime Minister such as Hugh Dalton, whom he described as 'that able but unattractive renegade'. (Tories continued to regard the old Etonian Dalton as a class traitor.)[13]

For Dalton himself the Polish issue was one of pressing urgency. Long a supporter of collective security, Dalton had thought that Halifax (or Eden, who had volunteered to go) should have been sent to Moscow in June and not a Foreign Office official like Strang. In the Foreign Affairs debate in the Commons on 31 July, Dalton had criticised Britain's 'dawdling diplomacy'. He had seen Halifax, he said at the Foreign Affairs Committee, as a 'Foreign Secretary in Chains', flanked on either side by the 'Man of Munich' and the 'Man of Manchukuo' (Simon). In the background, Dalton told the House, hovered the discredited Hoare.[14] He already much preferred Halifax to any of his colleagues but he flattered his abilities.

Some politicians, including Harold Macmillan, thought that the national emergency demanded a more broad-based National Government which would include Churchill, Eden and leaders of the Labour Party. Macmillan hoped that the *Daily Telegraph* owner, Lord Camrose, would be persuaded to start a campaign to that effect.[15] Chamberlain resisted all demands that 'Winston' should be included in his administration.

Over at the *Times*, Geoffrey Dawson still hoped that appeasement would carry the day and that a Polish settlement could be reached. He continued to ask whether Danzig was worth a war, replicating a French right-wing headline which demanded '*Mourir pour Danzig?*' The defection of Lothian was a blow, influenced perhaps by the fact that he had read the unexpurgated edition of *Mein Kampf*. Amongst the old Milner 'Kinder', Brand had always been resolutely anti-Nazi and he feared a repetition of Munich over Poland. He told Dawson of his fear that any surrender over Danzig would lead to war. 'Lately,' he told his old friend, 'I have had an uncomfortable feeling that the *Times* hates to face these facts.'[16]

In Warsaw Sir Howard Kennard, who had returned from leave on 30 July, was also convinced that the Poles must not be abandoned. The previous day, Halifax had underlined Britain's commitment in a speech at Chatham House in which he warned that Britain's 'immediate task ... is to resist aggression. I would emphasise that tonight with all the strength at my command, so that nobody may misunderstand it'.[17] The message for the Germans was clear-cut and unambiguous, but some felt that its tone might have been muffled by the alleged decision to offer the German representative, Dr Wohltat, a loan of £1000 million in exchange for an agreement on disarmament. Was economic appeasement compatible with the government's new search for security in Europe? In fact the loan was a myth.

Chamberlain had plainly not abandoned hope that agreement with Germany might still be possible. On 3 August, just as the British Military Mission to Moscow was setting out on its slow voyage to Leningrad, Sir Horace Wilson saw the German Ambassador, von Dirksen, and indicated British willingness to mediate over Danzig. But, at that very moment, a crisis was about to erupt in that city. On 4 August, the Poles learnt that the German authorities in Danzig intended to withdraw recognition of Polish customs inspectors and break treaty provisions by opening the border with East Prussia, that part of Germany which was isolated in the east by Polish territory. The Polish response was typically gritty. Should any such action be implemented, the Danzig Senate was told, Poland would regard it as an act of war. The orders must be withdrawn within twenty-four hours. London was not consulted before the Polish response was made. Kennard reminded Beck that His Majesty's Government must be consulted in future. On 5 April, the leader of the Danzig Senate, Arthur Greiser, telephoned the Poles to say that no such action had ever been contemplated. But by then the press in both Britain and France was talking about a 'climb down' by the Danzig

Senate. Hitler was furious and memories of the 'May Scare' of 1938 were stirred. The difference was that now, unlike in 1938, Hitler had already decided to strike. On 23 May, he had told his generals that Poland would always be on the side of Germany's enemies. The Reich needed living space and therefore 'it is not Danzig that is at stake'. In this context, Hitler had argued Poland must be attacked 'at the first suitable opportunity'.[18]

While a crisis blew up in Danzig, the House of Commons went on holiday on 4 August. Chamberlain's favourite pastime was fishing and he headed for the north of Scotland. The Foreign Office then heard on 10 August that Carl Burckhardt, the League of Nations High Commissioner, had agreed to go and talk to Hitler at Berchtesgaden about Danzig. Cadogan wanted to wait and see what emerged from this meeting, and Chamberlain and Halifax agreed. But things did not go well for Chamberlain even when he was on holiday. 'Everything is going wrong here from the fishing point of view',[19] he told his Principal Private Secretary, Syers, on 13 August. While he was away, a bizarre meeting took place on the Baltic island of Sylt between Göring and a deputation of British businessmen led by a Mr Charles F. Spencer, one of several unorthodox attempts that August to save the peace. Spencer dredged up the old chestnut of a four-power conference to settle the Danzig question, but the talks led nowhere. Did Chamberlain know about this meeting? There is no evidence that he did.

If Neville Chamberlain was finding it hard to catch fish in the Scottish Highlands, Professor Burckhardt found that his German adversary was starting to age. Burckhardt observed that Hitler 'looked ... much older and whiter. He gave the impression of fear, and seemed nervous, pathetic and almost shaken at times'. The Führer threatened the Poles with war if there were any further incidents in Danzig (now the subject of a ferocious Nazi press barrage), but told Burckhardt that he wished to 'live in peace with England' and even to guarantee its Empire. When he got back home to Basel, Burckhardt gave a description of his interview with Hitler to both the Foreign Office and the Quai d'Orsay.[20]

Hitler's assurances meant little without promises of good behaviour over Poland. Henderson told Cadogan on 15 August, 'We cannot yield, and I am afraid that I do not believe Hitler will either'.[21] This made war inevitable, despite Henderson's desperate efforts to prevent it. Ribbentrop's former aide, Spitzy, noted later how he met Henderson in the Dutch Legation in Berlin and how the British Ambassador begged him 'to make it clear to all my influential acquaintances that Britain would come in if Germany attacked Poland'.[22] As yet, however, the British government was not acting as if war was inevitable. The Cabinet Foreign Policy Committee, for example, did not meet at all between 1 August and 25 August. And the Under-Secretary of State at the Foreign Office, Butler, did not return from holiday until 24 August.

In Germany, Hitler's interpreter, Paul Schmidt, was also on holiday on the North Sea coast when a colleague from the Wilhelmstrasse phoned to order him to return to Berlin. He was not told why his services were required, and described how 'a sensation awaited me in the shape of a sealed envelope on my Foreign Office desk'.[23] The sensation was the news that Ribbentrop was to fly to Moscow to talk to Stalin and Molotov, and Schmidt would be going with him.

In England, 'Chips' Channon was staying at Kelvedon Hall when the news came through that the USSR and Germany were to sign a non-aggression pact. Channon's diary entry reflected the profound shock of the British establishment. In his view, 'The Russians have double-crossed us, as I always believed they would. They have been coquetting secretly with Germany, even as our negotiations proceeded. They are the foulest people on earth.'[24] There had, of course, been rumours about Soviet flirtations with the Germans, but the British government had convinced itself that the worst could not happen. The pact that was announced to the world on 23 August contained a secret protocol that provided for the division of Poland between the two powers along the line of the rivers Pissa, Narev, Vistula and San. The USSR was also given a free hand in Finland, Estonia and Latvia, and its interests in the Rumanian province of Bessarabia was recognised. Lithuania was to be part of the German zone of influence, although soon afterwards the primacy of the Soviet Union was recognised there also. The Nazi-Soviet Pact was nothing short of a diplomatic revolution. It sealed both the fate of the Poles and the European peace.

The shocking news accelerated R.A. Butler's return from his vacation. In Moscow, Molotov told Seeds that the German–Soviet rapprochement was entirely due to bad faith on the part of Britain and France. Poland was also to blame for refusing passage to Red Army troops in the event of war.[25] It was true that the biggest concession that the Poles were prepared to make (as late as 23 August) was that some form of Soviet–Polish cooperation could not be excluded in the event of a German attack. But by then, as the Frenchman Naggiar noted, this concession was not enough. It was also too late.[26]

Ribbentrop arrived with his entourage in Moscow that day, and the agreement was speedily concluded with Stalin playing a prominent part. He told Ribbentrop that the two sides had been 'pouring buckets of filth on each other for years' but now was the time for a new relationship. He also toasted the Germans and told their obnoxious Foreign Minister that he knew 'how much the German people loved their Führer'. (Rumour had it that Stalin even essayed a mock curtsey to the German delegation when he met them.) Ribbentrop was seen off with due pomp and ceremony at the railway station. Absurdly, he was to be lauded by Hitler as the greatest German statesman since Bismarck.

Halifax's reaction to the news from Russia was to underplay the extent of the catastrophe. Dining with a friend that night, he was reported as saying that 'in our agreement with Poland both we and they have always discounted Russia, so materially the situation is not so enormously changed'.[27] It is unlikely that Halifax can actually have been quite as sanguine as that. Chamberlain and he had only just drafted a letter to the Führer designed to make clear Britain's position if Hitler dared to attack Poland (this was in lieu of Henderson's other suggestion that General Ironside be sent to Berlin, presumably to overawe the Nazis with his imposing height). The letter was also designed to prevent a repetition of the 1914 scenario when Chamberlain believed that Sir Edward Grey had failed to make Britain's intentions clear.[28] News of the Nazi-Soviet Pact came through just as the draft, which had Cabinet approval, was about to be sent off to Germany. On 24 August, Chamberlain reassured the Commons about Britain's commitment to Poland, which neither Butler nor Henderson liked.

Were Chamberlain and his colleagues hopeless dupes where Stalin was concerned? It is clear from the evidence that the possibility of a Soviet-Nazi rapprochement was recognised, but it was ruled out as being beyond the bounds of practical politics. This was not unreasonable. Stalin and Hitler were dogmatists whose shrill propaganda had blasted their rivals for years, and the reluctance of the British to believe in such ideological apostasy should not surprise. Chamberlain had read enough about Nazi Germany to form the reasonable belief that hatred and animosity towards the USSR were the *sine qua non* of Hitler's foreign policy. How could anyone in British ruling circles have predicted that Fascists and Communists would bury the hatchet?

Stalin, after all, kept the Anglo-French in play until the last moment, when the territorial gains offered by Hitler proved too juicy a morsel to resist. The Anglo-French could not persuade the Poles to allow passage to the Red Army, but they also probably underestimated Stalin's problems in the Far East. In May and June 1939, there had been spasmodic fighting along the Soviet Mongolian frontier with Japanese Manchuria. The Japanese had been worsted by General Zhukov, but there was no certainty that hotheads in the Japanese Kwantung Army would not take advantage of the Red Army's involvement in a European war. Thus the Nazi-Soviet Pact, which has been portrayed as a Soviet Munich, was based on military calculation, just as Anglo-French policy had been a year earlier. If Britain and France needed time to rearm in 1938, so did the USSR in 1939.

As it was, even Churchill had to concede in his 1948 anti-appeasement polemic that whatever 'emotions the British Government may have experienced, fear was not among them'.[29] On 25 August, Hitler sent for Henderson and put forward a proposal which could not be deciphered back in London until the next day. Influenced, perhaps, by the vacillating behaviour of his ally Mussolini, who had reiterated his view that Italy was in no position to fight, he renewed his offer to guarantee the British Empire and declared that the German–Polish problem 'must be solved'.[30] Reaction to Hitler's initiative was mixed. Harvey thought the offer 'impudent' but Butler did not, wishing that the Foreign Office was less inhibited about putting pressure on the Poles to make concessions. Henderson had even taken to writing a letter to his *bête noire*, Ribbentrop, to prevent the greatest of all catastrophes.[31] But on that same day, 25 August, Chamberlain had transformed the guarantee to Poland into a full-blown military alliance. This at least had the result of forcing Hitler to postpone 'Case White' (the invasion of Poland) until 1 September. The 'little worms' as Hitler had called the British and French, were not, to his surprise, going to be intimidated by the pact with Stalin. Hitler would still have to fight a two-front war if he attacked the Poles.

Chamberlain's greatest critic, Churchill, had been oiling the wheels of the Entente Cordiale in mid-August. He flew to France on 14 August and was entertained by Gamelin's deputy, General Georges, before being taken to view sections of the Maginot Line, which had never been seen before by a foreigner. He was accompanied by the Tory MP Louis Spears, who had acted as a liaison officer with the French in the First World War and knew the country well (though some of the French military found him abrasive). On the way back to Paris a few days later, Churchill told his secretary, 'Before the harvest is gathered in – we shall be at war'.[32] He was back on London by 22 August before the news about the Nazi-Soviet Pact broke.

The last days of peace were beautiful and balmy in Britain, although a tremendous thunderstorm broke out with Wagnerian appropriateness over London on Saturday 2 September. Churchill had spent much of the preceding week wondering whether Chamberlain would now, with war imminent, offer him a job in the government. The Prime Minister had been back in London since 20 August giving consideration to the question of forming a War Cabinet, but also seemingly confident that the French army, even without Soviet help, could hold back the Wehrmacht in the west. But he also knew that, in the event of war, Britain would not have to fight Mussolini in the Mediterranean.

Parliament was recalled on 24 August and an Emergency Powers Bill was rushed through the House of Commons that day. Harold Nicolson speculated about whether Colonel Beck would 'lose his nerve and fly to Berchtesgaden'. He had heard that Chamberlain had offered to resign (this was untrue), but that King George had refused to accept his resignation. At the family home at Sissinghurst in Kent, Nicolson's wife, the writer Vita Sackville-West, wrote that the thought of air raids made her 'physically sick'. Nicolson thought Chamberlain 'dignified and calm' in the House of Commons (the source of the rumour about his resignation is a mystery).[33]

There was never any prospect of Beck going to Berchtesgaden. He, after all, had responded to a German accusation that Poland was negotiating at the point of a bayonet with a terse 'that is your method'. Instead, the last days of

August were marked by a round of amateur diplomacy, involving particularly the Swedish go-between, Birger Dahlerus, who was a friend of Göring's. On 27 August, Dahlerus visited 10 Downing Street with Halifax to tell Chamberlain that Göring was still working for peace. (It was true that of all the Nazi hierarchy, the Reichsmarshal seemed most disturbed by the prospect of war.) Dahlerus was soon followed by a harassed Nevile Henderson, who carried a message (flown over in a German plane) from Hitler offering yet another guarantee of the British Empire, in exchange for a renegotiation of the existing German–Polish Frontier. Chamberlain told Henderson to welcome the idea of renewed Polish–German talks without withdrawing Britain's guarantee of Polish integrity. The Poles were to be encouraged to talk about Danzig and the Corridor, but they knew (unlike the Czechs) that the guarantee was there as a safety net. They were adamant in their refusal to send a plenipotentiary to Berlin who might suffer the same fate as Hácha. This resolution alarmed Butler and Henderson, who felt that the Poles were being intransigent and dictating British policy.

Back came Dahlerus to Downing Street on 30 August to tell Chamberlain that Hitler would agree to a plebiscite in the Polish Corridor. But, given the way the Germans had manipulated plebiscites in the past, this was not an encouraging option. The offer was, in any case, coupled with the demand that the Poles must send a plenipotentiary to Berlin to accept Germany's terms over Danzig and the Corridor and the threat that, if they failed to do so, Poland would be invaded within twenty-four hours. Chamberlain told Dahlerus that this time limit was unreasonable but allowed the Swede to speak to Göring on the telephone. He thought the Poles ought to be prepared to go to Berlin, but would not try and coerce them into accepting Hitler's terms.

Real communication with Berlin had already broken down. On 29 August Hitler had a shouting match with Henderson, who had demanded that a Polish representative be sent by 30 August. The British were supposed to ensure this, which was plainly impossible as Henderson only got the German demand at 7.15 p.m. on 29 August. When Henderson pointed out that this demand sounded like an ultimatum, Hitler shouted that:

> I or His Majesty's Government did not give a row of pins whether Germans were slaughtered or not. I told him that I would not listen to such language from anybody ... I added [Henderson told the Foreign Office] a good deal more shouting of my own.

Two days later, Roger Makins of the Central Department minuted that Henderson was 'probably quite right to shout'.[34] Extreme provocation had been required to make Sir Nevile put aside old-world courtesy and raise his voice. His temper was to be sorely tested between 29 August and 3 September.

When the Cabinet met on 30 August, it was felt that, objectionable though Hitler's attitude was, it did not preclude further discussion with the Germans.[35]

Henderson saw Ribbentrop at midnight, but the German Foreign Minister gabbled through sixteen points at high speed (which included the demand that Danzig be returned, and the insistence on a plebiscite within the Corridor inside twelve months). Ribbentrop then refused to hand over the text of the document to Henderson, and shocked the British Ambassador by using the word 'damned'. Things got so heated that Paul Schmidt, present as ever as an interpreter, feared that Ribbentrop would throw the fifty-seven-year-old Henderson bodily out of the room.[36] Henderson himself was tempted to walk out but decided that it was his duty to try and extract more information from the pompous and irascible Ribbentrop. He failed.

For their part, the Poles remained determined not to send a plenipotentiary to Berlin. When their ambassador, Lipski, saw Ribbentrop at 1 p.m. on 31 August, he brought no new proposals, but when he tried to contact Warsaw afterwards he found that his telephone line had been cut. In March, German technology had failed when the wretched Hácha wanted to telephone Prague, now the Nazis wanted to ensure that Poland's representative in Berlin was isolated. The only common factor was the gangsterish breach of diplomatic convention and practice involved in the treatment of both men.

The British too had learnt from experience. There was to be no question of agreeing to Ciano's proposal for a great power conference on 5 September if this involved coercing the Poles. They themselves showed no interest in such a conference. In this sense, it has been rightly observed, 'Beck was the beneficiary of Beneš' calvary'.[37] And, one might add, that of Hácha. When Halifax suggested that Beck should get the text of Ribbentrop's sixteen points via Lipski in Berlin (this would plainly have been impossible as his telephone lines had been severed), he took no action. The crossing of Poland's borders by the Wehrmacht just before 5 a.m. on 1 September made such a move redundant in any case. When the news came through to Chamberlain, he convened a Cabinet meeting telling his colleagues that 'the event against which we had fought so long and so earnestly had come upon us'. Yet another message came through from the ultra-diligent Dahlerus saying that Hitler still wanted discussions. No one in the Cabinet took this message seriously, but Henderson was instructed to give Hitler a stern warning, without reference to a time limit about the consequences of German action.[38] Halifax had already confirmed to the Polish Ambassador in London, Raczynski, that German behaviour meant that the recently signed Anglo-Polish military agreement could be invoked. The Chiefs of Staff favoured an ultimatum by midnight on 1 September, but Chamberlain and Halifax laboured under the difficulty of trying to synchronise policy with the French.

The difficulties were a result of two factors. First, Bonnet was enthusiastic about Ciano's proposal for a conference and pleaded for one when the French Cabinet met on 31 August. (Daladier was so infuriated by his attitude that he turned his back on him.) Secondly, both Daladier and Gamelin wanted more time to mobilise the French forces and to evacuate the population from sensitive areas along the German border. Gamelin remarked, in a tone which was to be typical of Anglo-French acrimony ten months later, 'They want us to declare war today, but they are only going to send their aircraft tomorrow'. The French were unwilling to commit themselves to a time limit of less than forty-eight hours. Sir John Simon recorded later that Chamberlain and Halifax were involved over two days in an 'agonising struggle to get the French to take and announce contemporaneous action'.[39] As late as 1.30 p.m. on 2 September, the French government was still asking for a forty-eight hour time limit on any ultimatum to Germany. This opened Chamberlain to the accusation of foot-dragging when he tried to synchronise time limits and declarations of war. He and Halifax both thought it important that the Anglo-French declarations of war, when they came, should go out at the same time.

On the home front, there was one other important development on 1 September while German aircraft were pounding Warsaw and Cracow. This was Chamberlain's decision to offer Churchill a place in his War Cabinet (as yet without a portfolio), which he told the House of Commons about that evening. Throughout August London had been plastered with posters bearing the caption 'What Price Churchill?' No one seemed to know who was responsible, but the Prime Minister's decision owed nothing to any such pressure. Churchill was one of the few politicians available with real experience of running a war.[40]

At 4.30 p.m. on the afternoon of 2 September Chamberlain held another Cabinet meeting. He and Halifax still held off from sending an ultimatum with a time limit because of the problems with the French, preferring instead to send Henderson with another warning which would allow the Germans until midday on 3 September to reply without carrying the ultimate sanction of war. This was too much for a sizeable number of Cabinet Ministers led by Hoare, Kingsley Wood and Hore-Belisha, who were unhappy about the fact that no ultimatum had been sent to the Germans. It was also clear that the majority of the Cabinet were not prepared to extend a time limit to midnight on 3 September, as the Prime Minister and the Foreign Secretary then suggested. The mood of the dissidents was sharpened by a message from the Polish government demanding 'immediate fulfilment of British obligations to Poland', but they gave something of a hostage to fortune by allowing Chamberlain and Halifax to draft a statement to the Germans after consultations with the French. At 6.38 p.m. Halifax telephoned Ciano in Rome to let him know what the Cabinet had decided. There would be no British involvement in a conference without the withdrawal of German troops from Poland.

When Chamberlain spoke in the House of Commons that evening, however, his reference to consultations with the French went down very badly and the

mood turned ugly. Leo Amery made his famous interjection encouraging the
Labour Deputy Leader, Greenwood, to 'Speak for England', although it is generally forgotten that Greenwood's reply acknowledged Chamberlain's problem
with France by referring to 'reasons why instant action may not be taken'. The
Prime Minister had to get to his feet again to say that a definite statement about
a declaration of war would be made the next day, but that Britain and France
needed to keep in line.[41] Chamberlain's thinking here may have been influenced
by the memory of 1914, when at one point the French Ambassador Cambon
had become so indignant about what he regarded as British ambivalence
that he demanded that the word honour should be struck out of the English
dictionary.

Cabinet Ministers were also angry about what they (wrongly) took to be a
change of direction away from what had been agreed that afternoon. Chamberlain
found himself faced with what he described to his sister Ida as a 'sort of mutiny'
staged by some of those colleagues 'who always behave badly when there is
any trouble'.[42] This was not quite the case. The unlikely spokesperson for the
mutinous Ministers was John Simon, who met Stanley, MacDonald and others
in Simon's room in the House of Commons, where, forgetting that they had
agreed to Chamberlain and Halifax supervising links with Germany, they accused
Chamberlain of veering away from what was agreed in Cabinet. Chamberlain
then saw the disaffected Ministers at Downing Street, where he wisely refrained
from pointing out that they were in error. Simon delivered a letter after the
meeting which stated that the British ultimatum *must* expire at the latest by
twelve midday on 3 September. Chamberlain by now realised the seriousness
of the situation, and asked Simon to come and put the position to the French
Ambassador, Corbin, at 10 p.m. He then telephoned Daladier to tell him that his
parliamentary position might be in peril unless he went along with his colleagues.
Britain could not wait for a French ultimatum.

This done, Chamberlain called another Cabinet meeting for 11.30 p.m., where
the news that Britain would not wait for France defused the tension in the room.
It was agreed that Henderson should be instructed to present the British ultimatum to Ribbentrop at 9 a.m. on Sunday 3 September.[43] While all this was going
on, a frustrated Churchill had heard nothing further from Chamberlain about
his Cabinet post. At a meeting in his flat that night in Morpeth Mansions, Amery,
Eden, Duff Cooper, Bracken and Sandys urged him to go to the Commons next
day and 'break him [Chamberlain] and take his place'.[44] Churchill declined, as
this would effectively be a breach of the principle of Cabinet responsibility. He
must have known, in any case, as should his colleagues, that the Tories distrusted
him. If they ditched Chamberlain for anyone, it would be for Halifax not him.
Instead, Churchill wrote a letter to Chamberlain asking him, in the absence of
a further summons to Downing Street, how he stood. His position was clarified

the next day when Chamberlain offered him his old position as First Lord of the Admiralty.

The next morning, immaculately turned out as ever, Sir Nevile Henderson arrived at the Wilhelmstrasse on the stroke of nine o'clock. He was to be spared another confrontation with Ribbentrop, finding only the interpreter Schmidt there to receive the British ultimatum. Both men were in sombre mood. Schmidt expressed regret that they had to meet in such circumstances and spoke of his high regard for the British Ambassador. Henderson returned the compliment, but he was a bitterly disappointed man. His Embassy Third Secretary, Etherington Smith, recorded how, when he had taken him the telegram which included the text of the ultimatum, Henderson had remarked, 'they are only doing this to give them the satisfaction of kicking a dictator in the pants'.[45] It was the disillusionment of the moment. Shortly afterwards, Henderson was to tell an American journalist, William Hillman, that the 'people governing Germany today are utterly worthless'.[46] Henderson would have got some comfort, had he known about it, from Hitler's angry response when the British ultimatum was delivered to the Reich Chancellery later. Turning to Ribbentrop, who had convinced him that the British would never fight over Poland, he asked 'What now?'[47]

In London, Frank Roberts, the desk officer in the Central Department at the Foreign Office, received a phone call at 10.50 a.m., just ten minutes before the British ultimatum to Germany was to expire. It was the dogged Dahlerus now suggesting that Göring should fly to London (he had already ordered an aircraft to be on standby). Roberts used his authority flatly to reject the proposal.

The last act of the drama was played out in Downing Street. Chamberlain had checked that there was no response from Germany before telling the BBC that he would be ready to broadcast to the British people at 11.15 a.m. The BBC was not his favourite organisation, as it had made a number of attacks on him, normally in the form of selective reporting of speeches and debates. He had been sufficiently concerned about what he regarded as inaccurate BBC analysis of the significance of the Polish guarantee, Cadogan noted, to want Warsaw approached, so that there was no misunderstanding of its status (the BBC had implied that the Poles alone would decide when the guarantee was implemented). The former British Ambassador in Rome, Lord Perth, who knew something about broadcasting, also complained to Halifax in November 1938 about a 'scrappy and inadequate' BBC account of a speech Chamberlain had made in the House of Commons.[48]

This being a live broadcast, however, there was nothing the BBC could do to alter the record when he spoke that morning. He struck a very personal note from the outset. 'You can imagine', he said in a tone which conveyed the depth of his personal agony, 'what a bitter blow it is to me that all my long struggle to win the peace has failed.' Chamberlain told his people about the British ultimatum and how no German reply had been received, but he did not, as critics have alleged, indulge in maudlin self-pity. Instead the radio audience were rightly reminded of how Britain was going to the aid of Poland, which was 'so bravely resisting this wicked and unprovoked attack on her people. We have a clear conscience. We have done all that any country could do to establish peace'. The situation had been created, Chamberlain reminded his listeners, because 'no word given by Germany's ruler could be trusted and no people or country could feel themselves safe'. He finished by warning them that it would be 'evil things that we shall be fighting against – brute force, bad faith, injustice, oppression and persecution – and against them I am certain that right will prevail'. Even Churchill with all his rhetorical gifts could not have put it better.[49]

At noon on that fateful morning, Chamberlain went to the House of Commons to tell MPs about Hitler's unwillingness to compromise. Again he told of his personal distress that 'everything that I have worked for, everything that I have believed in during my public life has crashed into ruins'.[50] Chamberlain was speaking the truth, and he was entitled to remind his colleagues of his efforts to save the European peace. Britain was entering a long dark night of struggle and privation, and there was nothing ignoble about Chamberlain's desire to tell people of how supremely worthwhile his personal efforts had been, even though they ended in failure. But then, as Horace Rumbold had reminded Henderson in another context, no one could ultimately have succeeded with Hitler.

Later that day, Winston Churchill drove to Admiralty House to take up his new post. A message, the appropriately phrased 'Winston's back', had already been sent out to Royal Navy units across the globe and for Churchill new horizons beckoned. But in the Foreign Office, though events appeared to vindicate him, Vansittart was still marooned in his powerless post as Chief Diplomatic Adviser. He was sufficiently annoyed by Henderson's account of the 'circumstances leading to the termination of his mission to Berlin' to rouse himself for one last counterblast on 20 September. 'From the advent of the Nazi regime', Vansittart wrote, 'there was never the least chance that any course could or would be pursued other than that which was in fact pursued.'[51]

Henderson would not have agreed. He continued to see the war as a result of accident rather than design. He was back in England by 7 September, noting the lack of enthusiasm for war of the older generation of Germans as he passed out of their country for the last time. His offer to return to his old post in Belgrade was turned down by the Foreign Office, and he lost most of his belongings, which, for some unexplained reason, were interned in Berne for the duration of the war. He died in 1942. By a bizarre historical twist, Henderson's clothes were used by British escapees from Nazi imprisonment en route for home via Switzerland. (Clifford Norton, who had criticised Henderson's views on Poland, found himself wearing Henderson's carpet slippers when he became the British Minister in Switzerland in 1942.)[52]

Stanley Baldwin, who had warned Chamberlain about the great power that his post-Munich popularity had placed in his hands, had been in the United States in August 1939. He and his wife left New York on 20 August, intending to take their usual holiday in Aix-les-Bains. But from Le Havre their ship was diverted to Cork because of the outbreak of war. Even though he was seventy-two, Baldwin agreed to take in some evacuees from Britain's threatened cities.[53] His protégé Anthony Eden entered the War Cabinet as Secretary of State for War only when Churchill became Prime Minister in May 1940. Chamberlain extended an olive branch to the extent of making Eden Dominions Secretary outside the Cabinet on the outbreak of war. To that extent Eden's reluctance to distance himself from the government and appeasement paid off. Having been in government in the trying years after 1935, he had a greater sense of the difficulties Baldwin and Chamberlain had faced.

12

Verdict

On 11 May 1940, the day after Winston Churchill replaced Neville Chamberlain as Prime Minister, Sir Horace Wilson arrived for work at No. 10 Downing Street as usual. In 1937, Chamberlain had given him a room next to the Cabinet Room looking out over the Horseguards Parade. As he opened the door, he saw Randolph Churchill and Brendan Bracken sitting opposite him on the sofa. 'They stared at Sir Horace, but no one spoke or smiled. Then he withdrew, never to return to that seat most proximate to power.'[1] So wrote Hugh Dalton about the disappearance of Horace Wilson, Chamberlain's *éminence grise*, from the corridors of power. He is made to fall like Lucifer (although at the very least Wilson must have been back to collect his personal effects). The passage is used, characteristically, to finish *The Appeasers*, the 1963 polemic against Baldwin, Chamberlain and all they stood for.[2] After the dull (and incompetent) Roundheads, the glamorous and courageous Cavaliers rode in. And the English Civil War analogy is carried further. The 'decayed serving men' are pensioned off one by one. Hoare is exiled to the Embassy in Madrid, the dry and colourless Simon is retired to his natural home on the Woolsack, Halifax punished by being sent to the Washington Embassy while Chamberlain himself waits merely to die that November.[3]

Where Chamberlain is concerned at least, it is a travesty of the truth, and Halifax too has some claim to having had his reputation unfairly besmirched. For Chamberlain and Churchill worked well enough in government between September 1939 and May 1940, when Chamberlain was forced to stand down, largely because of Labour's old animosity against him, which made Attlee and his colleagues unwilling to serve in a National Government under Chamberlain's leadership. Ironically, it was Churchill's own failed Norway operation which brought about Chamberlain's fall, although he briefly considered soldiering on when the news came in of Hitler's offensive in the West on 10 May.

On his appointment as Prime Minister that day, Churchill memorably wrote that he felt as if he 'were walking with destiny, and that all my past life has been but a preparation for this hour and this trial'.[4] In a real sense this was true, and it can indeed be argued that Chamberlain, the man of peace, ought to have resigned on the outbreak of war. All his instincts were for peace, but he felt it was his duty to continue in office. Nevertheless, as he told the Archbishop of Canterbury that Christmas, he found 'war more hateful than ever and I groan in spirit over every life lost and every home blasted'.[5] But he found that, despite their former differences, Churchill was a loyal subordinate, albeit as ever one who wanted a finger in every pie. Chamberlain had always appreciated Churchill's brilliant qualities, but it was sometimes those very qualities which made him such a difficult colleague.

Loyalty was reciprocated when Churchill came to lead the government. Chamberlain became Lord President of the Council and would also have liked to have become Leader of the House of Commons (Churchill also wanted this, so that the experienced ex-Premier could relieve him of the burden of arranging day-to-day business in the Commons). But Labour was unwilling to put aside its partisan objection to Chamberlain and vetoed the suggestion. Nevertheless, and crucially, Chamberlain continued to be the Leader of the Tory Party.

Just why this was important was demonstrated when Churchill and Chamberlain sat together on the Front Bench for the first time on 13 May. Chamberlain received a great ovation from the Conservatives, whereas the cheers for Churchill came almost exclusively from the Labour benches. Channon, who had described Chamberlain's resignation on 10 May as 'perhaps the darkest day in English history', noted that when Churchill rose to speak, 'he was not well received'.[6] Thereafter, Churchill was only able to walk with destiny because Chamberlain was able to deliver the Tory Party. This was something that the new Prime Minister freely acknowledged. But by the autumn of 1940, Chamberlain was a grievously sick man with bowel cancer. He died at Heckfield Park in Hampshire on 9 November 1940, leaving poor Baldwin to suffer the brickbats and abuse of the anti-appeasers. Churchill, who could be generous when he did not feel impelled to doctor the historical record, gave the funeral oration in Church House, Westminster, as the House of Commons had suffered bomb damage.

> We can be sure [he said] that Neville Chamberlain acted with perfect sincerity according to his lights and strove to the utmost of his capacity and authority, to save the world from the awful, devastating struggle in which we are now engaged. This alone will stand him in good stead as far as what is called the verdict of history is concerned.[7]

For many years, in fact, Chamberlain's good faith and sincerity was questioned and traduced, as was that of Baldwin and Chamberlain's other colleagues.

One has to return here to the military disaster of 1940 for which the appeasers bore the odium. The extraordinary speed of that defeat, not Britain's alone, has been forgotten in the rush to judgement, just as has the fact that the application of Allied air power more judiciously might have prevented a smashing German triumph. Along with the Meuse and Dunkirk critics have tended to jettison the great British aerial victory in the summer of 1940, or at least the preparation for it, where Baldwin and Chamberlain deserve some praise.

Baldwin and Chamberlain (still less MacDonald) were not military men. They relied on the inexact science of military prediction by the Chiefs of Staff and other military advisers. In 1924, a British Cabinet Minister wrote: 'A war with Japan. But why a war with Japan? I do not believe there is the slightest chance of it in our lifetime ... She cannot menace our security in any way.'[8] That Minister was Winston Churchill, then occupying the key position of Chancellor of the Exchequer, which he used to insist on a reduction of one-third in the Admiralty's proposed expenditure on the Singapore base that was the linchpin of Britain's Far Eastern defences. Churchill *was* a military man who prided himself on his knowledge of military and naval matters. Yet he continued to ridicule the idea that the Japanese might be a threat, and in 1942 Singapore fell to the Japanese in the most humiliating of circumstances. It could also be argued that Churchill's slavish adherence to the notorious 'Ten Year Rule' made the task of his successors in the thirties infinitely more difficult.

All this means is that politicians in office sometimes get things wrong, something for which Baldwin and Chamberlain paid in full measure, whereas Churchill (rightly praised as a great war leader) has escaped similar castigation for numerous errors. As he himself recognised in a typically Churchillian aside: 'I have frequently been made to eat my words. I have always found them a most nourishing diet!'

The task that faced Baldwin and Chamberlain was a truly daunting one. At the heart of it, as the long-serving Cabinet Secretary Maurice Hankey recognised, was the problem of dealing with Hitler:

> Are we dealing with the Hitler of *Mein Kampf*, lulling his opponents to sleep with fair words ... Or is it a new Hitler, who has discovered the burden of responsible office, and wants to extricate himself, like many an earlier tyrant, from the commitments of his earlier irresponsible days?[9]

The situation would have been difficult enough had Britain only had to deal with Nazism, but the uncertain, unscrupulous policies of Mussolini and the Japanese also had to be contended with. And this at a time when Britain was an economic convalescent recovering from a depression more severe than the world had ever seen.

In the last phase of a long parliamentary career, Churchill himself was to recognise the virtues of appeasement:

> Those who are prone by temperament and character to seek sharp and clear-cut solutions of difficult and obscure problems, who are ready to fight whenever some challenge comes from a foreign power, have not been always right. On the other hand, those whose inclination is to bow their heads to seek patiently and faithfully for peaceful compromise are not always wrong.[10]

At the height of the Cold War, Churchill also recognised that 'jaw, jaw is better than war, war'.

The danger of generalisation about the appeasers remains apparent. Chamberlain, after the Fall of France, was just as doughty as Churchill about the need to fight on, while Hoare, decried as possessing the fighting qualities of a maiden aunt, was always the foremost advocate in Cabinet of that very alliance with the USSR which was the crux of Churchill's Grand Alliance. Baldwin was quick to understand the threat of air power to Britain's island security, and Halifax could go through a crisis of conscience about the Sudetenland which would never have troubled Stalin or Molotov. Examination of Churchill's record in 1938–39 also suggests that he was actually moving closer to the government position on rearmament, as it sought to deal with an increasingly complex and difficult global situation. Instead therefore of castigating Chamberlain, Baldwin and their colleagues for dereliction of duty on their watch, it is wiser to consider the context in which they operated when 'there were no good policies available ... only a choice between evils and dangers'.[11] Appeasement failed in the end because these evils were insurmountable without the use of force, but British statesmen recognised the need to try conciliation before they resorted to force, knowing as they did the terrible price in blood and treasure demanded in twentieth-century warfare. For this they can be accounted men of honour, cursed by the fact that, in the poet W.H. Auden's words, the 1930s was 'a low dishonest decade' in international relations.

Notes

Notes to Introduction

1   R. Graves and A. Hodge, *The Long Weekend* (London, 1940), p. 439.
2   A particularly bizarre example is A. Finkel and C. Leibovitz, *The Chamberlain–Hitler Collusion* (London, 1997).
3   See, for example, M. Gilbert and R. Gott, *The Appeasers* (London, 1963), recently issued in a new edition with no updating of its bibliography, let alone its perspective.
4   Dramatisations like *Winston Churchill: The Wilderness Years* (Southern Television, 1981) and *The Gathering Storm* (Channel Four Films, 2002) are typical of the way the Churchill perspective has become mainstream. There have, in addition, been numerous documentaries taking the same line.
5   See S. Aster, *1939: The Making of The Second World War* (London, 1973), and 'Guilty Men', in R. Boyce and E. Robertson, *Paths to War: New Essays on the Origins of the Second World War* (London, 1989); R.A.C. Parker's two titles are *Chamberlain and Appeasement* (London, 1993) and *Churchill and Appeasement* (London, 2000).
6   P. Kennedy, 'Appeasement', in G. Martel (ed.), *The Origins of the Second World War Reconsidered: The A.J.P. Taylor Debate after Twenty-Five Years* (London, 1986), p. 156.

Notes to Chapter 1: Armistice

1   M. Macmillan, 'Afterword', to J. Grigg, *Lloyd George: War Leader* (London, 2002), p. 638; with characteristic vengefulness the French were forced to sign the 1940 armistice in the same railway carriage by Hitler. Then transported to Germany, the carriage was later destroyed in an air raid.
2   House of Lords Record Office, Bonar Law Papers, box 70, 500, B 11/11/18.
3   D. Lloyd George, *War Memoirs* (London, 1938), pp. 3329–330.
4   A. Lentin, *Guilt at Versailles: Lloyd George and the Pre-History of Appeasement* (Leicester, 1984), p. 13.
5   Quoted in K. Middlemass and J. Barnes, *Baldwin* (London, 1969), pp. 70–71.
6   Neville Chamberlain to Ida Chamberlain, 16/11/18, Chamberlain Archive, University of Birmingham; a feature of Chamberlain's life was his regular correspondence with his sisters Ida and Hilda.

7   N. Chamberlain, *Norman Chamberlain* (Birmingham, 1923).

8   Lord Vansittart, *The Mist Procession* (London, 1958), p. 193.

9   Ibid., p. 220.

10 Sir N. Henderson, *Water under the Bridges* (London, 1945), pp. 88–89; Henderson's first memoir, *Failure of a Mission* (London, 1940), gives an account of his time as Ambassador in Berlin from 1937 to 1939.

11 Lord Avon, *Another World, 1897–1917* (London, 1976), p. 150.

12 A. Horne, *Macmillan*, i, *1894–1956* (London, 1988), p. 47.

13 Quoted in M. Gilbert, *Churchill: A Life* (London, 1991), p. 401.

14 A. Hitler, *Mein Kampf*, trans. Ralph Manheim with an introduction by D.C. Watt (London, 1973), pp. 185–87.

Notes to Chapter 2: The Birth of Appeasement

1   *Daily Mail*, 12/12/18.

2   D. Lloyd George, *The Great Crusade: Extracts from Speeches Delivered during the War* (London, 1918), pp. 180–81.

3   A. Lentin, *Guilt at Versailles* (Leicester, 1984), p. 19. The other seminal texts on Versailles are A. Sharp, *The Versailles Settlement: Peacemaking in Paris 1919* (London, 1991); A. Lentin, *The Versailles Peace Settlement: Peacemaking with Germany* (Oxford, 2003) (first published by the Historical Association, London, 1991); and M. Macmillan, *Peacemakers: The Paris Conference of 1919 and its Attempt to End War* (London, 2001).

4   In fact, the myth that the Allies were deliberately starving the German population had no substance. The Germans also refused to meet the Allied request that their merchant ships should be sent out to be filled with food. In the end, Allied merchant ships had to do the job and supplies arrived in March 1919 well before German supplies were exhausted. See E. Eyck, *A History of the Weimar Republic* (Cambridge, Massachusetts, 1962), pp. 88–89; Admiralty to Foreign Office, 19/4/19, m 10630, FO 371/3776.

5   J.M. Keynes, *The Economic Consequences of the Peace* (London, 1919).

6   M. Macmillan, *Peacemakers*, p. 46.

7   Lentin, *Guilt at Versailles*, p. 75.

8   K. Ingham, *Jan Christian Smuts: The Conscience of a South African* (London, 1986), p. 75.

9   Smuts to Lloyd George, 4/6/19, *Smuts Papers*, iv, ed., K. Hancock and van der Poel (Cambridge, 1966), pp. 219–21.

10 Quoted in C. Mee Jr, *The End of Order: Versailles 1919* (London, 1981), p. 194.

11 Quoted in N. Rose, *Harold Nicholson* (London, 2005), p. 97.

12 Ingham, *Smuts*, pp. 109–10.

13 Mee, *The End of Order*, p. 151.

14 A. Lentin, *Lloyd George and the Lost Peace: From Versailles to Hitler, 1919–40* (Basingstoke, 2001), p. 18.

15 N. Rose, *The Cliveden Set: Portrait of an Exclusive Fraternity* (London, 2001), p. 109.

16 J.R.M. Butler, *Lord Lothian* (London, 1960), p. 77.

17 Ibid., pp. 72–73; Macmillan, *Peacemakers*, pp. 271–72.

18 Lord Vansittart, *Lessons of My Life* (London, 1944), p. 21.

19 Sir N. Henderson, *Water under the Bridges* (London, 1945), pp. 93–94; for Henderson's later correspondence with Lothian, see Lothian to Henderson, 11/5/37, Lothian to Henderson 14/4/38, and Henderson to Lothian 22/4/38, Lothian Papers, National Archives of Scotland, GD 40/17/204, GD 40/17/32.

20 H. Nicolson, *Peacemaking 1919* (London, 1933), p. 321.

21 D. Lloyd George, *The Truth about the Peace Treaties* (London, 1938), p. 9.

22 Rose, *The Cliveden Set*, p. 109.

23 Lentin, *Lloyd George and the Lost Peace*, p. 71.

24 Ibid., p. 71.

25 D.C. Watt, 'Foreword', in *Chatham House and British Foreign Policy, 1919–45* (Edinburgh, 1994), i.

26 In 1922 Chatham House moved into its permanent home at 10 St James's Square, London.

27 Lentin, *Lloyd George and the Lost Peace*, p. 80.

28 N. Rose, *Churchill: An Unruly Life* (London, 1994), p. 143.

29 M. Gilbert, *Churchill: Companion Volume IV*, i, p. 603.

30 Ibid., ii, p. 1191.

31 Lentin, *Lloyd George and the Lost Peace*, p. 75.

32 See D. Lloyd George, *The Truth about the Peace Treaties and Memoirs of the Peace Conference* (New Haven, 1939).

33 M. Dockrill, *British Establishment Perspectives on France, 1936–40* (Basingstoke, 1999), p. 5.

34 Quoted in J. Ferris, *The Evolution of British Strategic Policy, 1919–26* (Basingstoke, 1989), p. 128.

35 Dilks, *Neville Chamberlain*, p. 304.

36 Baldwin to Ponsonby, 30/5/23, quoted in M. Cowling, *The Impact of Labour, 1920–4: The Beginning of Modern British Politics* (Cambridge, 1971), pp. 306–7.

37 Lord D'Abernon, *An Ambassador of Peace*, ii, p. 9 (3 vols, London, 1929–31); for the definitive study of D'Abernon, see G. Johnson, *The Berlin Embassy of Lord D'Abernon, 1920-26* (Basingstoke, 2002).

38 Lentin, *The Versailles Peace Settlement*, p. 16.

39 R.C. Self (ed.), *The Austen Chamberlain Diary and Letters* (Cambridge, 1995), p. 270; in making this remark, Chamberlain was paraphrasing Bismarck's statement that the Balkans were 'not worth the bones of a Pomeranian grenadier'.

40 E. Goldstein, 'The Evolution of British Diplomatic Strategy for the Locarno Pact, 1924–5', in M. Dockrill and B. McKercher (eds), *Diplomacy and World Power: Studies in British Foreign Policy, 1890–1950* (Cambridge, 1996), pp. 124-25.

41 Chamberlain to D'Abernon, 18/3/25, Documents on British Foreign Policy, 1/27/255.

42 G. Stewart, *Burying Caesar: Churchill, Chamberlain and the Battle for the Tory Party* (London, 1999), p. 201.

43 Ibid.

44 Norman Chamberlain to Neville Chamberlain, 20/5/17, quoted in *Norman Chamberlain: A Memoir* (Birmingham, 1923), p. 140.

Notes to Chapter 3: Hitler Comes to Power

1   For excellent detailed analysis of the decline and fall of the Weimar Republic, see I. Kershaw (ed.), *Weimar: Why Did German Democracy Fail?* (London, 1990), and D. Peukert, *The Weimar Republic* (Frankfurt, 1987).

2   Lord Vansittart, *The Mist Procession* (London, 1958), p. 279.

3   'The United Kingdom and Europe', 1/1/1932, CP 4 (32), CAB 24/227.

4   Ibid.

5   T. Jones, 7/2/33, *A Diary with Letters, 1931–50* (Oxford, 1954), p. 89.

6   Ibid., 3/8/34, p. 137.

7   Ibid., 17/5/36, p. 199.

8   Ibid., 15/1/37, p. 304.

9   Lentin, *Lloyd George and the Lost Peace*, p. 92.

10 P. Schmidt, *Hitler's Interpreter* (New York, 1950), p. 56.

11 Ibid.; Schmidt's account is supported by Ribbentrop's aide, R. Spitzy, see *How We Squandered the Reich*, trans. G.T. Waddington (Norwich, 1997), p. 123, who wrote that Lloyd George had been 'much taken with the Führer and his ideas'.

12 Lentin, *Lloyd George and the Lost Peace*, p. 98.

13 Sylvester, *The Real Lloyd George* (London, 1947), p. 148.

14 Ibid., p. 204.

15 'Notes of a Conversation between Lloyd George and Hitler at Berchtesgaden, 4 September 1936', appendix to M. Gilbert, *The Roots of Appeasement* (London, 1966), p. 198.

16 Jones, *A Diary with Letters*, p. 251.

17 Ibid.

18 Ibid., p. 250.

19 P. Rowland, *Lloyd George* (London, 1975), p. 736.

20 Lentin, *Lloyd George and the Lost Peace*, p. 157 n. 82.

21 Frances Lloyd George (Stevenson), *The Years That Are Past* (London, 1967), p. 257.

22 Lloyd George to Conwell Evans, 17/12/37, quoted in Rowland, *Lloyd George*, p. 745.

23 W.S. Churchill, *The Gathering Storm* (London, 1948), p. 211.

24 Ibid.

25 The two men later fell out, and Hanfstaengl was lucky to escape Germany with his life.

26 M. Gilbert, *Churchill: A Life* (London, 1991), p. 508.

27 W.S. Churchill, *Great Contemporaries* (London, 1935), p. 203.

28 Quoted in N. Rose, *The Cliveden Set: Portrait of an Exclusive Fraternity* (London, 2001), p. 152.

29 Dawson had dropped his original name of Robinson.

30 Dawson to Lothian, 23/5/37, unpublished letter, Lothian Papers, Scottish Public Record Office, Edinburgh.

31 As is clearly demonstrated in Rose, *The Cliveden Set*.

32 Lord Astor to Garvin, 8/5/37, Garvin Papers, Astor File, University of Texas at Austin, Texas.

33 Although Astor was enthusiastic when Garvin published pro-appeasement articles in *The Observer* and urged him to do so. See R. Cockett, *Twilight of Truth: Chamberlain: Appeasement and the Manipulation of the Press* (London, 1989), pp. 25–26.

34   B. Granzow, *A Mirror of Nazism: British Opinion and the Emergence of Hitler, 1929–33* (London, 1964), pp. 56–57.
35   Ibid.
36   A. Howard, *RAB: The Life of R.A. Butler* (London, 1987), p. 76.
37   R. Blythe, *The Age of Illusion: England in the Twenties and Thirties* (London, 1963), p. 291.
38   Ibid., p. 287.
39   K. Harris, *Attlee* (London, 1982), p. 115.
40   B. Pimlott, *Dalton* (London, 1985), p. 227.
41   *Dalton Diaries*, 29–30/4/33 (London School of Economics).
42   Blythe, *The Age of Illusion*, p. 286.
43   Ibid.
44   An accusation which has been most effectively demolished by his latest biographer. See P. Williamson, *Stanley Baldwin* (Cambridge, 1999), pp. 294–99.
45   Jones, *A Diary with Letters*, 18/9/35.
46   K. Middlemass and J. Barnes, *Baldwin: A Biography* (London, 1969), p. 722.
47   H. Montgomery Hyde, *Neville Chamberlain* (London, 1976), p. 78.
48   Final Report of the Defence Requirements Committee, 28/2/34, CP 64 (34) CAB 24/247.
49   A. Horne, *Macmillan*, i, *1894–1956*, the first volume of the official biography (London, 1988), p. 112.
50   R. Rhodes James, *Bob Boothby: A Portrait* (London, 1991), p. 147.
51   Ibid.
52   House of Commons Debates, 270, CC 632–38, November 1932.
53   *'Chips': The Diaries of Sir Henry Channon*, ed. R. Rhodes James (London, 1967), 16/3/35, p. 28.
54   Lord Templewood, *Nine Troubled Years* (London, 1954), p. 159.
55   A. Roberts, *Eminent Churchillians* (London, 1994), p. 5.
56   For detail on such German aspirations, see J. Weiss, *Hitler's Diplomat: The Life and Times of Joachim von Ribbentrop* (New York, 1992), pp. 137–38.
57   P. Ziegler, *King Edward VIII* (London, 1990), p. 392.
58   Ibid.
59   Ibid.
60   Ibid., p. 210.
61   D. Clemens, *Herr Hitler in Germany: Wahrnehmung und Deutungen des Nationalsozialismus in Grossbrittannien, 1920 bis 1939* (Göttingen, 1995), p. 289.

Notes to Chapter 4: Four Appeasers

1   The definitive works on Baldwin are K. Middlemass and J. Barnes, *Baldwin* (London, 1969), and P. Williamson, *Stanley Baldwin* (Cambridge, 1999). Less scholarly, but with his usual literary polish, is R. Jenkins, *Baldwin* (London, 1987), while a family perspective is provided in A.W. Baldwin, *My Father: The True Story* (London, 1955).

2   Jenkins, *Baldwin* (London, 1987), p. 32.
3   Middlemass and Barnes, *Baldwin* (London, 1969) p. 15; for additional speculation about the importance of this episode, see Jenkins, *Baldwin*, p. 32, and F. Williams, *A Pattern of Rulers*.
4   Quoted in T. Jones, *A Diary with Letters, 1931–50* (Oxford, 1954), p. 155.
5   Jenkins, *Baldwin*, p. 37.
6   Baldwin Papers, Cambridge University Library, 42, fos 3–10.
7   R. Jenkins, *The Chancellors* (London, 1998), p. 247.
8   Williamson, *Stanley Baldwin*, p. 29.
9   M. Gilbert, *Winston S. Churchill*, iv, *1916–22* (London, 1975), pp. 59–60; Williamson, *Stanley Baldwin*, p. 33; Jones, WD II, 8 November 1924.
10   HNKY 1/7, Hankey diary 22/3/1925.
11   E. Goldstein, 'The Locarno Pact, 1924–5', in M. Dockrill and B. McKercher (eds), *Diplomacy and World Power: Studies in British Foreign Policy, 1890–1950*, p. 132.
12   Ibid., p. 135.
13   S. Baldwin, *On England* (London, 1926).
14   Ibid., p. 83.
15   Ibid., p. 84.
16   Ibid.
17   Ibid., p. 85.
18   Lord Templewood, *Nine Troubled Years* (London, 1954), p. 34.
19   Ibid.
20   G.M. Young, *Baldwin* (London, 1952), p. 152.
21   Templewood, *Nine Troubled Years*, pp. 32–33.
22   Stanley Baldwin to Thomas Jones, *A Diary with Letters*, 14/9/33.
23   Williamson, *Stanley Baldwin*, pp. 313–14.
24   House of Commons Debates, 289 c 2139, 18/5/34.
25   *Times*, 31/10/35.
26   W.S. Churchill, *The Gathering Storm* (London, 1948), index 607.
27   The Andros episode is described in detail in D. Dilks, *Neville Chamberlain*, i, *1869–1929*, pp. 39–54. Other biographies of Chamberlain include K. Feiling, *Neville Chamberlain* (London, 1946); I. Macleod, *Neville Chamberlain* (London, 1961); and H. Montgomery Hyde, *Neville Chamberlain* (London, 1976). R.A.C. Parker, *Chamberlain and Appeasement* (Oxford, 1993), has a valuable chapter on Chamberlain's personality and outlook, while D. Dutton, *Neville Chamberlain* (London, 2001) is a must for an evaluation of the historical debate about Chamberlain.
28   Montgomery Hyde, *Neville Chamberlain*, pp. 87–89.
29   Neville Chamberlain to A. Greenwood, 13/6/08.
30   D. Dilks, *Neville Chamberlain*, p. 113.
31   Quoted in Hyde, *Neville Chamberlain*, p. 27.
32   Neville Chamberlain Diary, 17/2/18. Chamberlain made his entry when the circumstances of Norman's death had been confirmed.
33   For the complexities surrounding these appointments, see Dilks, *Neville Chamberlain*, pp. 399–400.

34   S. Ball (ed.), 'Parliament and Politics in the Age of Baldwin and MacDonald', *The Headlam Diaries, 1923–35* (London, 1992), p. 203.

35   Important studies of Eden include D. Carlton, *Anthony Eden* (London, 1981); D. Dutton, *Anthony Eden: A Life and a Reputation* (London, 1997); and A.R. Peters, *Anthony Eden at The Foreign Office, 1931–38* (Aldershot, 1986). Eden's own memoir (by then he had become Lord Avon) on the 1930s, *Facing The Dictators*, published in 1962, has to be treated with caution because of Eden's transparent attempts at self-justification.

36   D. Carlton, *Anthony Eden*, p. 11.

37   A.R. Peters, *Anthony Eden at the Foreign Office, 1931–39*, p. 3.

38   Lord Vansittart, *The Mist Procession* (London, 1958), p. 429.

39   A. Roberts, *'The Holy Fox': A Biography of Lord Halifax* (London, 1991), p. 6.

40   Hickleton Papers, 20/10/1892.

41   The Earl of Birkenhead, *Halifax: The Life of Lord Halifax* (London, 1965), p. 54.

42   Roberts, *'The Holy Fox'*, p. 8.

43   Birkenhead, *Halifax*, p. 106.

44   A. Roberts, *Eminent Churchillians* (London, 1994), p. 12; Roberts's error is even more reprehensible because he is also a biographer of Halifax! On page 11 of *'The Holy Fox'*, he *does* mention Halifax's military service, although revealingly not the fact that he was mentioned in despatches. The error referred to above is repeated in *'The Holy Fox'* on p. 50.

45   Charmley, *Chamberlain and the Lost Peace*, p. 14.

46   Roberts, *'The Holy Fox'*, p. 16.

47   A.J.P. Taylor, *Beaverbrook* (London, 1972), p. 270.

48   India Office Library and Records, C152/18 13/11 29.

49   Ibid., C152/27 10/3/31.

Notes to Chapter 5: Italy and Japan

1   N. Rose, *Churchill: An Unruly Life* (London, 1994), p. 236.

2   R. Bosworth, *Mussolini* (London, 2002), p. 184.

3   *DBFP*, first series, xxiv, pp. 1046–47.

4   D. Mack Smith, *Mussolini* (London, 1981), p. 61.

5   Duff Cooper to K. Rutland, Easter, 1934; J. Charmley, *Duff Cooper: The Authorised Biography* (London, 1986), p. 76; Duff Cooper, *Old Men Forget* (London, 1955), pp. 172–73.

6   Wrench, *Geoffrey Dawson and Our Times* (London, 1955), p. 247.

7   Lothian to H.V. Hodson, 16/8/35, GD40/17/34.

8   Rose, *Churchill*, p. 236.

9   E. Wiskemann, *The Rome–Berlin Axis* (London, 1966), p. 53.

10   Vansittart, *The Mist Procession* (London, 1958), p. 297.

11   Curzon to Cecil, 17/9/23, quoted in R. Lamb, *The Drift to War, 1922–39* (London, 1987), p. 31.

12   Ibid., p. 32.

13   TNA (PRO), FO 371/19158.

14   R.A.C. Parker, *Chamberlain and Appeasement* (Oxford, 1993), p. 45.

15   Vansittart minute 8/6/35, *DBFP*, second series, xiv, p. 281.

16   Jones, *A Diary with Letters*, p. 155.

70   Templewood, *Nine Troubled Years* (London, 1954), p. 170.

18   Ibid., p. 188.

19   Williamson, *Stanley Baldwin*, p. 52; for a detailed analysis of the Ethiopian Crisis, see R.A.C. Parker, 'Britain, France and the Ethiopian crisis, 1935–36', *English Historical Review*, 89 (1974), pp. 293–332.

20   Templewood, *Nine Troubled Years*, p. 168.

21   Mussolini to Grandi, 4/122/35, *I documenti diplomatici italiani*, series 8, ii.

22   Manchester Guardian, 10/10/35.

23   D. Maclachlan, *In the Chair: Barrington-Ward of 'The Times', 1891–1948* (London, 1971), p. 164.

24   Dawson to Curtis, 17/12/35, MSS Curtis 10.

25   Templewood, *Nine Troubled Years*, p. 185.

26   TNA (PRO), CAB 23 (90b), FO 4–10, 13.

27   Templewood, *Nine Troubled Years*, p. 188.

28   D.C. Waley, *British Public Opinion and the Abyssinian War, 1935–36* (London, 1975), p. 69; *HCD*, vol 307, cols 2030–39.

29   R.R. James (ed.), *Winston S. Churchill: His Complete Speeches, 1897–1963*, vii (New York, 1974), p. 5654.

30   R.A.C. Parker, *Churchill and Appeasement* (London, 2000), p. 76.

31   P. Neville, *Mussolini* (London, 2004), p. 141.

32   Jones, *A Diary with Letters*, 30/4/36, p. 191.

33   Wiskemann, *The Rome–Berlin Axis*, pp. 78–83; E.M. Robertson, *Mussolini as Empire-Builder: Europe and Africa, 1932–36* (London, 1977), pp. 186-88.

34   M. Thomas, *Britain, France and Appeasement: Anglo-French Relations in the Popular Front Era* (London, 1996), p. 94.

35   Jones, *A Diary with Letters*, 5/8/36, pp. 230–31.

36   *HCD*, fifth series, vol 317, cols 282–83; see also Avon, *Facing the Dictators*, pp. 425-26.

37   The text of the agreement can be seen in *Documents on International Affairs, 1937* (London, 1939), pp. 87–89.

38   Quoted in Avon, *Facing the Dictators*, p. 428.

39   Parker, *Chamberlain and Appeasement*, p. 89.

40   Ibid.

41   TNA (PRO), CAB 23/92, 12/3/38; Neville to Hilda Chamberlain, 15/1/39, Chamberlain Papers, NC, 18/1/1082.

42   For an overview of this issue, see G. Bruce Strang, 'Mussolini's Road to Munich', in I. Lukes and E. Goldstein (eds), *The Munich Crisis, 1938: Prelude to World War II* (London, 1999), pp. 161–90.

43   C. Thorne, *The Approach of War, 1938–39* (London, 1967), p. 82.

44   *DBFP*, third series, iii, appendix ii, no 285.

45   K. Feiling, *Neville Chamberlain* (London, 1946), p. 393.

46   *Ciano Diaries*, 11/1/39 (London, 2002).

47   D. Cameron Watt, *How War Came* (London, 1989), p. 97.

48   *Ciano Diaries*, 15/3/39.

49   *DBFP*, third series, iv, p. 402.

50   Neville to Hilda Chamberlain, NC 18/1/1094, Chamberlain Papers.

51   Watt, *How War Came*, pp. 527–28.

52   Jones, *A Diary with Letters*, 8/6/40, p. 460; Balbo was one of Mussolini's oldest Fascist comrades and a celebrated aviator.

53   Sir O. O'Malley, *The Phantom Caravan* (London, 1954), p. 220.

54   CU5, i, pp. 442–43.

55   Quoted in E. Behr, *Hirohito: Behind the Myth* (Harmondsworth, 1989), p. 164.

56   *DBFP*, second series, ix, nos 636 n. 2, 238 n. 2.

57   Parker, *Chamberlain and Appeasement*, p. 38; Vansittart, *The Mist Procession*, p. 437.

58   For a notable attempt to redress the balance, see D. Dutton, *Simon: A Political Biography* (London, 1992).

59   For an explanation of why the term Fascist does not fit well into the Japanese scenario, see A. Best, 'Imperial Japan', in R. Boyce and J. Maielo (eds), *The Origins of World War Two: The Debate Continues* (London, 2003), p. 55.

60   Parker, *Chamberlain and Appeasement*, p. 36.

61   *DBFP*, second series, x, no 228.

62   I. Nish, *Japanese Foreign Policy, 1862–1942* (London, 1977), p. 218; M. Maruyama, *Thought and Behaviour in Modern Japanese Politics* (London, 1963), p. 97.

63   *Channon Diaries*, 20/5/38, p. 156.

64   Chamberlain Diary, 6/6/43, quoted in Feiling, *Neville Chamberlain*, p. 253.

65   Feiling, *Neville Chamberlain*, p. 413.

66   Best, 'Imperial Japan', p. 66.

67   For discussion of Emperor Hirohito's responsibility, see E. Behr, *Hirohito: Behind the Myth* (London, 1989), and D. Bergamini, *Japan's Imperial Conspiracy* (London, 1971).

68   TNA (PRO), CAB 23/83, Cabinet 11 (36) 5, 26/2/36.

69   Feiling, *Neville Chamberlain*, p. 296.

Notes to Chapter 6: Three Crises

1   W.S. Churchill, *The Gathering Storm* (London, 1948), p. 174.

2   Ibid., pp. 152–53; Churchill relied here on the eyewitness testimony of Wigram's devoted wife Ava, later Countess of Waverley.

3   Wigram was Counsellor at the British Embassy in Paris from 1924 to 1933, and Head of the Central Department at the Foreign Office from 1934 to 1936; a more accurate and vivid assessment of him is given in V. Lawford, *Bound for Diplomacy* (London, 1963).

4   TNA (PRO), CAB 2 (35), 14/1/35.

5   Wigram minute, 27/3/35, TNA (PRO), FO 371/18828, C1804/20/18.

6   TNA (PRO), CAB 27/599.

7   *DBFP*, second series, xv, pp. 624–96.

8   M. Thomas, *Britain, France and Appeasement* (London, 1996), p. 27; Corbin to Handin, 30/1/36, Centre des Archives Diplomatiques de Nantes, Londres, 267, tel. 153.

9   TNA (PRO), CAB 23, Cabinet 15 (36), 5/3/36.

10 B.J. Bond (ed.), *Chief of Staff: The Diaries of Sir Henry Pownall*, 2 vols (London, 1972), i, 8/3/36, p. 104.

11 H. Dalton, *Memoirs, 1931–45: The Fateful Years* (London, 1957), p. 88.

12 Ibid.

13 M. Dockrill, *British Establishment Perspectives on France 1936–40* (Basingstoke, 1999), p. 28.

14 N. Jordan, 'The Cut Price War on the Peripheries: The French General Staff, the Rhineland and Czechoslovakia', in R. Boyce and E. Robertson (eds), *The Paths to War: New Essays on the Origins of the Second World War* (London, 1989), p. 142; M. Alexander, *The Republic in Danger: General Maurice Gamelin and the Politics of French Defence, 1933–40* (Cambridge, 1992), p. 76.

15 S.A. Schuker, 'France and the Remilitarisation of the Rhineland in 1936', *French Historical Studies*, 14 (1986).

16 TNA (PRO), CAB 18 (36), 11/3/36.

17 For German reactions to the Rhineland coup, see I. Kershaw, *Hitler*, i, *Hubris, 1889–1936*, pp. 591–92.

18 TNA (PRO), C1817/4/18, 13/3/36; see also C1533/4/18, 8/3/36 and C1658/4/18, 10/3/36.

19 *Documents on International Affairs* (London, 1937), p. 251.

20 A.J. Crozier, *The Causes of the Second World War* (London, 1997), p. 128. The definitive study about Britain's colonial appeasement policy is Crozier's *Appeasement and Germany's Last Bid for Colonies* (London, 1988).

21 K. Hancock, *Smuts*, p. 197.

22 Smuts to Lothian, 7/4/37, Lothian Papers, appendix III.

23 Documents on German Foreign Policy, series D, i, no 19, Hossbach Memorandum, 5/11/37.

24 Hitler–Halifax meeting 11/37, *DGFP*, series D, i, no 31.

25 TNA (PRO), CAB 23/90 cc 43 (57) 3, 24/11/27.

26 P. Neville, *Appeasing Hitler: The Diplomacy of Sir Nevile Henderson, 1937–39* (London, 2000), p. 49.

27 TNA (PRO), CAB 27/623, Foreign Policy Committee Minutes 3/2/38; Henderson to Eden, 26/1/38, FO 371/21678 C522/184/18.

28 For details about the Blomberg affair, see Kershaw, *Hitler*, i, pp. 52–60.

29 Sir N. Henderson, *Failure of a Mission*, p. 115.

30 Crozier, *Appeasement and Germany's Last Bid for Colonies*, p. 239.

31 *Akten zur Deutschen Auswärtigen, 1918–45*, series D, i, nos 80, 106.

32 G. Weinberg, *The Foreign Policy of Nazi Germany: Starting World War Two* (Chicago, 1980) pp. 261–68.

33 Lamb, *The Drift to War*, p. 224.

34 Palairet to Halifax, 9/3/38, *DBFP*, third series, i, no 2.

35 Ibid., no 8.

36 H. Nicolson, *Diaries and Letters, 1930–39*, ed. N. Nicolson (London, 1966), 10/3/38.

37 Neville to Ida Chamberlain, 13/3/38, NC 18/1/1041.
38 TNA (PRO), CAB 23/92 CAB 12 (38).
39 *Nicolson Diaries*, 14/3/38.
40 Cited in A. Adamthwaite, *France and the Coming of the Second World War* (London, 1977), p. 75.
41 Palairet to Halifax, 13/3/38, *DBFP*, third series, i, no 65.
42 Halifax to Palairet, 11/3/38, ibid., no 25.
43 Sargent memorandum, 16/1/38, TNA (PRO), FO 371/22311/01502.
44 P. Demetz, *Prague in Black and Gold: The History of a City* (Harmondsworth, 1997), p. 353.
45 Templewood, *Nine Troubled Years* (London, 1954), p. 285.
46 Ibid.
47 Ibid., p. 287.
48 Ibid., p. 288.
49 A.H. Broderick, *Near to Greatness: A Life of Earl Winterton* (London, 1965), p. 229.
50 Ibid.
51 Broderick, *Near to Greatness*, p. 229.
52 George S. Messersmith (US Legation Vienna) to the Secretary of State, 4/6/38, Foreign Relations of the USA.
53 Vansittart minute, 23/2/37, *DBFP*, second series, xviii, no 185, n. 5.
54 Sargent memorandum on Czech–German talks, 9 February 1937, ibid., no 160.
55 Ibid.
56 M. Cornwall, 'The Rise and Fall of a "Special Relationship": Britain and Czechoslovakia, 1930–48', in B. Brivati and H. Jones (eds), *What Difference Did the War Make? 1930–1946* (London, 1993), p. 132; for further detail on the Addison–Beneš relationship, see I. Lukes, *Czechoslovakia between Stalin and Hitler: The Diplomacy of Edvard Beneš in the 1930s* (Oxford, 1996), pp. 55–57.
57 Cornwall, *The Rise and Fall of a Special Relationship*, p. 136; ibid., p. 138.
58 Lord Avon, *The Eden Memoirs: Facing the Dictators* (London, 1962), p. 503.
58 The extent of Beneš's unpopularity was underlined to the writer by the late Sir Frank Roberts, then a desk officer in the Central Department of the Foreign Office, interview, 10/10/96.
60 Eden to Hadow, 23/2/36, *DBFP*, second series, xviii, no 200; Avon, *Facing the Dictators*, pp. 502–3.
61 Eden minute, 15/9/36, TNA (PRO), R 5216/32/12, FO 371/20375.
62 R. Kee, *Munich: The Eleventh Hour* (London, 1988), pp. 38-39.
63 R. Smelser, *The Sudeten Problem, 1933–38* (London, 1975), pp. 201–2.
64 I. Lukes, *Czechoslovakia between Stalin and Hitler: The Diplomacy of Edvard Beneš in the 1930s* (Oxford 1996), p. 35.
65 Eisenlohr to the Wilhelmstrasse, 21/12/37, *DGFP*, series D, i, no 93.
66 TNA (PRO), CAB 27/623, fos 114–25.
67 W.S. Churchill, *The Gathering Storm* (London, 1948), p. 172.
68 Neville Chamberlain to Ida Chamberlain, 20/3/38, Chamberlain Papers, 18/1/1042.
69 *DGFP*, series D, ii, p. 198.

70   *Documents on International Affairs*, ii (London, 1942), pp. 130–37.
71   Newton to Halifax, 15/3/38, *DBFP*, third series, i, no 86.
72   TNA (PRO), CAB 27/263, FP (36) 26, 18/3/38.
73   Henderson to Halifax, 30/3/38, *DBFP*, third series, i.
74   Henderson to Halifax, 25/8/38, *DBFP*, third series, i, no 613.
75   *Cadogan Diaries*, 30/3/38, p. 63.
76   TNA (PRO), CAB 27/627, fos 35–42.
77   Neville to Ida Chamberlain, 24/3/38, Chamberlain Papers, University of Birmingham, 18/1/1042.
78   Anglo-French Conference, 28–29 April 1938, *DBFP*, third series, i, pp. 227–232.
79   R. Rhodes James (ed.), *'Chips': The Diaries of Sir Henry Channon* (London, 1993), 20/3/38, 21/3/38 and 3/5/38.
80   *Nicolson Diaries*, 29/3/38, p. 332.
81   Dalton, *The Fateful Years*, p. 162.
82   Henderson to Halifax, 19/5/38, *DBFP*, third series, i, no 234.
83   *DBFP*, third series, i, p. 340; Henderson, *The Failure of a Mission*, pp. 135–37.
84   Henderson, *The Failure of a Mission*, p. 135.
85   Lukes, *Czechoslovakia between Stalin and Hitler*, p. 157.
86   *DGFP*, series D, ii, no 175.
87   Ibid., no 221.
88   A. Duff Cooper, *Old Men Forget* (London, 1955), p. 211.
89   TNA (PRO), CAB 23/93; *DBFP*, third series, i, appendix 2; see also G. Weinberg, *The Foreign Policy of Hitler's Germany Starting World War Two, 1937–39* (Chicago, 1980), p. 391 n. 57.
90   Henderson to Halifax, 27/8/98, no. 701.

Notes to Chapter 7: Munich

1   Halifax minute, 8/8/38, TNA (PRO), FO 371/21723 C5297/ 1941/18.
2   Addison continued to attack the Czechs even in retirement. In April 1938, he had sent in a memorandum saying that Anglo-French assistance to Czechoslovakia would 'merely be attempting to bolster up an injustice'. Memorandum to Sir A. Cadogan, 21/4/38, TNA (PRO), FO 371/21717 C3745/1941/18.
3   A. McCulloch, 'Franklin Roosevelt and the Runciman Mission to Czechoslovakia, 1938: A New Perspective on Anglo-American Relations in the Era of Appeasement', *Journal of Transatlantic Studies*, 1 (2003), pp. 152–74.
4   Wilson to Halifax, 22/26/38, PREM 1/265.
5   A. McCulloch, *Franklin Roosevelt and the Runciman Mission*, p. 156; I. Lukes, *Czechoslovakia between Stalin and Hitler*, p. 181.
6   Lukes, *Czechoslovakia between Stalin and Hitler*, p. 192.
7   Ibid., p. 183.
8   K. Feiling, *Neville Chamberlain*, p. 325.
9   Runciman to Baldwin, 8/2/37, 'Conversations with President Roosevelt and Mr Hull', PREM, i, vol 291; see also TNA (PRO), FO 371/20656/1059/93/45.

10 McCulloch, *Franklin Roosevelt and the Runciman Mission*, p. 159.
11 Speech by Roosevelt, 18/8/38, Queen's University, Kingston, Ontario.
12 Churchill, *The Gathering Storm* (London, 1948), p. 199.
13 Neville to Hilda Chamberlain, 29/8/37, 18/1/1038, Chamberlain Papers.
14 Lukes, *Czechoslovakia between Stalin and Hitler*, p. 185.
15 J. Harvey (ed.), *The Diplomatic Diaries of Oliver Harvey, 1937–40*, 6/9/38; *DBFP*, third series, ii, no 587.
16 Lukes, *Czechoslovakia between Stalin and Hitler*, pp. 185–86.
17 *DBFP*, third series, ii, no 758.
18 J.H. Wheeler Bennett, *Munich: Prologue to Tragedy* (New York, 1964), p. 92.
19 30/8/38, TNA (PRO), CAB 23/94.
20 Henderson to Wilson, 9/9/38, TNA (PRO), FO 800/371/269, Henderson Papers.
21 Neville to Hilda Chamberlain, 13/3/38, NC 18/1/1015.
22 *DBFP*, second series, ii, no 262.
23 Templewood, *Nine Troubled Years*, p. 300.
24 *Channon Diaries*, 14/9/28, p. 166.
25 P. Schmidt, *Hitler's Interpreter* (New York, 1951), p. 91.
26 Feiling, *Neville Chamberlain*, p. 366.
27 Notes by Mr Chamberlain of his conversation with Herr Hitler at Berchtesgaden on 15 September 1938, *DBFP*, third series, ii, no 895.
28 Feiling, *Neville Chamberlain*, p. 367.
29 D. Dutton, *Neville Chamberlain* (London, 2001), p. 50.
30 *Harvey Diary*, 15/9/38, p. 180.
31 *Nicolson Diary*, 19/9/38, pp. 360–61.
32 Phipps to Halifax, 10/9/38, *DBFP*, second series, ii, no 843.
33 *Inskip Diary*, 13/9/38, Inskip MSS, i, 1/1.
34 'Record of an Anglo-French Conversation at No. 10 Downing Street on September 18 1938', *DBFP*, third series, ii.
35 *Dalton Diary*, 17/9/38, Dalton MSS, i, vol 19, London School of Economics.
36 TNA (PRO), CAB 27/646.
37 H. Dalton, *High Tide and After: Memoirs, 1931–45* (London, 1957), pp. 188–89.
38 Ibid., p. 188.
39 *DBFP*, third series, ii, pp. 464–65.
40 Schmidt, *Hitler's Interpreter*, p. 96.
41 *DBFP*, third series, ii, pp. 465–66.
42 Schmidt, *Hitler's Interpreter*, p. 96.
43 *DGFP*, Series D, i, pp. 870–79.
44 Feiling, *Neville Chamberlain*, p. 369.
45 Henderson, p. 156; *DBFP*, third series, ii, p. 483.
46 Lukes, *Czechoslovakia between Stalin and Hitler*, p. 234.
47 *Times*, 24/9/38.
48 For Mason-MacFarlane's personal account of his adventures, see E. Butler, *Mason-Mac: The Life of Lieutenant-General Sir Noel Mason-MacFarlane* (London, 1972).
49 Minute by R. Speaght, 26/9/38, TNA (PRO), FO 371/217141.

50 TNA (PRO), CAB 23/95, fos 195–233.
51 J. Charmley, *Duff Cooper: The Authorised Biography* (London, 1986), p. 119; TNA (PRO), CAB 23/95; PREM 1/266A.
52 *Harvey Diary*, 24/9/38, p. 195.
53 TNA (PRO), CAB, 23/95.
54 Halifax Papers, Borthwick Institute, University of York, A4/410/10/3/7.
55 *Documents on International Affairs* (1938), ii, pp. 236–38.
56 Lukes, *Czechoslovakia between Stalin and Hitler*, p. 240.
57 Record of an Anglo-French conversation held at Downing Street, 25/9/38, DBFP, II, no 1093; Dockrill, *British Establishment Perspectives on France*, p. 104; Sir John Simon's own memoirs are singularly unhelpful about this important meeting. See Viscount Simon, *Retrospect: The Memoirs of the Rt Hon. Viscount Simon* (London, 1952), pp. 246–47.
58 TNA (PRO), CAB 23/95.
59 A. Duff Cooper, *Old Men Forget*, p. 237.
60 Henderson to Halifax, 26/9/38, *DBFP*, third series, iii, no 1126.
61 *DBFP*, third series, iii, no 1121.
62 Schmidt, *Hitler's Interpreter*, p. 104.
63 Ibid., p. 105.
64 Duff Cooper, *Old Men Forget*, p. 229.
65 M. Alexander, *The Republic in Danger: General Maurice Gamelin and the Politics of French Defence, 1933–1940* (Cambridge, 1992), p. 285; N. Jordan, 'The Cut-Price War on the Peripheries: The French General Staff, the Rhineland and Czechoslovakia', in R. Boyce and E.M. Robertson (eds), *Paths to War* (London, 1989), p. 154.
66 G. Stewart, *Burying Caesar: Churchill, Chamberlain and the Battle for the Tory Party* (London, 1999), p. 305.
67 Henderson to Halifax, 27/9/38, *DBFP*, third series, ii, no 1143.
68 Quoted in Feiling, *Neville Chamberlain*, p. 372.
69 Eisenlohr to the Wilhelmstrasse, 21/12/37, *DGFP*, series D, ii, no 38.
70 W.J. West, *Truth Betrayed* (London, 1987), pp. 142–43.
71 *Harvey Diary*, 27/9/38, p. 200.
72 Smuts to Lothian, 20/25/38, *Smuts Papers*, vii, pp. 127–30.
73 H. Montgomery Hyde, *Neville Chamberlain* (London, 1976), pp. 122–23; Simon, *Retrospect*, p. 247.
74 Feiling, *Neville Chamberlain*, p. 374.
75 *Channon Diary*, pp. 170–71; *Nicolson Diaries and Letters*, 28/9/38, p. 371.
76 Montgomery Hyde, *Neville Chamberlain*, p. 123.
77 A. Horne, *Macmillan*, i, p. 116; Lukes, *Czechoslovakia between Stalin and Hitler*, p. 237.
78 S. Grant Duff, *The Parting of Ways: A Personal Account of the Thirties* (London, 1982), p. 183.
79 C. Thorne, *The Approach of War, 1938–39* (London, 1967), p. 82.
80 Quoted in T. Taylor, *Munich: The Price of Peace* (London, 1979), p. 29; see also Kee, *Munich, The Eleventh Hour* (London, 1988), p. 199, and H. Noguères, *Munich*, trans. P. O'Brien (London, 1965), p. 263.
81 Noguères, *Munich*, p. 265.

82 Ibid., p. 266.

83 Kee, *Munich*, p. 201; Lamb, *The Ghosts of Peace* (Salisbury, 1987), p. 259.

84 Lamb, *The Ghosts of Peace*, p. 87.

85 Neville to Hilda Chamberlain, 2/10/38, 18/1/1070.

86 Ibid., Chamberlain Papers, 18/1/1070.

87 Anglo-German Declaration, 30/9/38, Imperial War Museum.

88 R. Spitzy, *How We Squandered the Reich* (Norwich, 1997), p. 254.

89 *Proceedings of the International Military Tribunal, Nuremberg*, testimony of Dr Schacht, part 13, p. 5, HMSO (London, 1946).

90 Lord Home of the Hirsel, *The Way The Wind Blows* (London, 1976), p. 66.

91 Lukes, *Czechoslovakia between Stalin and Hitler*, pp. 253–55.

92 Lídové noviny, Prague, 1/10/38.

93 Feiling, *Neville Chamberlain*, pp. 381–82.

94 Neville to Hilda Chamberlain, 15/10/38, Chamberlain Papers, 18/1/1072.

95 Henderson, *Failure of a Mission*, p. 168.

96 Duff Cooper, *Old Men Forget*, p. 239.

97 Ibid.; House of Commons Debates, 5/10/38.

98 D. Dutton, *Neville Chamberlain*, pp. 54–55.

99 Noguères, *Munich*, p. 304; the first version is attributed to the journalists André Stibio and Geneviève Tabuois, the second to J. Debu-Bridel Daladier.

100 A.J.P. Taylor, *The Origins of the Second World War* (London, 1961), p. 235.

101 Feiling, *Neville Chamberlain*, p. 382.

102 Ibid., p. 392.

103 The strongest proponent of this viewpoint in recent years has been the Canadian scholar S. Aster. See his 'Guilty Men', in R. Boyce and E. Robertson (eds), *Paths to War*, pp. 233–68.

104 Ripka memorandum on his meeting with Churchill in June 1938 in U. Kral (ed.), *Das Abkommen von Munchen, 1938: Tschecko slowakische diplomatische Dokumente, 1937–39* (Prague, 1968), no 94.

105 G. Weinberg, 'Reflections on Munich after Sixty Years', in I. Lukes and E. Goldstein (eds), *The Munich Crisis, 1938, Prelude to World War Two* (London, 1999), p. 6. The best and most recent appraisal of Munich.

106 Ibid., p. 9.

107 Chamberlain to Halifax, 19/8/38, *DBFP*, third series, ii, appendix 4, p. 686.

108 P. Neville, *Appeasing Hitler: The Diplomacy of Sir Nevile Henderson, 1937–39* (London, 2000), p. 106.

109 For a study that suggests that it *was* the task of the British Government to encourage such opposition, see P. Meehan, *The Unnecessary War: Whitehall and the German Resistance to Hitler* (London, 1992).

110 Lamb, *The Drift to War*, p. 264.

111 Much of my account here has relied heavily on the admirable analysis in I. Lukes, *Czechoslovakia between Stalin and Hitler*, pp. 195–96, 246, 257–58, and the same author's 'Stalin and Czechoslovakia in 1938–39: An Autopsy of a Myth', in Lukes and Goldstein, *The Munich Crisis, 1938*, pp. 35–37; for the material about Rumania, see Lamb, *Drift to War*, p. 264.

112 Parker, *Chamberlain and Appeasement*, p. 324.

113 Weinberg, 'Reflections on Munich', pp. 6–7.

114 Lukes, 'Stalin and Czechoslovakia in 1938–39', p. 38.

115 Weinberg, 'Reflections on Munich', p. 8.

116 Earl of Halifax, *Fullness of Days* (London, 1957), p. 198; for other defences of Munich by Cabinet Ministers, see Templewood, *Nine Troubled Years*, pp. 322–24, and Simon, chapter 13.

117 There are a number of good summaries of the impact of Munich in addition to the perceptive analysis by Weinberg mentioned above. See, for example, J. Charmley, *Chamberlain and the Lost Peace* (London, 1989), ch. 14; D. Cameron Watt, *How War Came* (London, 1989), pp. 76–83; R. Kee, *Munich*, pp. 202–13; Parker, *Chamberlain and Appeasement*, pp. 182–86.

Notes to Chapter 8: The Armed Forces

1 There was much speculation at the time about who the author of 'Guilty Men' was. In fact, three men were responsible, Michael Foot, Frank Owen and Peter Howard, all of them journalists with the *Evening Standard*.

2 Cato, *Guilty Men* (London, 1940), p. 110; House of Commons Debates, 28/11/34.

3 Ibid., p. 16.

4 Ibid., p. 38.

5 Ibid., p. 125; for a critique of appeasement which focuses on 'Guilty Men', see S. Aster, 'Guilty Men', in R. Boyce and E. Robertson (eds), *Paths to War* (London, 1989), pp. 233–268.

6 P.M.H. Bell, *The Origins of the Second World War* (London, 1986), p. 176.

7 D.C. Watt, *Too Serious a Business* (London, 1975), p. 89.

8 Viscount Simon Papers, MS 70, Bodleian Library, Oxford University.

9 TNA (PRO), CAB, 4/23.

10 S. Newton, *Profits of Peace: The Political Economy of Anglo-German Appeasement* (Oxford, 1996), p. 73.

11 R. Shay Jr, *British Rearmament in the Thirties* (Princeton, 1977).

12 G.C. Peden, 'Keynes, The Economics of Rearmament and Appeasement', in W. Mommsen and L. Kettenacker (eds), *The Fascist Challenge and the Policy of Appeasement* (London, 1983), p. 143.

13 G.C. Peden, 'A Matter of Timing: The Economic Background to British Foreign Policy', *History*, 69 (1984), p. 16.

14 Chamberlain Papers, 2/24 A, December 1936.

15 B. Bond (ed.), *Chief of Staff: The Diaries of Lieutenant-General Sir Henry Pownall*, i, *1933–1940* (London, 1972), 25/9/38, p. 161.

16 Neville Chamberlain to Lord Lothian, 10/6/37, NC, 7/7/4.

17 TNA (PRO), CAB 23/95.

18 Newton, *Profits of Peace*, p. 68.

19 Chamberlain Papers, 18/1/993.

20 B. Bond, *France and Belgium, 1939–40* (London, 1975), p. 33.

21 TNA (PRO), CAB 75 (36) 3, 'The Role of the British Army'.

22 *Pownall Diaries*, i, pp. 126–29.

23 Bell, *The Origins of the Second World War*, pp. 175–76.

24 Quoted in G.C. Peden, *British Rearmament and the Treasury* (Edinburgh, 1979), pp. 134–35.

25 Ibid.

26 Chamberlain Papers, 19/1/36, NC, 2/23.

27 Parker, *Churchill and Appeasement*, p. 287.

28 Vansittart, *The Mist Procession*, p. 499.

29 Disappointingly, Professor Lindemann's biographer makes no reference to these nefarious night-time activities. See the Earl of Birkenhead, *The Prof in Two Worlds: The Official Life of Professor E. Lindemann, Viscount Cherwell* (London, 1961).

30 M. Gilbert, *Churchill: The Wilderness Years* (London, 1981), p. 127.

31 N. Rose, *Churchill. An Unruly Life* (London, 1994), p. 189.

32 Parker, *Churchill and Appeasement*, p. 133.

33 J. Charmley, *Churchill: The End of Glory. A Political Biography* (London, 1993), p. 313.

34 *Companion to the Official Churchill Biography*, M. Gilbert (ed.), vol v, pt 3, iii, p. 218.

35 Ibid., ii, pp. 1207–8, and iii, p. 325.

36 Rose, *Churchill*, p. 225.

37 C. Ponting, *Churchill* (London, 1994), p. 362.

38 Rose, *Churchill*, p. 225.

39 Quoted in R.J. Overy, 'German Air Strength, 1933–39: A Note', *Historical Journal*, 28 (1984).

40 C. Andrew, *Secret Service* (London, 1985), p. 390.

41 For details of the Arras action, see the classic study by A. Horne, *To Lose a Battle: France 1940* (London, 1969), pp. 440–45.

42 J. Jackson, *The Fall of France: The Nazi Invasion of France* (Oxford, 2003), p. 13. The author points out that the Popular Front announced a fourteen billion franc rearmament programme in September 1936.

43 Ibid., p. 19.

44 See, for example, M. Gilbert and R. Gott, *The Appeasers* (London, 1963), chapter 22.

45 Quoted in Horne, *To Lose a Battle*, p. 191.

Notes to Chapter 9: The Foreign Office

1 Sir N. Henderson, *Water under the Bridges* (London, 1945), p. 23.

2 For details about the merger, see Lord Strang, *The Foreign Office* (London, 1955), pp. 214–22.

3 Chirol to Hardinge, 10/8/1904, Hardinge Papers, Cambridge University Library.

4 D. Dilks (ed.), *The Diaries of Sir Alexander Cadogan, 1938–1945* (London, 1971), 30/10/1940, p. 333.

5 Lord Avon, *Facing the Dictators* (London, 1962), p. 242.

6   Vansittart to Phipps, 23/2/35, TNA (PRO), FO 371/18828 C1834/55/18.
7   For detail on Sargent's anti-Soviet prejudices, see M. Carley, 'A Fearful Concatenation of Circumstances: The Anglo-Soviet Rapprochement, 1934–36', Contemporary European History, 5 (1996).
8   Memorandum, 21/11/35, TNA (PRO), FO 371/18851 C7522/55/18.
9   N. Rose, Vansittart: Study of a Diplomat (London, 1978), p. 200.
10 W.S. Churchill, The Gathering Storm (London, 1948), pp. 152–53.
11 Lord Vansittart, The Mist Procession (London, 1958), p. 550.
12 Stumm to Dirksen, 2/5/38, Dirksen Papers, ii, appendix 1.
13 Vansittart minute, 28/2/35, TNA (PRO), FO 371/19287/F4811.
14 Vansittart minute, 5/2/34, TNA (PRO), F0 371/17593.
15 For further detail on Vansittart's attitude to the Japanese problem, see John R. Ferris, 'Indulged In All Too Much: Vansittart, Intelligence and Appeasement', Diplomacy and Statecraft, 6 (1995), p. 132; P. Neville, 'Lord Vansittart, Sir Walford Selby and the Debate about Treasury Interference in the Conduct of British Foreign Policy in the 1930s', Journal of Contemporary History, 36, no 4, October 2001, pp. 623–33.
16 Quoted in R. Lamb, The Drift to War, 1922–37 (London, 1989), p. 138.
17 For details about Vansittart's relationship with Henlein, see Rose, Vansittart, pp. 222–26, and P. Neville, Appeasing Hitler: The Diplomacy of Sir Nevile Henderson, 1937–39 (London, 2000), pp. 86–87.
18 The most recent exponent of this viewpoint is P. Meehan, The Unnecessary War: Whitehall and the German Resistance to Hitler (London, 1992).
19 Chamberlain Papers, NC 18/1/993.
20 The Diaries of Hugh Dalton, London School of Economics, 12/4/38.
21 Lord Gladwyn, Memoirs (London, 1972), p. 70.
22 Cadogan Diaries, 15/9/38, p. 98.
23 Ibid., 8/9/39, p. 215.
24 Ibid., 14/3/39, p. 151.
25 Ibid., 1/4/39, p. 168 and 11/8/38, p. 194.
26 Ibid., 1/10/38, p. 11.
27 Rose, Vansittart, p. 209.
28 Cadogan Diaries, 7/4/39, p. 170.
29 Ferris, 'Indulged In All Too Little', p. 168; evidence for the view that Chamberlain perceived Van as a potential external threat is provided by a conversation the two men had in December 1937. When Chamberlain offered Van the post of Chief Diplomatic Adviser, he replied, 'I don't know whether I will accept or not'. When Chamberlain asked him what else he might do, he said 'I may stand for Parliament'. An alarmed Prime Minister then said, 'What. You can't do that! You know too much', I. Colvin, The Chamberlain Cabinet (London, 1971), pp. 171–72.
30 Neville Chamberlain to Ida Chamberlain, 12/12/38.
31 Henderson to Halifax, 10/1/38, A4 410 3, Hickleton Papers, Borthwick Institute.
32 Cadogan Diaries, 30/1/38, p. 43.
33 J. Harvey (ed.), The Diplomatic Diaries of Oliver Harvey, 1937–40 (London, 1970), p. 66.
34 Cadogan Diaries, 15/2/38, p. 47.

35 Ibid., 11/3/38, p. 60.

36 Sargent memorandum, 16/2/38, TNA (PRO), F0 371/2231 C1502.

37 Ibid.

38 *Cadogan Diaries*, 30/3/38, p. 63. A view endorsed by Britain's military leaders. See R. Macleod and D. Kelly (eds), *Ironside Diaries*, 22/9/38 (London, 1962), p. 62.

39 *Cadogan Diaries*, 24/9/38, pp. 103–4.

40 Ibid.

41 Notably A. Roberts in *'The Holy Fox': A Biography of Lord Halifax* (London, 1991), p. 117; for further detail about this episode, see P. Neville, 'Sir Alexander Cadogan and Lord Halifax's "Damascus Road" Conversions over the Godesberg Terms 1938', *Diplomacy and Statecraft*, 11 (November, 2000), pp. 81–90.

42 Cadogan minute, 14/10/38, TNA (PRO), FO 371/21659.

43 Cadogan minute, 10/10/38, TNA (PRO), FO 371/22185.

44 Cadogan to Henderson, 26/2/39, TNA (PRO), 800/294, Cadogan Papers.

45 *Cadogan Diaries*, 15/3/39, p. 163.

46 *DBFP*, third series, v, p. 642.

47 M. Cowling, *The Impact of Hitler: British Politics and British Policy 1933–40* (Cambridge, 1975), pp. 283–84.

48 Rumbold to Simon, 14/3/33, *DBFP*, second series, v, no 452.

49 Rumbold to Simon, 28/6/32, second series, no 3.

50 Rumbold to Simon, 22/2/33, second series, no 423.

51 Quoted in M. Gilbert, *Sir Horace Rumbold: Portrait of a Diplomat* (London, 1973), p. 383.

52 Rumbold to Simon, 30/6/33, second series, no 229.

53 Rumbold to Henderson, 15/4/40, TNA (PRO), FO 800/270, Henderson Papers.

54 Orme Sargent, *Dictionary of National Biography*, 1959.

55 Sir Frank Roberts to author 7/8/90.

56 Phipps to Hankey 29/12/40, Phipps Papers, Churchill College Cambridge, 2/19.

57 M. Gilbert and R. Gott, *The Appeasers* (London, 1963), p. 49.

58 Phipps to Simon 26/10/33, *DBFP*, second series, v, no 495.

59 These remarks were made in a conversation Phipps had with the US Ambassador in Paris, Bullitt (who had become a colleague in 1937), 30/4/37, *Foreign Relations of The United States 1937*, i, p. 84.

60 For more detail on Phipps's career, see J. Herman, *The Paris Embassy of Sir Eric Phipps, 1937–39* (1998), and Professor D. Cameron Watt, 'Chamberlain's Ambassadors', in M. Dockrill and B. McKercher (eds), *Diplomacy and World Power: Studies in British Foreign Policy* (London, 1996), pp. 136–70.

61 Vansittart to Cleverly, 31/3/36, Baldwin Papers 124, University Library Cambridge.

61 Gilbert and Gott, *The Appeasers*, p. 64; Lewis Namier, *Diplomatic Prelude* (London, 1948), p. 218; Namier, *Europe in Decay: A Study in Disintegration* (London, 1950), p. 175.

63 This select band includes Maurice Cowling, John Charmley, Vaughan B. Baker (unpublished Ph.D. thesis, 1975, University of Southwestern Louisiana) and the author.

64 T. Jones, *A Diary with Letters* (London, 1954), p. 314.

65 For the controversy surrounding Henderson's appointment, see A. Goldman, 'Two Views of Germany: Nevile Henderson and Vansittart', *British Journal of International Studies*, 6

(1980); P. Neville, 'The Appointment of Sir Nevile Henderson 1937: Design or Blunder?', *Journal of Contemporary History*, 33 (1998), pp. 609–20; *Harvey Diaries*, 23/4/37, p. 41.

66 Henderson, *Failure of a Mission*, p. 13.

67 Ibid., p. 17.

68 Vansittart minute, 5/6/37, TNA (PRO), F0 800/268, Henderson Papers.

69 Henderson to Sargent, 20/7/37, TNA (PRO), FO 371/20736/ 5377/270/86. In a covering note, Henderson told Sargent that the memorandum 'is dated May 10th 1937'.

70 J. Wedgwood, *Memoirs of a Fighting Life* (London, 1941), p. 225.

71 Henderson to George VI, 2/10/38, TNA (PRO), FO 800/269, Henderson Papers.

72 For a general assessment of Henderson's diplomatic career, see Neville, *Appeasing Hitler*, pp. 168–76.

73 Most notably by P. Meehan in *The Unnecessary War: Whitehall and the German Resistance to Hitler* (London, 1992); see also J. Fest, *Plotting Hitler's Death* (London, 1996).

74 Sargent minute, 15/4/39, TNA (PRO), FO 371/22958 C4897/13/18.

75 M. Cornwall, 'The Rise and Fall of a "Special Relationship": Britain and Czechoslovakia, 1930–1948', in B. Brivati and H. Jones (eds), *What Difference Did the War Make?* (London, 1993), p. 133.

76 S. Grant Duff, *The Parting of Ways: A Personal Account of the Thirties* (London, 1982), p. 96.

77 Rumbold to Lindsay, quoted in M. Gilbert, *Sir Horace Rumbold: Portrait of a Diplomat* (London, 1973), p. 319.

78 S. Aster, *1939: The Making of the Second World War* (London, 1973), p. 154.

79 For further discussion of Vansittart's views on Far Eastern policy, see S. Bourette Knowles, 'The Global Micawber: Sir Robert Vansittart, the Treasury and the Global Balance of Power 1933–1935', *Diplomacy and Statecraft*, 6 (1995), pp. 91–92.

80 D. Cameron Watt, *Chamberlain's Ambassadors*, p. 165.

81 Memorandum by Orde, 4/9/34, *DBFP*, third series, viii, no 15.

82 Ibid.

83 Bourette Knowles, *The Global Micawber*, p. 96; Fisher memorandum, 21/1/35, T721/31.

84 Neville Chamberlain to Hilda Chamberlain, 15/7/39, Chamberlain Papers, NC 19/1/1107.

85 For Craigie, see Watt, *Chamberlain's Ambassadors*, pp. 163–69; see also A.M. Best, *Avoiding War: The Diplomacy of Sir Robert Craigie and Shigemitsu Mamoru, 1937–1941* (London, 1992).

Notes to Chapter 10: Poland

1 C. Andrew, *Secret Intelligence: The Making of the British Intelligence Community* (London, 1985), p. 414; I. Kirkpatrick, *The Inner Circle* (London, 1959), pp. 136–38; Kirkpatrick went on to become Permanent Under-Secretary at the Foreign Office in the 1950s.

2 Makins to Strang, 6/10/38, *DBFP*, third series, iii, no 150. Makins was sent out to Berlin after Munich in somewhat mysterious circumstances, and thereafter to the Commission. Interview with Lord Sherfield, 16/5/96.

3 'Chips', The Diaries of Sir Henry Channon, (London, 1967), 15/11/38, p. 177.

4 Neville to Hilda Chamberlain, 13/11/38, 18/1/1076.

5 Peake Papers, 19/11/57, quoted in A. Roberts, 'The Holy Fox': A Biography of Lord Halifax (London, 1991), p. 128.

6 A. Horne, MacMillan, i, p. 119.

7 W. Wark, The Ultimate Enemy (Oxford, 1986), p. 113; TNA (PRO), FO 370/22344 R8690/94/67, 31/10/38 (the Jebb Memorandum).

8 P. Neville, Mussolini (London, 2003), p. 154.

9 Ciano's Diary, 1937–43, 11/1/39 (London, 1947), p. 176.

10 J. Zay, Carnets Secrets (Paris, 1942), pp. 53–54. The remark was made by Georges Mandel.

11 O. Bullitt, For the President: Personal and Secret Correspondence between Franklin D. Roosevelt and William C. Bullitt (1973), p. 310.

12 D.C. Watt, How War Came (London, 1989), p. 75.

13 Halifax to Henderson, 13/3/39, TNA (PRO), Henderson Papers, 800/270; Parker, Chamberlain and Appeasement (London, 1993), p. 195.

14 P. Schmidt, Hitler's Interpreter (London, 1951), p. 124.

15 Ibid.

16 Ibid., p. 126. Watt, How War Came, pp. 153–54.

17 Nicolson Diary, 16/3/39.

18 Channon Diary, 15/3/39.

19 H. Dalton, The Fateful Years, 1931–1945 (London, 1957), p. 227.

20 House of Commons Debates, 15/3/39, fifth series, cols 435–40.

21 Cmd 6106, Documents Concerning ... the Outbreak of Hostilities (1939), document 9.

22 Ibid.

23 E. Crampton, Eastern Europe in the Twentieth Century (London, 1994), p. 41.

24 Ibid., p. 39.

25 Quoted in R. Mackray, Poland, 1914–31 (London, 1932), p. 359.

26 Watt, How War Came, p. 58.

27 Ibid., p. 59.

28 Quoted in M. Gilbert, Sir Horace Rumbold (London, 1973), p. 187.

29 M. MacMillan, Peacemakers (London, 2001), p. 227.

30 Quoted in B. Pimlott, Hugh Dalton (London, 1985), p. 194.

31 H. Dalton, Towards the Peace of Nations: A Study in International Politics (1928), pp. 24–25.

32 Vansittart, The Mist Procession, p. 326.

33 The two best sources on the Tilea affair are Watt, How War Came, pp. 169–77, and S. Aster, 'Viorel Virgil Tilea and the Origins of the Second World War: An Essay in Closure', Diplomacy and Statecraft, 13 (September 2002), no 3. Also useful is A. Prazmowska, Britain, Poland and the Eastern Front, 1939 (Cambridge, 1987), pp. 40, 51 and 62.

34 Cadogan Diaries, 17/3/39.

35 Watt, How War Came, p. 175.

36 Channon Diary, 18/3/39; see also Aster, 'Viorel Virgil Tilea', pp. 155–57.

37 Cadogan minute, 18/3/39, TNA (PRO), FO 371/23060, C3538/3356/18.

38 Ibid.
39 Aster, 'Viorel Virgil Tilea', p. 170.
40 Ibid.
41 Watt, *How War Came*, pp. 178–79; A.M. Cienciela, *Poland and the Western Powers, 1938–39* (London, 1968), pp. 216–17.
42 Documents on German Foreign Policy, third series, 5, nos 293 and 295.
43 *DGFP*, series D, v, nos 399 and 400.
44 *DBFP*, third series, iv, nos 458 and 484.
45 Minutes, TNA (PRO), CAB (12) 39 18/3/39, CAB 23/98.
46 TNA (PRO), FO 371/22967 C3858–9/5/18; Neville to Ida Chamberlain, 19/3/39, Chamberlain Papers.
47 *Ciano's Diary*, 15/3/39, p. 201.
48 Minutes, TNA (PRO), CAB (13) 39, 20 March, CAB 23/98.
49 Ibid.
50 Neville to Hilda Chamberlain, 26/3/39, Chamberlain Papers.
51 For accounts of the Colvin interview, see Watt, *How War Came*, pp. 182–84, and S. Aster, *1939: The Making of The Second World War* (London, 1973), pp. 99–101.
52 Watt, *How War Came*, p. 184.
53 Hansard, 345, *HCD*, fifth series, col 2415.
54 Ibid., fifth series, col 2417.
55 Aster, *Second World War*, p. 115.
56 Gilbert, *Companion*, iii, pp. 1038–39.
57 Ibid.
58 TNA (PRO), FO 371/23016 C4622/54/18.
59 TNA (PRO), COS 872 (JP) 3/4/39.
60 R. Mallett, *Mussolini and the Origins of the Second World War, 1933–1940* (London, 2003), p. 196.
61 *Channon Diary*, 7/4/39, pp. 192–93.
62 Quoted in Feiling, *Neville Chamberlain*, p. 404.
63 *Harvey Diaries*, 7/4/39, p. 275.
64 Ibid., 4/4/39, p. 273.
65 TNA (PRO), CAB 23/98, CAB 18/39 5/4/39.
66 *Channon Diary*, 13/4/39, p. 193.
67 Ibid., p. 194.
68 Prazmowska, *Britain, Poland and the Eastern Front*, p. 65.
69 Ibid., p. 56.
70 Litvinov to Merekalov, 4/4/39, *Dokumenty uneshnei politiki USSR*, 23 vols (Moscow, 1958).
71 TNA (PRO), FO 371/22969 C5460/15/18.
72 R.A. Butler, *The Art of the Possible* (London, 1971), pp. 78–79.
73 M. McCauley, *The Soviet Union, 1917–1991* (2nd edn, London, 1993), p. 106.
74 Quoted in M. Carley, *1939: The Alliance That Never Was and the Coming of the Second World War* (London, 2000), p. 120.
75 *DBFP*, third series, v, no 201.

76 Henderson to Cadogan, 31/5/39, TNA (PRO), FO 800/294, Cadogan Papers.

77 TNA (PRO), CAB 27/624; *DBFP*, third series, iv, no 76; *Foreign Relations of the United States 1939*, i, pp. 139–40.

78 G. Weinburg, *The Foreign Policy of Hitler's Germany Starting World War Two, 1937–39* (Chicago and London, 1980), p. 571.

79 Bullitt to Hull, 5/5/39, FRUS.

80 *Nicolson Diaries*, 4/5/39, p. 401.

81 Ibid., 2/5/39.

82 Malcolm and Kelly (eds), *The Ironside Diaries*, p. 77.

83 Quoted in Mallett, *Mussolini and the Origins of the Second World War* (London, 2003), p. 201.

84 *Ciano Diaries*, 27–28/5/39.

85 TNA (PRO), CAB 23/100/187, 19/7/39.

86 Molotov to Maisky, 16/6/39, *Soviet Peace Efforts on the Eve of World War II* (September 1938–August 1939, i and ii, ed. V. Falin (Moscow, 1973).

87 Templewood, *Nine Troubled Years* (London, 1954), p. 357.

88 P. Bell, *France and Britain, 1900–1940: Entente and Estrangement* (London and New York, 1996), pp. 224–25.

89 *DBFP*, third series, vi, nos 279, 281–82.

90 TNA (PRO), CAB 23/100 and CAB 27/625.

91 For an excellent compilation of essays on the United States in the thirties, see I. Leighton (ed.), *The Aspirin Age* (London, 1963).

92 R.A. Divine, *The Reluctant Belligerent: American Entry into World War Two* (New York, 1969), p. 262.

93 D. Dimbleby and D. Reynolds, *Oceans Apart* (London, 1988), p. 122.

94 Watt, *How War Came*, p. 268.

95 M.A. Jones, *The Limits of Liberty: American History, 1607–1992* (2nd edn, Oxford, 1995), p. 490.

Notes to Chapter 11: The Coming of War

1 D.C. Watt, *How War Came* (London, 1989), p. 383.

2 Haslam, *The USSR and the Struggle for Collective Security in Europe, 1933–39* (London, 1984), p. 225, but the source quoted is a member of the American Embassy.

3 'Anglo-French-Soviet negotiations', Skrine Stevenson minute 25/7/39, TNA (PRO), FO 371/23071 C10634/3356/18; for accusations about British 'complacency', see also M. Carley, *The Alliance that Never Was* (London, 2000), p. 185.

4 Watt, *How War Came*, p. 382.

5 Templewood, *Nine Troubled Years* (London, 2000), p. 358.

6 Haslam, *The Struggle for Collective Security*, p. 225.

7 Committee on Imperial Defence, Deputy Chiefs of Staff Sub-Committee 16/8/39, TNA (PRO), FO 371/23072 C11506/3356/18.

8 Schnurre memorandum, 27/7/39, *DGFP*, series D, vi, no 729.

9   Vansittart, *The Mist Procession* (London, 1958), p. 536.
10 Halifax to Norton, 5/7/39, *DBFP*, third series, vi, no 231.
11 *Nicolson Diary*, 20/7/39 (London, 1967), pp. 406–7.
12 Ibid.
13 *Channon Diaries*, 29/6/39 (London, 1967), p. 203; 31/7/39, p. 206.
14 Dalton, *The Fateful Years, 1931–45* (London, 1957), p. 255.
15 *Harvey Diaries*, 30/6/39 (London, 1970), p. 300.
16 N. Rose, *Cliveden Set* (London, 2001), p. 195.
17 *Documents Concerning German-Polish Relations and the Outbreak of Hostilities*, Cmd 6106, London, 1939, no 25.
18 *DGFP*, series D, vi, no 43; S. Aster, *The Making of the Second World War* (London, 1973), pp. 320–21.
19 K. Feiling, *Neville Chamberlain* (London, 1946), p. 410; Chamberlain to Syers, 13/8/39, TNA (PRO), PREM, 1/331.
20 Minute by R. Makins, 14/8/39, *DBFP*, third series, vi, no 659; Makins to Walters, 14/8/39; Strang to Nesbitt, 17/8 in TNA (PRO), FO 371/23025–6 C11266/54/18.
21 Henderson to Cadogan, 115/8/39, *DBFP*, third series, vi, nos 609–10.
22 R. Spitzy, *How We Squandered the Reich* (Norwich, 1997), pp. 285–86.
23 P. Schmidt, *Hitler's Interpreter* (London, 1951), p. 133.
24 *Channon Diaries*, 22/8/39, p. 208.
25 *Harvey Diaries*, 23/8/39, p. 304.
26 M. Carley, *The Alliance That Never Was and the Coming of World War II* (London, 2000) p. 207.
27 Quoted in A. Roberts, '*The Holy Fox*' (London, 1991), p. 167.
28 J. Charmley, *Chamberlain and the Lost Peace* (London, 1989), p. 200.
29 W.S. Churchill, *The Gathering Storm* (London, 1948), p. 319.
30 Henderson to Halifax, 25/8/39, Blue Book no 68.
31 Henderson to Ribbentrop, 26/8/39, TNA (PRO), FO 371/22975 C12238/15/18.
32 Quoted in M. Gilbert, *The Wilderness Years* (London, 1981), p. 260.
33 *Nicolson Diary*, 24/8/39, p. 413.
34 Henderson to the Foreign Office, 29/8/39, TNA (PRO), FO 371/22975 C12401/15/18; N. Henderson, *Failure of a Mission* (London, 1940), pp. 268–69; Makins minute, 31/8/39, TNA (PRO), FO 37/122975 C1240/15/18.
35 TNA (PRO), CAB 23/100, 46/39, 30/8/39.
36 P. Neville, *Appeasing Hitler* (London, 2000), pp. 164–65; Schmidt, *Hitler's Interpreter* (London, 1951), p. 157; Henderson, *Failure of a Mission*, pp. 293–94.
37 Charmley, *Chamberlain and the Lost Peace*, p. 205.
38 TNA (PRO), CAB 23/100, 47 (39), 1/9/39.
39 A. Adamthwaite, *Grandeur and Misery: France's Bid for Power in Europe, 1914–40* (London, 1995), p. 222; Viscount Simon, *Retrospect* (London, 1952), p. 252.
40 *Nicolson Diary*, 1/9/39, pp. 416–18.
41 *HCD*, 2/9/39, cols 280–85.
42 Neville to Ida Chamberlain, 10/9/39, NC 18/1/1116.
43 TNA (PRO), CAB 23/100 49 (39) 1/9/39.

44 R. Rhodes James, *Bob Boothby: A Portrait* (London, 1991), p. 232.
45 Schmidt, *Hitler's Interpreter*, p. 158; Etherington Smith to author, 2/5/97.
46 TNA (PRO), FO 371/800/270, Henderson Papers.
47 Schmidt, *Hitler's Interpreter*, p. 158.
48 W.J. West, *Truth Betrayed* (London, 1987), p. 166 n. 101; *Cadogan Diaries*, 2/5/39, p. 178; Perth to Halifax, 3/11/38, TNA (PRO), P3248/3250/3404/5/150.
48 Neville Chamberlain, BBC Radio Broadcast 3/9/39, *The Penguin Book of Twentieth-Century Speeches*, ed. B. MacArthur (London, 1992), pp. 176–78.
50 *HCD*, 3/9/39, fifth series, cols 291–92.
51 Vansittart Memorandum, TNA (PRO), FO 371/22986 C19495/15/18.
52 N. Wylie, *Britain, Switzerland and the Second World War* (Oxford, 2003), p. 274; I am indebted to Rosie Alison, a relative, for the interesting titbit about Sir Clifford Norton, who kept Henderson's slippers for many years! Letter to author, 23/11/2000.
53 Middlemass and Barnes, *Baldwin* (London, 1969), pp. 1051–52.

Notes to Chapter 12: Verdict

1 H. Dalton, *The Fateful Years, 1931–45* (London, 1957), p. 321.
2 M. Gilbert and R. Gott, *The Appeasers* (London, 1963), p. 352.
3 Ibid.
4 Churchill, *The Gathering Storm* (London, 1948), p. 532.
5 H. Montgomery Hyde, *Neville Chamberlain* (London, 1976), p. 154.
6 *Channon Diaries*, 10/5/40 and 13/5/40, pp. 248–52.
7 *HCD*, 12/11/40.
8 M. Gilbert, *Churchill Companion*, v, p. 76.
9 Note by Hankey, 24/10/33 quoted in P. Bell, *Chamberlain, Germany and Japan, 1933–34* (Basingstoke, 1996), p. 31.
10 P. Neville, *Winston Churchill: Statesman or Opportunist?* (London, 1996), p. 60.
11 P.W. Schroeder, 'Munich and the British Tradition', *Historical Journal*, 19 (1976), pp. 223–43.

Bibliography

PRIMARY SOURCES

CHURCHILL COLLEGE, CAMBRIDGE

Cadogan Papers
Phipps Papers
Vansittart Papers

NATIONAL ARCHIVE OF SCOTLAND

Lothian Papers

NATIONAL ARCHIVES

CAB 23 Cabinet Minutes.
CAB2 Minutes and Reports of the Committee of Imperial Defence.
Cadogan Papers, Foreign Office, 800 series.
Halifax Papers, Foreign Office, 800 series.
Henderson Papers, Foreign Office, 800 series.
Orme Sargent Papers, Foreign Office, 800 series.

UNIVERSITY OF BIRMINGHAM

Chamberlain Papers

SECONDARY SOURCES

OFFICIAL PAPERS

Documents on British Foreign Policy, second series, volume xviii; third series, volumes i–vii (London, 1949–55).
Documents on German Foreign Policy, 1938–39, series D, volumes i–vii (London, 1949–56).
Documents Diplomatiques Français, 1936–39, série 2 (Paris, 1963–86).
Foreign Relations of the United States, 1919–39, published by the State Department, Washington, 1934–56.

DIARIES AND PAPERS

Bond, B.J., *Chief of Staff: The Diaries of Sir Henry Pownall*, 2 volumes (London, 1972).
Dilks, D. (ed.), *The Diaries of Sir Alexander Cadogan* (London, 1971).
Harvey, J. (ed.), *The Diplomatic Diaries of Oliver Harvey* (London, 1970).
Hassell, U. von, *The Von Hassell Diaries* (New York, 1946).
Jones, T., *A Diary with Letters* (London, 1954).
Nicolson, N., (ed.), *Harold Nicolson Diaries and Letters, 1930–39* (London, 1966).
Nicolson, N., (ed.), *Harold Nicolson Diaries and Letters, 1939–45* (London, 1967).
Rhodes James, R., (ed.), *Chips: The Diaries of Sir Henry Channon* (London, 1967).

BOOKS

Alexander, M., *The Republic in Danger: General Maurice Gamelin and the Politics of French Defence, 1933–40* (Cambridge, 1992).
Andrew, C., *Secret Service: The Making of the British Intelligence Community* (London, 1985).
Aster, S., *The Making of the Second World War* (London, 1973).
Avon, Lord, *Facing the Dictators* (London, 1962).
Bell, P.M.H., *France and Britain 1900–1940: Entente and Estrangement* (London, 1996).
Bell, P.M.H., *The Origins of the Second World War in Europe* (London, 1986).
Blythe, R., *The Age of Illusion* (London, 1963).
Boyce, R., and Maiolo, J. (eds), *The Origins of World War Two: The Debate Continues* (London, 2003).

Boyce, R., and Robertson, E.M. (eds), *Paths to War: New Essays on the Origins of the Second World War* (London, 1989).

Brendon, P., *The Dark Valley: A Panorama of the 1930s* (London, 2000).

Broderick, A.H., *Near to Greatness: A Life of Earl Winterton* (London, 1965).

Bruegel, J.W., *Czechoslovakia before Munich: The German Minority Problem and British Appeasement Policy* (Cambridge, 1973).

Bullock, A., *Hitler: A Study in Tyranny* (London, 1952).

Butler, E., *Mason-Mac: The Life of Lieutenant General Noel Mason-MacFarlane* (London, 1972).

Carley, M., *1939: The Alliance that Never Was and the Coming of the Second World War* (London, 2000).

Carlton, C., *Anthony Eden* (London, 1981).

Charmley, J., *Duff Cooper: The Authorised Biography* (London, 1989).

Churchill, W.S., *The Gathering Storm* (London, 1948).

Cockett, R., *The Twilight of Truth* (London, 1989).

Colville, J., *The Fringes of Power* (London, 1985).

Colvin, I., *Vansittart in Office* (London, 1965).

Craig, G. and Gilbert, F., *The Diplomats 1919–39*, ii, *The Thirties* (New York, 1968).

Crozier, A.J., *Appeasement and Germany's Last Bid for Colonies* (London, 1988).

Crozier, A.J., *The Causes of the Second World War* (London, 1997).

Dalton, H., *Memoirs*, ii, *The Fateful Years, 1939–45* (London, 1957).

Dockrill, M., *British Establishment Perspectives on France, 1936–40* (London, 1999).

Dutton, D., *Anthony Eden* (London, 1998).

Dutton, D., *Neville Chamberlain* (London, 2001).

Emmerson, J.T., *The Rhineland Crisis, 7 March 1936* (London, 1977).

Feiling, K., *Neville Chamberlain* (London, 1946).

Fest, J., *Plotting Hitler's Death: The German Resistance to Hitler, 1933–45* (London, 1996).

François-Poncet, A., *The Fateful Years* (London, 1949).

Gilbert, M., *Sir Horace Rumbold: Portrait of a Diplomat* (London, 1973).

Gilbert, M., *Winston Churchill: The Wilderness Years* (1981).

Gilbert, M. and Gott, R., *The Appeasers* (London, 1963).

Gill, A., *An Honourable Defeat: A History of the German Resistance to Hitler* (1994).

Gillies, C., *Radical Diplomat: The Life of Archibald Clark Kerr, Lord Inverchapel, 1882–1951* (London, 1999).

Jebb, Gladwyn, *The Memoirs of Lord Gladwyn* (London, 1972).

Grant Duff, S., *The Parting of Ways* (London, 1982).

Halifax, Earl of, *Fullness of Days* (London, 1957).

Haslam, J., *The Soviet Union and the Struggle for Collective Security in Europe, 1933–39* (London, 1984).

Henderson, Sir N., *Failure of a Mission* (London, 1940).

Howard, A., *RAB: The Life of R.A. Butler* (London, 1986).

Jackson, J., *The Fall of France: The Nazi Invasion of 1940* (London, 2003).

Kee, R., *Munich: The Eleventh Hour* (London, 1988).

Kershaw, I., *Hitler, i, Hubris, 1889–1936* (London, 1998).

Kershaw, I., *Hitler, ii, Nemesis, 1936–45* (London, 2000).

Kershaw, I., *Making Friends with Hitler: Lord Londonderry and Britain's Road to War* (London, 2004).

King, C., *With Malice towards None* (London, 1970).

Kirkpatrick, Sir I., *The Inner Circle* (London, 1959).

Klemperer, K. von, *German Resistance against Hitler* (Oxford, 1994).

Lamb, R., *The Drift to War, 1922–39* (London, 1989).

Lentin, A., *Guilt at Versailles: Lloyd George and the Pre-History of Appeasement* (London, 1984).

Lentin, A., *Lloyd George and the Lost Peace: From Versailles to Hitler, 1919–40* (London, 2001).

Lukes, I., *Czechoslovakia between Stalin and Hitler: The Diplomacy of Eduard Beneš in the 1930s* (Oxford, 1996).

Lukes, I. and Goldstein, E. (eds), *The Munich Crisis 1938: Prelude to World War Two* (London, 1999).

MacMillan, M., *Peacemakers: The Paris Conference of 1919 and its Attempt to End War* (London, 2001).

Martel, G. (ed.), *The A.J.P. Taylor Debate after 25 Years* (London, 1986).

Meehan, P., *The Unnecessary War* (London, 1992).

Namier, L., *Diplomatic Prelude* (London, 1948).

Namier, L., *Europe in Decay: A Study in Disintegration* (London, 1950).

Neville, P., *Appeasing Hitler: The Diplomacy of Sir Nevile Henderson, 1937–39* (London, 2000).

Neville, P., *Mussolini* (London, 2003).

Newman, S., *The British Guarantee to Poland* (Oxford, 1976).

Newton, S., *The Profits of Peace: The Political Economy of Anglo-German Appeasement* (London, 1996).

O'Malley, Sir O., *The Phantom Caravan* (London, 1954).

Papen, F. von, *Memoirs* (London, 1952).

Parker, R.A.C., *Chamberlain and Appeasement* (London, 1993).

Parker, R.A.C., *Churchill and Appeasement* (London, 2000).

Peters, A.R., *Anthony Eden at the Foreign Office* (Aldershot, 1986).

Prazmowska, A., *Britain, Poland and the Eastern Front* (Cambridge, 1987).

Roberts, A., *'The Holy Fox': A Biography of Lord Halifax* (London, 1991).

Roberts, Sir F., *Dealing with Dictators: The Destruction and Revival of Europe* (London, 1991).

Rose, N., *Churchill: An Unruly Life* (London, 1994).

Rose, N., *The Cliveden Set: Portrait of an Exclusive Fraternity* (London, 2001).

Rose, N., *Vansittart: Study of a Diplomat* (London, 1978).

Schlabrendorf, F. von, *The Secret War against Hitler* (Oxford, 1994).

Schmidt, P., *Hitler's Interpreter* (London, 1951).

Spitzy, R., *How We Squandered the Reich* (Norwich, 1997).

Stewart, G., *Burying Caesar: Churchill, Chamberlain and the Battle for the Tory Party* (London, 1999).

Taylor, A.J.P., *The Origins of the Second World War* (London, 1963).

Taylor, T., *Munich: The Price of Peace* (London, 1979).

Templewood, Lord, *Nine Troubled Years* (London, 1954).

Thielenhaus, M., *Zwischen Anpassung und Widerstand: Deutsche Diplomaten, 1938–41* (Munich, 1985).

Vansittart, Lord, *The Mist Procession* (London, 1958).

Vyšný, P., *The Runciman Mission to Czechoslovakia 1938: Prelude to Munich* (London, 2003).

Waley, D., *British Public Opinion and the Abyssinian War, 1935–36* (London, 1975).

Watt, D. Cameron, *How War Came* (London, 1989).

Watt, D. Cameron, *Too Serious a Business* (London, 1975).

Wark, W., *The Ultimate Enemy* (Oxford, 1986).

Weinberg, G., *The Foreign Policy of Hitler's Germany: Starting World War II, 1937–39* (Chicago, 1980).

West, W.J., *Truth Betrayed* (London, 1978).

Wheeler-Bennett, J., *The Nemesis of Power* (London, 1964).

Williamson, P., *Stanley Baldwin* (Cambridge, 1999).

Young, R., *In Command of France: French Foreign Policy and Military Planning, 1933–40* (Cambridge, Massachusetts, 1978).

ARTICLES

Aster, S., 'Viorel Vergil Tilea and the Origins of the Second World War: An Essay in Closure', *Diplomacy and Statecraft*, 13 (2002) pp.153–74.

Aulach, H., 'Britain and the Sudeten Crisis 1938: The Evolution of a Policy', *Journal of Contemporary History*, (1983) pp. 246–76.

Bourette Knowles, S., 'The Global Micawber: Sir Robert Vansittart, the Treasury and the Global Balance of Power, 1933–35', *Diplomacy and Statecraft*, 6 (1995), pp. 91–110.

Carley, M.J., 'A Fearful Concatenation of Circumstances: The Anglo-Soviet

Rapprochement 1934–36', *Contemporary European History*, 5 (1996) pp. 29–54.

Cornwall, M., 'The Rise and Fall of "A Special Relationship": Britain and Czechoslovakia, 1930–48', in Brivati, B. and Jones, H. (eds), *What Difference Did the War Make* (London, 1983).

Douglas, R., 'Chamberlain and Appeasement', in Mommsen, W. and Kettenacker, L. (eds), *The Fascist Challenge* (London, 1983), pp. 79–88.

Goldman, A., 'Two Views of Germany: Nevile Henderson versus Vansittart and the Foreign Office', *British International Studies*, 6 (1980), pp. 247–77.

McCulloch, A., 'Franklin Roosevelt and the Runciman Mission to Czechoslovakia, 1938: A New Perspective on Anglo-American Relations in the Age of Appeasement', *Journal of Transatlantic Studies*, 1 (2003), pp. 152–74.

Neville, P., 'Lord Vansittart, Sir Walford Selby and the Debate about Treasury Interference in the Conduct of British Foreign Policy in the 1930s', *Journal of Contemporary History*, 36, (2001), pp. 623–33.

Neville, P., 'Sir Alexander Cadogan and Lord Halifax's "Damascus Road" Conversion over the Godesberg Terms 1938', *Diplomacy and Statecraft*, 2 (2000), pp. 81–90.

Neville, P., 'The Appointment of Sir Nevile Henderson 1937: Design or Blunder?', *Journal of Contemporary History*, 4 (1998) pp. 609–19.

Overy, R.J., 'German Air Strength 1933–39: A Note', *Historical Journal*, 28 (1984), p. 469.

Parker, R.A.C., 'British Rearmament 1936–39: Treasury, Trade Unions and Skilled Labour', *English Historical Review*, (1983) pp. 306–43.

Parker, R.A.C., 'Great Britain, France and the Ethiopian Crisis', *English Historical Review*, (1974), pp. 269–97.

Watt, D. Cameron, 'British Intelligence and the Coming of the Second World War in Europe', in May, E.R. (ed.), *Knowing One's Enemies* (1986) pp. 123–51.

Index

CPSIA information can be obtained
at www.ICGtesting.com
Printed in the USA
LVHW061808070119
603023LV00003B/10/P